THE OWL
AT DAWN

SUNY Series in Radical Social and Political Theory
Roger S. Gottlieb, Editor

THE OWL
AT DAWN

A Sequel to Hegel's
Phenomenology of Spirit

Andrew Cutrofello

State University of New York Press

Published by
State University of New York Press, Albany

© 1995 State University of New York

For information, address State University of New York Press, State University
Plaza, Albany, N.Y., 12246

Production by Diane Ganeles
Marketing by Dana Yanulavich

Library of Congress Cataloging-in-Publication Data

Cutrofello, Andrew, 1961–
    The owl at dawn : a sequel to Hegel's Phenomenology of spirit/
Andrew Cutrofello.
        p.   cm.—(SUNY series in radical social and political
theory)
    Includes bibliographical references and index.
    ISBN 0-7914-2583-5 (CH : alk. paper).—ISBN 0-7914-2584-3 (PB :
alk. paper)
    1. Philosophy.   2. Radicalism.   3. Knowledge, Theory of.
4. Passive resistance.   5. Hegel, Georg Wilhelm Friedrich,
1770–1831. Phänomenologie des Geistes.   6. Absolute, The-
-Controversial literature.   7. Philosophy, Modern—19th century.
8. Philosophy, Modern—20th century.   I. Hegel, Georg Wilhelm
Friedrich, 1770–1831. Phänomenologie des Geistes.   II. Title.
III. Series.
B945.C872095   1995
190—dc20   94-24303
                                                             CIP

10 9 8 7 6 5 4 3 2 1

This book is for Megan

• Contents

———————————————————————— • Acknowledgments

An earlier draft of the first part of the Preface appeared in *The Owl of Minerva*. An earlier draft of Chapter 4, Section BBB.b, "Actualization of structural reason's self-consciousness," did as well. I am grateful to the editor of this journal, Lawrence Stepelevich, for permission to use these. An earlier draft of the second part of the Preface is to be presented at the American Philosophical Association in December 1994. My proleptic thanks to Tina Chanter for the comments she is to prepare. A still earlier draft of this paper was presented before the Philosophy Department at Loyola University of Chicago in January 1994. I am grateful to my colleagues at Loyola for the exemplary critical discussion which this presentation occasioned.

An earlier draft of the third part of the Preface was presented at a meeting of the Radical Philosophy Association in October 1992. I would like to thank those who attended and offered their thoughts.

I am particularly grateful to Alison Brown, William Desmond, Kelly Oliver, Heidi Ravven, and an anonymous reviewer, all of whom gave their time in reading an earlier draft of this book. Their comments and suggestions were of great value to me and helped me to get a better sense of the shape of this writing project and of the stakes involved in shaping it one way rather than another. My thanks as well to Clay Morgan, my editor at State University of New York Press, for supporting this project, despite its somewhat strange character. My thanks also to Roger Gottlieb.

I learned how to read Hegel from the late Bill Earle and from John McCumber, exemplary philosophers and teachers both. I am also grateful for many dialectical and non-dialectical philosophical encounters with students, colleagues, and other friends, some of whom I would like to mention here: Alison Brown, Angela Capodivacca, Mary Caputi, Ann Clark, Elizabeth Hayes, David Ingram, Kathleen League, Bill Martin, Alan Rosiene, Dianne Rothleder, Hans Seigfried, Tom Sheehan, Kelli Skehan, and Cynthia Willett.

As always, my thanks go out to my parents and to the rest of my family. Indefinitely many thanks go out to Dianne Rothleder and to Megan Rose Cutrofello. Gratitude, like confession, is difficult, if not impossible, to express in the public sphere. But neither can perhaps suffice in the private sphere. Both belong to the work of friendship, the idea and practice for which I thank Dianne Rothleder.

• Conceptual Personae

(in order of appearance, with the names of philosophers
who have invented or assumed them)

absolute knowers: G. W. F. Hegel, F. W. Schelling
absolute master: Hegel
philosophical apprentices
philosophical missionary: Victor Cousin
usurper: Arthur Schopenhauer
philosophical equal
philosophical reformers
preservers of the master's legacy: Old Hegelians
philosophical radicals: Young Hegelians
philosophical revolutionaries: Arnold Ruge
philosophical anthropologist: Ludwig Feuerbach
philosophical egoist: Max Stirner
philosophical loner: Søren Kierkegaard
communists: Karl Marx, Frederick Engels
statists
anarchists: Michael Bakunin
nihilists: Nicholas Chernyshevsky
Christian humanist: Fyodor Dostoevsky
psychologist of Christianity: Friedrich Nietzsche
true lover of humanity: Lou Salomé
antipsychologist: Gottlob Frege
defender of the subject
linguistic idealist: F. H. Bradley
logical realists: Bertrand Russell, G. E. Moore
logical positivists: Rudolf Carnap, A. J. Ayer
logical mystic: Ludwig Wittgenstein
ordinary language theorist: J. L. Austin, John Searle
ontological relativist: W. V. O. Quine
multiple world theorist: Thomas Kuhn
radical interpreter: Donald Davidson

transcendental phenomenologist: Edmund Husserl
phenomenologist of revelation: Martin Heidegger
existentialist: Jean-Paul Sartre
phenomenologist of otherness: Emmanuel Levinas
psychoanalyst: Sigmund Freud
ego psychologist: Alfred Adler
psychoanalyst of the absolute: C. G. Jung
feminist psychoanalyst: Nancy Chodorow
radical feminist: Mary Daly
masculine psychoanalyst of gender: Jacques Lacan
feminine psychoanalyst of gender: Julia Kristeva
structuralists: Claude Lévi-Straus, Noam Chomsky, Patricia Churchland
antistructuralist: Michel Foucault
utilitarian: Jeremy Bentham
liberal lawgiver: John Rawls
sociologists: Max Weber
state socialists: Bolsheviks
father of the revolution: V. I. Lenin
defender of the people: Rosa Luxemberg
tyrant of the revolution: Josef Stalin
antitotalitarianist: Hannah Arendt
defenders of the tyrant: Louis Althusser
new sociologists: Talcott Parsons
macho-individualists: American men
totalitarian democrat: Joe McCarthy
libertarian: Robert Nozick
pragmatists: John Dewey
liberal ironist: Richard Rorty
love generation
defenders of masculine myths
reformed youth: Jerry Rubin on Wall Street
"me"-generation
fraternity of sociology: Georges Bataille
feminine theorist of difference: Luce Irigaray, Hélène Cixous
liberal feminist: Betty Friedan
deconstructive consciousness: Jacques Derrida
queer theorist: Eve Kosofsky Sedgwick
exemplary others advocate: Gayatri Chakravorty Spivak
multiculturalist
subversive terrorist
postmodernist: Jean Baudrillard
theorist of communicative action: Jürgen Habermas
critical feminist: Nancy Fraser
traditionalist: Alisdair MacIntyre
consciousness of the differend: Jean-François Lyotard
antidialectician: Gilles Deleuze
Satyagrahi: Baruch Spinoza

I. Why Hegel's *Phenomenology of Spirit* Requires a Sequel

> There is also a Catholic church here, or several, I believe. I already saw
> many a dirty Capuchin running about. But they seem to me stricter father
> confessors than the one to whom you usually confess, and I do not believe
> that you would get off so cheaply here. They are also probably stricter than
> you yourself, who have absolved me without inflicting a penance. (Hegel,
> in a letter to Nanette Endel, dated February 9, 1797).[1]

The act of confession plays a crucial and recurring role in the *Phenomenology of Spirit*. Alienation between individuals, Hegel suggests, can be overcome only through a mutual confessing and forgiving between distinct alienated consciousnesses. Thus the dramatic climax of the text occurs at the close of the section on Spirit, with the breaking of the hard heart and the reciprocal acts of confession and forgiveness on the parts of the acting and judging consciousnesses. (The rest of the *Phenomenology* is, as has been frequently noted, an anticlimax). Leading up to this act of mutual confession are a series of confessional scenes, whose insufficiency arises from one of two failings: either they fail to be direct (*unmittelbar*), or they fail to be mutual. The paradigmatic cases of each of these types of failure can be found, respectively, in the section on the unhappy consciousness and in the section on the ethical realm. The unhappy consciousness's admission of misery to the mediating consciousness is a type of confession. Presumably, both the lord and the bondsman confess at this point. However, they do not confess directly to each other; they confess only to the mediator. Thus, the gesture of confessing *to the other* remains something

---

1. G. W. F. Hegel, *Hegel: The Letters*, trans. Clark Butler and Christiane Seiler (Bloomington: Indiana University Press, 1984), p. 58.

merely intended and not yet carried out in the deed. This failure is compensated for at the level of the ethical realm, where the defender of the divine law performs a double deed: first, she carries out the deed of violating the human law, and then she carries out the deed of confessing directly to the antagonist from whom she is alienated. However, the defender of the human law does not recognize his own guilt and so he refuses either to confess or to forgive. The structure of this latter scene of confession is eventually repeated at the level of spirit. For so long as the judging consciousness refuses to recognize his own evil, he remains stubbornly Creonic. Only when he recognizes that he, too, is evil does the hard heart reciprocate the confession of the other. Mutual and direct confessing takes place.

The problem, though, is that the one to whom the Creonic hard heart confesses is not the one who confessed her crime of violating the human law. Antigone has been brushed aside; it is to a living Polyneices, in effect, that Creon is willing to confess. This gender elision raises all kinds of questions about whether the *Phenomenology* leaves us with an uncompleted dialectic of confession. Just as Hegel himself suggests that *Oedipus Rex* needed to be supplemented by *Antigone*, we might very well ask whether the *Phenomenology of Spirit* needs a sequel as well.

In her provocative essay, "Has Hegel Anything to Say to Feminists?"[2] Heidi Ravven shows that, if we read Hegel's treatment of gender and gender relations as social rather than as natural, then the *Phenomenology* can be useful for thinking through certain feminist issues. In order to extend an Hegelian analysis of gender relations, I think, it would be necessary to begin from Ravven's *reading* of Hegel's narrative and then to continue this narrative by *writing* a sequel, the telos of which would be a mutual confessing and forgiving between masculine and feminine subjects. Here, I want to prepare the way for the sequel I have written by analyzing the stakes that are involved in the type of confessional narrative which the *Phenomenology* itself—insofar as it denies its own intrinsic need for a sequel—purports to be. Toward this end, it will be illuminating to examine the concept of confession as it appears in Hegel's other texts as well—particularly in his religious and political writings.

Confession, for Hegel, is in part an act of self-sacrifice. Were the confessing individual to expect something in return for his or her confession, it would not be a true confession. Yet for confession to advance the dialectic, this act of self-sacrifice must be transformed into some sort of return-to-self. Having given up everything for nothing, the confessing individual must receive everything back: thus, the structure of this movement recalls the Kierkegaardian transition from the pure loss of the act of infinite res-

2. Heidi M. Ravven, "Has Anything to Say to Feminists?" in *The Owl of Minerva*, volume 19, no. 2 (Spring 1988).

ignation to the return of what was lost in the leap of faith. It also recalls the Lacanian structure of symbolic castration, especially as Slavoj Žižek has drawn out its Hegelian filiation.[3]

As is well known, Hegel thinks that individuals can attain a sense of self-identity only by risking death. However, the most extreme risk of death occurs not in the battle to the death, but in the act of self-sacrifice which takes place in confession. The unhappy consciousness brings *itself* to Mount Moriah and raises the sword—only to find himself delivered from death by the mediator to whom he has confessed. The renunciation of self-identity in confession is the only mechanism which enables the individual to achieve a sense of self-identity in a "meaningful" way. In psychoanalytic terms, Hegelian confession would function as a kind of symbolic castration meant to ward off the threat of real castration. The act of voluntarily confessing would be a way of becoming "Oedipalized"; by renouncing one's imaginary claim to be identical with the universe, the confessing individual enters the symbolic realm as one *gendered* individual among many.

The confessing unhappy consciousness does not realize that it is sacrificing itself in order to prevent its being sacrificed. We—the audience—see it, but the confessing subject does not. But after having experienced the return to self, the individual now understands the structure of how confession works. Subsequent confessions will no longer be acts of pure self-sacrifice; on the contrary, individuals will consciously confess in order to be forgiven. In some sense, they will only pretend to "sacrifice" themselves, retaining all the while their self-certainty, and *knowing* that reciprocal confession will lead to a fuller actualization of self-identity.

---

3. See Slavoj Žižek, *Tarrying with the Negative*, (Durham: Duke University Press, 1993). The parallels between Hegel and Lacan are many and complex. It is worth noting here some surface similarities in their reception. Critics of both Hegel and Lacan object to what is taken to be the politically reactionary and phallocentric orientations of their texts. Hegel and Lacan are both said to be politically conservative because they seem to defend the ethical norms and institutions of their respective societies. Thus, Hegel's apparent attack on the achievements of the French Revolution, as well as his articulation of the rationality of various features of the Prussian state, the institution of private property, and so forth have been criticized in precisely the same ways as have Lacan's apparently one-sided condemnation of "May '68" and his view of psychoanalytic practice as helping individuals to achieve successful Oedipalization. Again, Hegel and Lacan are said to be phallocentric to the extent that they appear to defend gender hierarchies—Hegel, by relegating women to the realm of the family, and Lacan with his privileging of the phallus and his description of woman as a castrated subject. That the charges of political conservatism and phallocentrism go hand in hand is clear, and the crucial place where they meet are in those specific processes whereby individual subjects attain a sense of self-identity as masculine members of a patriarchal society. In Hegel, I want to suggest, the primary mechanism at work here is the act of confession, and more specifically, the scene of mutual confession which is expected to take place between two morally self-certain individuals.

Hegel does not explicitly treat the absolution of the confessing unhappy consciousness as a gendering of the subject. At this point in the text, at least, he does not pause to indicate that there are two possible results of this symbolic entry into a gendered world—one can become a "she" or one can become a "he." In effect, individuals seem to remain gender-neutral "rational" subjects, at least up until the point where the dialectic of "Reason" gives way to that of "Spirit." But it is possible that these apparently gender-neutral subjects are essentially masculine, an assumption that would not only anticipate, but to some extent explain, the fact that Hegel's eventual hero—the subject who will rise to the level of the absolute standpoint—will be explicitly identified as masculine. That this is so can be seen by the fact that the scene of explicitly gendered confession, which takes place at the level of the ethical world, is important only as a setting-up of the form of mutually masculine confession that will take place between two "he's" at the level of morality. In other words, despite the fact that there are *three* important confessional scenes in the *Phenomenology*, only *two* of these play any significant role in articulating the movement toward mutual recognition.

What then is the relationship between these two masculine scenes of confession? In Hegelian language, we might describe the first as symbolic castration "in itself," the second as symbolic castration "in and for itself." But what exactly is being sacrificed in each of the two cases? Does the second confession merely represent the *completion* of the original movement, or can it be read, in some respect, as a *reversal* of the original movement? That is, if the original scene of confession introduces gender identities, does the final act of confession acknowledge, or abolish, these identities? Or is this question irrelevant? For even if we can detect some sort of challenge to gender hierarchies from the absolute standpoint, would not the fact that it is an explicitly masculine subject who here champions feminine subjectivity suggest that Hegel's larger narrative is incomplete? Must there not remain a gap between the certainty of mutual recognition achieved at the end of the text and the truth with which Hegel leaves us? Put otherwise: can the *Phenomenology* do without a sequel—a sequel that must have a feminine subject as one of its chief protagonists?

The unhappy consciousness is the individual who belongs to a community in which no one recognizes anyone else; being unable to recognize the other is here equivalent to not being recognized *as* an other. The position of the unhappy consciousness is even lower than that of mere solipsistic despair, for its sense of "I" is as lost as is its sense of the existence of others. Completely alienated from itself as well as from others, the unhappy consciousness sees no way of repairing its damaged sense of self. It confesses its utter misery to the mediator not in the expectation of a return of a sense of self, for this seems utterly impossible. This is why the confession constitutes a "pure" sacrifice; the act of confession functions as pure gift-giving, for the subject expects nothing in return. To underscore this point, Hegel insists that the sacrifice would not have worked had it been merely feigned, noting that, "Only through this *actual* sacrifice could it demonstrate this self-renunciation."[4] The result of this actual sacrifice is the very foundation of the state—in its first stage of an ethical community of rational agents.

But this gift-giving confession turns out not to suffice for building a genuine community of mutually recognizing selves. The process must be recapitulated later, with the confessing subject consciously aware of the symbolic significance of its sacrifice. This occurs in the section on morality, where the individual who sees himself as evil must confess his wickedness (*Böse*) to another. This time there is no mediator between the two mutual confessors. Each confronts the other directly, knowing the roles that they are to play in the process.

This second scene of now self-consciously masculine confession does not arise so much out of despair as out of a sense of dignity and strength of self. The one who initiates the confession asks explicitly for recognition by the other:

> His confession (*Geständnis*) is not an abasement (*Erniedrigung*), a humiliation (*Demütigung*), a throwing-away of himself in relation to the other; for this utterance is not a one-sided affair, which would establish his disparity with the other: on the contrary, he gives himself utterance solely on account of his having seen his identity with the other; he, on his side, gives expression to their common identity in his confession. (405/490)

Here, the confession is not a gift, it is an offering which expects something in return. The individual recognizes himself in his act of confession, and if the one to whom he confesses refuses the exchange, he will rescind the offer. This other, however, at first sees no advantage in the terms of the contract. As judging consciousness, he refuses to reciprocate by confessing himself in return:

> But the confession (*Eingeständnis*) of the one who is wicked, "I am so", is not followed by a reciprocal similar confession (*Geständnisses*). This

4. G. W. F. Hegel, *Hegel's Phenomenology of Spirit*, trans. A. V. Miller (New York: Oxford University Press, 1977), p. 137. "Die Verzichtleistung auf sich konnte es allein durch diese *wirkliche* Aufopferung bewähren." (*Phänomenologie des Geistes* (Frankfurt: Suhrkamp, 1970), p. 176. All further references to Hegel's *Phenomenology* will appear in parentheses in the body of the paper, with the English pagination followed by the German.

was not what the judging consciousness meant: quite the contrary. It repels this community of nature, and is the hard heart that is *for itself*, and which rejects any continuity with the other. (405/490)

The hard heart refuses to make the exchange, seeing nothing to gain. He withdraws into himself much as did the unhappy consciousness, but now as the self-satisfied "beautiful soul" who thinks he needs no other. The position of the beautiful soul is untenable, though, as he himself well knows, for recognition of the other is necessary for true self-recognition. Eventually, therefore, he seeks out the other and confesses himself. Mutual confession now must culminate in mutual forgiveness, and each achieves what it knew it could get from the movement of mutual confession and forgiveness.

This movement might be characterized as self-conscious symbolic castration. Each now might be said to be thoroughly reconciled to the symbolic order. This would imply that their mutual otherness has been swallowed up in the unity of the religious community. Yet in fact, each is posited as a particular member of a spiritual community which recognizes their particular differences—in other words, a community which is constituted through the irreducible, and recognized, *otherness* of its members.

At least this is how Hegel presents it, describing the religious community as "the 'I' which has expanded into a duality." (409/494) But here, precisely, arises the crucial question: is there genuine otherness in the Hegelian religious community or not? How we answer this question would depend, in part, on how we view the second confession (symbolic castration) in relation to the first. Is the religious community formed by a completion of the original movement of symbolic castration? If so, then each will identify himself solely as an individual member of the universal community, and not equally in terms of irreducible otherness. Or is it, rather, that genuine otherness is achieved in the religious community in a way that it was not in the state? Has the movement into the religious community negated the symbolic order of the state? If so, then the second confession would not be a mere completion of the first symbolic castration, but might instead be viewed as a purportedly feminine negation of the symbolic order itself.

But is the symbolic order really sacrificed in the second movement of mutual confession and forgiveness? Is the state negated or preserved in its *Aufhebung* into the religious community? The answers to these questions depend upon a reading of the dialectic which leads from the transformation of the state into the religious community. The section of the *Phenomenology* which culminates in this mutual confession and forgiveness involves a dialectic of private and public spheres. The conflict between divine law and human law which appears at the beginning of this section is an opposition between the realm of the family and that of the state. The family is at first simply sacrificed to the universal, but the opposition between private and public resurfaces at the level of culture, where the private is subsumed under the public, and then at the level of morality, where the hierarchy is inverted. The eventual resolution of the entire movement—the mutual confession which leads to the "I" that is a "we"—presumably marks the overcoming of the opposition between private and public spheres. We might therefore expect to find some sort of overcoming of the conflict between the imaginary and the symbolic orders. But what sort of overcoming? What kind of *Aufhebung*? Does the domain of the family simply disappear in the self-transparency of the religious community, or does the religious community represent a community reclaimed by the family?

The second scene of confession clearly raises to the level of self-awareness a symbolic castration that occurred at the beginning of social interaction. Castration must occur twice. But why? It is important to notice that only the first movement of confession was necessary for the establishment of the state. Is it not the state which calls forth the second confession? If not, then what does call for this repetition?

In many places, Hegel makes quite clear that a true religious community is not only different from the state, but diametrically opposed to it. In his early work, "The Positivity of Christian Religion," he had characterized the transformation of Christianity into a state religion as a kind of perversion. A sign of this perversion can be found in what the state does to confession.

> Originally, everyone was free to choose a friend whom he respected and to make him the confidant of his secrets and faults, but instead of this the rulers of the spiritual state now arranged that these confessors should be officials to whom everyone had to have recourse.
>
> Confession of one's faults was originally voluntary, but now it is the *duty* of every citizen of the spiritual state, a duty over whose transgression the church has pronounced its supreme punishment, eternal damnation.[5]

In this text, Hegel clearly endorses a social order modeled on a religious community of friends rather than on a religious state. What is noble and good among friends becomes perverted in the state. He thus refers to the admirable "traits which are found in a circle of trusted friends, united for the purpose of truth-seeking or moral improvement" and then notes:

---

5. G. W. F. Hegel, "The Positivity of the Christian Religion," trans. T. M. Knox, in *Early Theological Writings* (Philadelphia: University of Pennsylvania Press, 1971), p. 104.

> These same traits are met later on a large scale in the Christian church once it has become universal; but because this church has become a church which is universal throughout a state, their essence is disfigured, they have become contradictory and unjust, and the church is now a state in itself.[6]

The state represents the perversion of the religious community. Confession, praiseworthy when it is voluntary and among friends, becomes contradictory and unjust when it is made a mandatory obligation of the state. The religious community of the *Phenomenology* is meant to be a reclaiming of what the state had distorted.

Yet although Hegel insists on the value of voluntarism and privacy in religious confession, he presents a somewhat different view with regard to the subject of *criminal* confession. In his Jena lecture notes of 1805–1806, Hegel seems to approve of the view that it is the nature of law to require, in certain circumstances, that criminals confess their crimes. At first, the suggestion is merely pragmatic: "The criminal's confession is needed— since we mistrust the inference from external circumstances to inner motive."[7] Hegel also notes, though, the difficulty if not impossibility of relying on criminals to confess to their crimes: "The law should know that obstinacy against such expression is not to be overcome."[8]

A truly dramatic departure from his earlier critique of the state is suggested in the *Philosophy of Right*, where Hegel suggests that the legal requirement that criminals be made to confess their crimes is done mainly *for the sake of the criminal*. Still more striking is Hegel's argument that *voluntary* confession is best of all, for in voluntarily confessing, the criminal "attains a measure of satisfaction" by choosing to "chime in with the judge's sentence":

> The demand, commonly made in German law, that a criminal should confess his guilt (*Die Forderung des Eingeständnisses von seiten des Verbrechers*), had this to be said for it, that the right of self-consciousness thereby attains a measure of satisfaction; consciousness must chime in with the judge's sentence, and it is only when the criminal has confessed that the judgment loses its alien character so far as he is concerned.[9]

---

6. Ibid.

7. G. W. F. Hegel, *Hegel and the Human Spirit*, trans. Leo Rauch (Detroit: Wayne State University Press, 1983), p. 149.

8. Ibid.

9. G. W. F. Hegel, *Hegel's Philosophy of Right*, trans. T. M. Knox (New York: Oxford University Press, 1967), p. 275.

Of course: "a difficulty arises here, because the criminal may lie, and the interest of justice may be jeopardized"![10]

The value placed on truth-telling arises from the notion that confession—*to the state*—is beneficial *for the criminal*. By confessing, the criminal accuses himself and thereby gets reconciled to the universal. He finds himself guilty, as if the verdict were not something imposed upon him by an external force. By refusing to accuse himself, the criminal suffers more than the state, for either way the state has found him guilty, but only by confessing will he "save" himself. Criminal confession is the bizarre paradox of "forced" yet "voluntary" self-sacrifice.

Yet it was precisely this—the notion of a mandatory but supposedly voluntary confession *to the state*—which Hegel had objected to in his much earlier "Positivity of the Christian Religion." To be sure, the latter spoke of religious confession rather than criminal confession. But is there really, for Hegel, an essential difference between the two? While both involve admission of guilt, religious confession might be said to concern private wrongdoing, whereas criminal confession concerns public wrongdoing. But is this really so? The crime of Antigone cuts across these easy distinctions. Her crime was clearly a crime against the state. Yet it was a crime waged in the name of what was then the religious community—the family. But there, a crime against the state and a crime against the divine law are opposed to each other. Indeed, the origin of crime *as such* arises in the conflict between the divine law and the law of the state:

> guilt . . . acquires the meaning of *crime* (*Verbrechens*); for as simple, ethical consciousness, it has turned towards one law, but turned its back on the other and violates the latter by its deed. (282/346)

By deciding to bury her brother, Antigone violates the human law in the name of the divine law—she pits the crime of the family against the law of the state. This, however, only makes Antigone all the more eager to confess her crime against the state, in celebration of her revolutionary act. It is because she knowingly violated the law of the state that she is willing to confess. (284/348)

Now, when the mutually confessing and forgiving individuals initiate a religious community, they can be seen as overthrowing the state, thereby retrospectively declaring Antigone the winner in her battle against the state. Hegel is quite clear in presenting the religious community as a higher level of spirit than can be achieved in the state because the conflict between the

---

10. Ibid.

private and public spheres cannot be resolved in the ethical realm. Antigone's criminal activity will turn out to have been a necessary condition to bring about the overthrow of the state. Her crime—and her confession—are both heroic deeds. They prefigure the possibility of a self-conscious act of symbolic castration which now, in dialectical reversal, negates the state rather than instituting it (as did the confession between the unhappy consciousnesses). Can we relate Antigone's situation to that of the criminal in the *Philosophy of Right*, who is required to voluntarily confess? Is the criminal simply being asked to make the same movement as Antigone, proudly acknowledging that she has violated the law of the state?

Hegel might think so, but we might be suspicious. Antigone's confession was mandated not by the state but by her allegiance to a higher law which she herself voluntarily acknowledged. But the criminal whose "voluntary" confession is extracted is forced by the state to confess to the state. There is no dialectical *other* who would oppose the state in Hegel's *Rechtsphilosophie*; the requirement of confession is meant, on the contrary, to confirm the state's omnipotence and self-sufficiency. Or does there lurk, in the criminal's "satisfaction" with "chiming in" with the law of the state a secret pleasure—ready to burst into revolutionary mirth—akin to that enjoyed by the eternally ironic feminine subject whom Hegel represents as the state's other?

Our options for reading Hegel divide here along familiar lines. But rather than simply choosing between the either/or alternatives of Hegel-the-patriarch and Hegel-the-philosopher whom feminists should take seriously, let us leave Hegel for a minute to consider the political stakes. The post-Hegelian, postmodern skepticism which thinks that any notion of community is totalitarian will inevitably see any self-sacrifice as a sign of the will-to-docility which power trains bodies to adopt. The problem with this view, of course, is that it indiscriminately throws out solidarity with totalitarianism, communities of resistance with oppressive communities.

In his critique of the "repressive hypothesis," Michel Foucault shows that confession can sometimes *appear* to be more radical than it in fact is. According to the repressive hypothesis, we have been living under a prohibition against discourse about sexuality for the past few hundred years. "For a long time, the story goes, we supported a Victorian regime, and we continue to be dominated by it even today. Thus the image of the imperial prude is emblazoned on our restrained, mute, and hypocritical sexuality."[11] But in fact, "when one looks back over these last three centuries . . . things appear in a very different light: around and apropos

---

11. Michel Foucault, *The History of Sexuality, Volume One: An Introduction*, trans. Robert Hurley (New York: Vintage, 1978), p. 3.

of sex, one sees a veritable explosion."[12] Foucault argues that we live in the age of "bio-power," an age characterized (among other things) by an imperative requiring the production of discourse about sexuality. In tracing the history of confession, Foucault shows how confession of sin in the Church came to be supplanted by confession of one's sexuality on the psychiatrist's couch. To many French intellectuals, it had long appeared that "confession" about one's sexuality was a way of subverting power; Foucault shows that such apparent subversion is in fact a confirmation of the power it would subvert.

Foucault's cautionary tale might lead us to conclude that any apparently subversive confession in Hegel is itself not genuinely subversive at all. But is this too hasty? In Hegel, the act of confession is nothing less than a condition for the possibility of social group formation. Were we to refuse the act of confession altogether, we would undermine the possibility for friendships, solidarity, communities of resistance. More importantly, the second level of confession is undertaken by members of a state who consciously see that mutual self-sacrifice is the only means to forging a community adequate to resist the dominating forces of the state. Foucault, perhaps excessively suspicious of group identification, is notoriously vague when it comes to articulating a positive account of the conditions for formulating communities of resistance, a vagueness which is obviously related to his suspicion that every act of confession is a form of complicity with power.[13] To be sure, with every action that founds a community comes the risk that the community will become a means for controlling individuals, for disfiguring their communal confession into something perverted. Hegel is not unaware of this problem—we see clearly the evils of the state in Hegel as surely as we see his hopeful vision of a community that would overcome these evils.

The *Phenomenology of Spirit* perhaps can itself be read as a confession of—and an invitation to—a crime. A crime against the symbolic order, the confession of which must be addressed, above all, to friends. The state demands confessions so as to justify its punishment of criminals. Friends, on the other hand, forgive—exorbitantly, even, out of all proportion to the symbolic laws of exchange.

Yet have we achieved, as Hegel thought, the conditions for the possibility of such friendship? Can there be, for Hegel, a genuine friendship for women? Between women and men? "Certainly!" we are assured by Stuart Swindle, who echoes the certainty of the masculine founders of the

---

12. Ibid., p. 17.
13. Cf. Andrew Cutrofello, *Discipline and Critique: Kant, Poststructuralism, and the Problem of Resistance* (Albany: SUNY Press, 1994).

religious community in Hegel's own text.[14] But has this certainty been actualized? Or do we not await the scene of confession and forgiveness that must take place directly between gendered subjects?

II. Why *We* Need a Sequel to Hegel's *Phenomenology of Spirit*

The development of recent French philosophy has been governed by what I call "the problematic of the givenness of others." The word "givenness" is deliberately ambiguous here. First, what is at issue is "givenness" in an epistemic sense, and as such the problem concerns the knowability of others. Construed in this way, the problem of the givenness of others links together all of modern French philosophy, as it first emerges as a problem in the work of Descartes. For Descartes, my certainty of my own existence is something that I am *immediately* aware of as soon I reflect on the fact that I am thinking. Because this certainty of self is not mediated by any thing or anyone other than me, there is no other whose existence is guaranteed merely by my awareness of my own thinking. Only subsequent to my certainty of my own existence can I, according to Descartes, come to know the existence of others. This purely epistemic problem of the givenness of others persists in *Being and Nothingness*, where Sartre criticizes the Anglo-American tradition for not taking the problem of solipsism seriously enough.

In marked contrast to the Cartesian approach to this epistemic question of whether or not a thinking subject can be certain of the existence of others stand two very different strategies within the continental tradition for undercutting it—those of Hegel and Heidegger. In the *Phenomenology*, Hegel maintains that a thinking subject can become certain of its own existence only through an equiprimordial recognition of the existence of another subject. This is why the ensuing struggle for recognition can reach a stable conclusion only with the mutual recognition of two independently existing subjects. Similarly, Heidegger—although he rejects the Hegelian construal of human subjectivity as consciousness—also attempts to rule out the very possibility of solipsism by demonstrating that Dasein is always already revealed to itself as being-in-the-world-alongside-others.[15]

---

14. Stuart Swindle, "Why Feminists Should Take the *Phenomenology of Spirit* Seriously," *The Owl of Minerva*, vol. 24, no. 1 (Fall 1992), pp. 41–54.

15. "By reason of this *with-like* [*mithaften*] Being-in-the-world, the world is always the one that I share with Others." Martin Heidegger, *Being and Time*, trans. John Macquarrie and Edward Robinson (New York: Harper & Row, 1962), p. 155.

One of the most decisive influences on the post-Sartrean French philosophical scene was Alexandre Kojéve's attempt to situate Heidegger's conception of human Dasein in an Hegelian dialectical framework. It is from Kojéve that contemporary French philosophy derives its reorientation of the problem of the givenness of others. The problem is no longer, as it was for Descartes, merely epistemic; it is now also ethical. This, then, is the *second* problematic: to what extent are others "given" to me as objects that are "available" to be "used" in some sense or other? It is important to note that in the work of contemporary French philosophers, we do not here simply shift from an epistemic problem to an ethical problem; we lay the groundwork for a radical reconception of the epistemological problem itself. That is, with the Hegelian-Heideggerian reorientation of the question, the focus of the epistemic problem itself shifts. With Descartes, the risk was that others might not be given to me, in which case I could never know of their existence. But now the risk is that the givenness of others might lead me to fail to recognize that it is precisely the fact that others *transcend* whatever can be given to me in my experience that defines *both* the epistemic *and* the ethical character of my relation to them.

Recast in this way, Descartes' problematic of the givenness of others now concerns the question of how my certainty of self might lead to a recognition of and obligation to others whose existence is, in a certain sense, *not* given to me. Contemporary French thought is united by a shared strategy for addressing this problematic by reversing the Cartesian primacy of the subject. Put schematically, this reversal can be stated as a rejection of the "I think, therefore I am" in favor of a certain "I think, therefore you are."

This reversal can be seen most clearly in the work of Emmanuel Levinas. In some of his earliest phenomenological work, Levinas was concerned with the theme of the "*il y a*." In contrast to the Heideggerian conception of the "*es gibt*," Levinas presents the "*il y a*" in terms of the subject's awareness of an indeterminate "rumbling" of being. That "there is" something other than the subject is beyond questioning; to this extent Levinas is already "beyond" the problem of solipsism. But the precise nature of what "there is" remains unknown, and to this extent the primordial awareness of the world is not yet the recognition of the existence of determinate others. But, the theme of the "*il y a*" quickly gives way in Levinas to an analysis of being-for-the-other as the most primordial way in which a subject comes to a consciousness of itself. "Prior" to any conception of the indeterminacy of what there is outside the subject is the subject's "certainty," to retain the Cartesian notion, of the existence of others. For me to become aware of myself is to disclose that I am in a relation to others: I think, therefore the other is—therefore *you* are.

This is "a point of almost absolute proximity" (to borrow a phrase from Derrida) between Hegel and Levinas. Yet there is also a divergence between the types of phenomenological exegesis which Hegel and Levinas engage in. In Hegel, we might say, the "I think" wants to resolve itself immediately into "therefore I am." Hence the "therefore you are" is an interpellation, an interference on the part of the other in my otherwise solitary attempt to determine my own existence. The other becomes an obstacle which the subject now sets out to remove in the famous struggle to the death. If, eventually, the subject can come to determine its own existence only by acknowledging and being acknowledged by the other, this appears to have the character of a compromise, a second-best solution for the subject.

For Levinas, by contrast, we could say that the fact that the "I think" leads to the conclusion "therefore you are" demonstrates that the ultimate telos of the subject is not to determine its own existence but to be responsible for the other. Thus, recognizing the other is not a necessary but unfortunate means to my own end; it is, rather, the only "proper" end that I myself can be said to have. Right away, therefore, the very notion of what can be "proper" to a subject is problematized in a way it does not appear to be in Hegel.

At issue here, it would seem, is a question of what actually is the "most primordial" relationship in which the subject stands in relation to others. On this issue it is important, I think, to invoke Aristotle's distinction between two senses of primordiality. In the *Nicomachean Ethics* Aristotle says, "Let us not fail to notice . . . that there is a difference between arguments from and those to the first principles. . . . For, while we must begin with what is evident, things are evident in two ways—some to us, some without qualification. Presumably, then, *we* must begin with things evident to *us*."[16] An important difference between Hegelian and Levinasian phenomenology can be drawn, it would seem, on precisely these lines. When Levinas describes the subject's responsibility for the other as being primordial, he means that it is so "without qualification." By contrast Hegelian phenomenology—again, leaving aside for now the question of what, ultimately, will be first "without qualification" for Hegel—begins with what is first "for us." Hegelian phenomenology is thus on the way *to* first principles; it is only with his *Logic* that Hegel will start—as Levinas does—*from* first principles.

Of course, it could be argued that, because the Hegelian subject's intrinsic telos is the "therefore I am," whereas the Levinasian subject's telos

---

16. Aristotle, *The Nicomachean Ethics*, book I, chapter 4, trans. David Ross, revised by J. L. Ackrill and J. O. Urmson (New York: Oxford University Press, 1980), p. 5.

is the "therefore you are," that they cannot reach a point of agreement. But again on a deeper level, both Hegel and Levinas are trying to arrive at a conception of "we" who constitute ourselves as mutually recognizing one another. For both, therefore, the distinction between the "therefore I am" and the "therefore you are" could be described as a false dichotomy which each tries to overcome.

It is precisely at this point of proximity between Hegel and Levinas that Derrida problematizes both of their attempts to "solve" the problem of recognition. Derrida, it would seem, agrees that Levinas has presented the "ideal" form of the relationship of a self to an other, but he wonders if this ideal is in fact ever realizable. In "Violence and Metaphysics," Derrida points to the paradoxical requirement that the other's transcendence—that is, non-givenness—would itself have to be given to the subject in order for the subject to recognize the other.[17] Elsewhere, Derrida re-raises this concern, but by reversing the problem. Instead of working within the problematic of the givenness of the other to the subject, Derrida tries to think through Levinasian ethics in terms of the subject's givenness *to* the other. He does this by inquiring into the conditions for the possibility of gift-giving: what would have to be the case for a subject to give (itself) to an other? Can I give to another without my giving constituting what Heidegger analyzes as a "sending"—that is, a giving that turns out not to be pure because it in some way involves a return to self?[18] For a gift to be a gift and not something exchanged in some form of economic circulation, Derrida argues, it cannot even be recognized *as* a gift; for this recognition would itself be that which is "returned" in exchange for the gift. But this then leads to the question of whether we can say that there is such a thing as gift-giving. Related to the paradox that the giver cannot give to another without receiving something in return is the parallel paradox that, on Levinas' description of ethical obligation, the other *obliges* me to give to him or her. If I am obligated to give, then my giving is also not pure. Derrida concludes that the conditions for the possibility of gift-giving are paradoxically the conditions for its impossibility as well.[19] However, his point is not to "overturn"

---

17. Jacques Derrida, "Violence and Metaphysics," in *Writing and Difference*, trans. Alan Bass (Chicago: The University of Chicago Press, 1978).

18. "A giving which gives only its gift, but in the giving holds itself back and withdraws, such a giving we call sending." Martin Heidegger, *On Time and Being*, trans. Joan Stambaugh (New York: Harper and Row, 1972), p. 8.

19. "These conditions of possibility of the gift (that some "one" gives some "thing" to some "one other") designate simultaneously the conditions of the impossibility of the gift. And already we could translate this into other terms: these conditions of possibility define or produce the annulment, the annihilation, the destruction of the gift." Jacques Derrida, *Given Time: 1. Counterfeit Money*, trans. Peggy Kamuf (Chicago: The University of Chicago Press, 1992), p. 12.

the Levinasian ideal of giving oneself to the other but to demonstrate the aporias involved in this ideal. He writes, "The gift *is not*. One cannot ask 'what is the gift?'; yet it is only on that *condition* that there will have been, by this name or another, a gift."[20] To some extent, there is a trace here of the Kantian suggestion that it may be impossible but nonetheless necessary to act from duty, or of Kierkegaard's suggestion that it may be impossible but necessary to make the leap of faith.[21] It might be noted here that the double sense of the problematic of the "givenness" of others arises in Derrida with the twofold questioning of the "metaphysics of presence"—the epistemic question of givenness—and the ethics of the gift—the ethical question of givenness. Derrida himself calls attention to the fact that in both French and English the word "present" carries a double meaning, and he stresses the connection of these two meanings in his own questioning.[22]

In both his early and later reflections on the work of Levinas, Derrida in effect argues that the attempt to define the subject's absolute responsibility to its other does not completely escape the Hegelian trap of inscribing this responsibility in the name of the subject itself. Once again, this is not to say that Derrida rejects the Levinasian ideal, but it is to show the difficulty of advancing beyond the Hegelian speculative dialectic whereby the subject "gives" to the other only for the subject's own sake—even if this is not its "intention." So for instance, in his essay "At this very moment in this work here I am," Derrida highlights the problem of otherness as a problem of gender, asking in effect if Levinas' attempt to give to the other may not itself fall prey to philosophy's essentially phallocentric failure to recognize a feminine other. Derrida is not trying to "trump" Levinas by showing that he, Derrida, is "more open" to a feminine other than is Levinas; on the contrary, Derrida tries to show, self-referentially, how his own attempt to mark the exclusion of a feminine other will itself be "guilty" of failing to give to the other. As it turns out, both Levinas and Derrida have been accused of excluding feminine otherness at the very places in their texts where they try to let a feminine other speak. Luce Irigaray, for instance, suggests that "Levinas does not perceive the feminine as other."[23]

---

20. Jacques Derrida, "At this very moment in this work here I am," in *Re-Reading Levinas*, eds., Robert Bernasconi and Simon Critchley (Bloomington: Indiana University Press, 1991), p. 15.
21. Here, though, it would be important to keep in mind Derrida's own emphasis of the differences between Levinas and Kierkegaard. See Jacques Derrida, "Donner la mort," in *L'éthique du don: Jacques Derrida et la pensée du don*, eds., Jean-Michel Rabaté and Michael Wetzel (Paris: Métailié-Transition, 1992).
22. "That a gift is called a present, that 'to give' may also be said 'to make a present,' 'to give a present' (in French as well as in English, for example), this will not be for us just a verbal clue, a linguistic chance or *alea*." Derrida, *Given Time 1.: Counterfeit Money*, p. 10.
23. Luce Irigaray, "Questions to Emmanuel Levinas," in *Re-Reading Levinas*, op.cit., p. 111.

This kind of objection would seem, in one way, to confirm Derrida's point about the impossibility of giving to the other. But in another way I think that the gender critique of Levinas is instructive for a way of further developing the Levinasian notion of ethics as first philosophy—by way of Hegel.

Here, it is necessary to say a few words about psychoanalysis and recent French-language critiques of Freud's analysis of gender. In *The Enigma of Woman* and in other writings, Sarah Kofman reflects on the ambiguity in Freud's attempt to think through questions of gender.[24] On the one hand, Kofman shows, Freud breaks with the traditional phallocentric way in which masculine philosophers have defined gender in essentialist terms. By construing "masculine" and "feminine" as denoting types of drives which can be found in both men and women, Freud opens the way to a social reading of gender which can then be used to undermine traditional readings of the "natural" superiority of men over women.[25] Yet at the same time, Freud also defines libido as essentially masculine. If libido, the basic energy behind all erotic drives, is somehow inherently masculine, then masculine behavior becomes the "normal" mode of behavior for all human subjects.[26] The problem for psychoanalytic theory would then be to figure out where feminine impulses come from—thus we have Freud's famous "riddle of femininity."[27] Hence Freud continues to privilege masculine subjectivity over feminine subjectivity.

When we now raise the question of what it is that distinguishes masculinity from femininity for Freud, and what it therefore means to define libido as essentially masculine, we come up with the following. Roughly, we can say that for Freud, masculine drives express something like what Nietzsche calls the "will to power." Their telos is self-enhancement; in this way they are self-centered. By contrast, feminine drives are oriented toward others. From the time of his early analyses of hysteria through his last writings on the "riddle of femininity," Freud associates femininity with the phenomenon of hysterical identification.[28] In identification, a subject comes

---

24. Sarah Kofman, *The Enigma of Woman: Woman in Freud's Writings*, trans. Catherine Porter (Ithaca: Cornell University Press, 1985).
25. "In one sense, against every metaphysical tradition, Freud strives to differentiate between active and masculine, passive and feminine, emphasizing that, for example, the opposition active/passive arises earlier than the opposition masculine/feminine. . . . Therefore, active and passive are no longer the essential property of either sex." Sarah Kofman, *"Ca Cloche,"* in *Derrida and Deconstruction*, ed. Hugh J. Silverman (New York: Routledge, 1989), p. 114.
26. Ibid., p. 155.
27. On this question, see also Teresa Brennan, *The Interpretation of the Flesh: Freud and Femininity* (New York: Routledge, 1992).
28. As Teresa Brennan notes, for Freud "hysteria is the archetype of femininity." Ibid., p. 189.

to identify herself so closely with the desires of another subject, that her very sense of self is undermined.

Insofar as he construes masculine self-centered drives as normal and feminine other-oriented drives as abnormal, Freud remains tied not only to the traditional masculine denigration of femininity, but also thereby to the traditional failure to rise to the level of what Levinas calls the "primordial responsibility to the other." By reducing the phenomenon of hysterical identification to a disorder, Freud in effect denigrates the Levinasian understanding of ethical obligation to others. In the *Interpretation of Dreams*, Freud writes, "Identification is a highly important factor in the mechanism of hysterical symptoms. It enables patients to express in their symptoms not only their own experiences but those of a large number of other people; it enables them, as it were, to suffer on behalf of a whole crowd of people."[29] Now to be sure, Levinas' emphasis on the transcendence of the other in one sense precludes and in fact deliberately forestalls a more Hegelian logic of identification with others. Yet at the same time there is for Levinas a going-beyond-oneself-toward-the-other which is "selfless" in the same way that essentially feminine hysteria is as described by Freud. Thus, for Levinas my responsibility for others itself transcends the limits of my own freedom.[30]

It would be a short step to associate Freud's picture of "normal" masculine selfishness with the Hegelian view according to which the proper telos of the "I think" is its return to self in the "therefore I am." We could similarly relate Freud's picture of femininity and the logic of hysterical identification with the Levinasian model according to which the "proper" telos of the "I think" would be the "therefore you are." In this sense, we could read Levinas as the ultimate transvaluator of masculine values. Although Levinas has been questioned by some feminists about his apparent equation of femininity with maternity, this criticism is usually tempered by an acknowledgment that Levinas opens the way to a critique, as Catherine Chalier puts it, of "the virility of being."[31]

But at this point, Derrida's question comes up again—namely, is there such a thing as a "pure" gift? This same question can now be reformulated as a question of gender—namely, is there such a thing as a "pure" femininity? But this question can also be turned around: is there such a thing as

29. Sigmund Freud, *The Interpretation of Dreams*, trans. James Strachey (New York: Avon Books, 1965), pp. 182–183.

30. "To be obliged to responsibility overflowing freedom, that is, responsibility for the others." Emmanuel Levinas, "Humanism and An-archy," in *Collected Philosophical Papers*, trans. Alphonso Lingis, (Boston: Martinus Nijhoff Publishers, 1987), p. 136.

31. "We have to encounter this failure in the virility of being in order to understand the meaning of Other. . . . But we have to take note of the fact that, according to Levinas, ethics in its feminine achievement means to be a mother and nothing else." Catherine Chalier, "Ethics and the Feminine," in *Re-Reading Levinas*, op.cit., p. 127.

a "pure" masculinity? If the answer to both questions is no, then perhaps what we need is a phenomenological description of the relation between self and other that would take into account both the Hegelian moment of the struggle for recognition, along with the Levinasian moment of the structure of absolute ethical obligation to the other. Perhaps the "I think" cannot take us either to the "therefore I am" or "therefore you are" because there is no pure "I am" or "you are." If so, then we would have to articulate the conditions for the possibility of how the "I think" might arrive at the telos "therefore *we* are" in a way that does not represent a veiled reduction of the "we" to the individual subject's own self-understanding. How to articulate these conditions, I think, is the problem given to us by contemporary French philosophy—a problem which takes us back to Hegel.

In an interview, Derrida once said that, "We will never be finished with the reading or rereading of Hegel, and, in a certain way, I do nothing other than attempt to explain myself on this point."[32] This curious statement has to be understood in terms of two other recurring Derridean themes: the iterability of writing and the ethical necessity of constantly returning to the question, "Who, 'we'?" To say that writing—that is, all language, including speech—is iterable is simply to say that every text can always be placed in a new context.[33] Because meaning is determined by context, the iterability of every text indicates that its meaning is never fixed once and for all; in different contexts, a text will mean different things. In one sense, therefore, to say that we will never be finished with the rereading of Hegel is to say something that could be said of every text—namely, that we can never be finished reading them because there is no end to the possible contexts we might find ourselves and it in. In another sense, however, the necessity of rereading *Hegel*—and here I take Derrida to be thinking of the *Phenomenology* above all, though he seems to have the *Science of Logic* in mind as well—is singularly connected to the Hegelian project of thinking through the conditions for the possibility of saying "we."

Suppose we view Hegel's *Phenomenology* as an attempt to show how we get from the "I think" to the "therefore we are." An obvious objection that is always lying in wait for Hegel is the question which Derrida raises explicitly: "Who, 'we'?" The possibility always remains that the "we" might be based on an exclusion of others.[34] From Derrida's perspective, this is not

---

32. Jacques Derrida, *Positions*, trans. Alan Bass (Chicago: The University of Chicago Press, 1981), p. 77.

33. Jacques Derrida, "Signature Event Context," in *Margins of Philosophy*, trans. Alan Bass (Chicago: The University of Chicago Press, 1982).

34. For a systematic discussion of the political issues raised by the open-endedness of the "we," see Bill Martin, *Matrix and Line: Derrida and the Possibilities of Postmodern Social Theory* (Albany: State University of New York Press, 1992).

a contingent possibility which we could get around by writing the "perfect" *Phenomenology of Spirit*. Directly connected to the essential possibility that every text can be read differently in another context is the equally irreducible possibility that every "we" is exclusive of otherness in some way. Ironically, therefore, feminist critics who charge Derrida with excluding feminine voices would seem to confirm Derrida's point here. Thus, Derrida's claim that "we will never be finished rereading Hegel" can be read as cautioning us not to return to the Hegelian project.

But here, two objections to Derrida might be raised. First, the need to say—or to *write*—"we" might be as ineluctable as the need to reread every inscription of the word "we." Obviously, it is no accident that Derrida says "*we* will never be finished rereading Hegel." Perhaps too it is necessary to transform Derrida's claim—or at least add to it the additional claim—that "we will never be finished *rewriting* Hegel." Instead of trying to arrive at some kind of absolute standpoint where the identity of a "we" would be self-transparent to the mutually recognizing members of a community, a revised version of the *Phenomenology* might bring the narrative to a close at precisely that point where it *perhaps* becomes possible for the mutually recognizing members of a community to acknowledge both the necessity of writing "we" and the necessity of deconstructing—rereading and rewriting—every written "we." To put this in Levinasian terms, we would envision a face-to-face encounter in which the work of *saying* "we" must be constantly renewed. Or, to put Levinas and Derrida together here, we would construct an Hegelian narrative that would break where, instead of reaching closure, we would take up the dual task of writing and reading: writing, understood as the *work* of *saying* "we;" reading, understood as the responsibility to critique every *said* "we." In short, we would take up the standpoint of a Satyagrahi. If such a standpoint is possible.

III. Satyagraha and the Absolute Standpoint

Parallels have been drawn between Mohandas K. Gandhi's politics of Satyagraha and the politics of discourse ethics, and it is easy to view Gandhi as a discourse ethicist *avant la lettre*.[35] Of course, the phrase "discourse ethics" is a very broad one. Philosophers as different as Seyla Benhabib, Nancy Fraser, Jürgen Habermas, John McCumber, John Rawls, and Richard Rorty might all be called discourse ethicists of a sort. If we were to look for

---

35. Cf. Thomas Pantham, "Habermas' Practical Discourse and Gandhi's *Satyagraha*," in Bhikhu Parekh and Thomas Pantham, eds., *Political Discourse: Explorations in Indian and Western Political Thought* (New Delhi: Sage Publications, 1987).

a common thread that unites these disparate thinkers, it might be, simply, that they all view ethical and political questions as having some irreducible bearing on fundamental questions about the nature of discourse. However, were we to define discourse ethics in this way, it would be hard to imagine *any* social and political thinkers who would *not* count as discourse ethicists of some sort or other. Alison Brown, Drucilla Cornell, Jacques Derrida, Michel Foucault, Julia Kristeva, Bill Martin and other non-Habermasian "poststructuralists" are philosophers who see political questions as essentially "about" discourse in one way or another. It would be too hasty, therefore, to reduce the discursive politics of Satyagraha to a theory of communicative action.

An important difference between Habermas and Gandhi might be expressed in words borrowed from Lenin: Habermas might be described as something like a revolutionary philosopher, but Gandhi was a philosophical revolutionary. For Habermas's theory of communicative action draws a sharp line between a communicative model of conflict resolution and a revolutionary model. By contrast, Gandhi's discursive politics was *itself* a way of making revolution.

For Habermas, the ideal conditions for communicative action involve an absence of discursive constraints other than basic shared commitments to sincerity and rationality. In emphatically rejecting Foucault's power/ knowledge equation, he denies that conversation is inevitably coercive. In one sense, Gandhi would not have disagreed with Habermas on this point; he believed that a sincere commitment to truth was the only route to conflict resolution and to freedom. But Gandhi also believed that truth claims were weapons in an agonistic struggle, and—I will return to this point—that there are no universal standards of rationality.

Gandhi's carefully chosen word "Satyagraha" explicitly allies the commitment to truth with the use of a certain kind of force:

> Truth (Satya) implies love and firmness (Agraha) engenders and therefore serves as a synonym for force. I thus began to call the Indian movement "Satyagraha," that is to say, the Force which is born of Truth and Love or non-violence.[36]

A Satyagrahi (one who practices Satyagraha) not only fights *for* the truth, he or she fights *with* the truth. However farfetched the comparison might seem at first blush, Gandhi was like Nietzsche in that he viewed truth claims as expressions of force. To be sure, there are important differences

---

36. M. K. Gandhi, "The Advent of Satyagraha," in *The Gandhi Reader: A Sourcebook of his Life and Writings*, ed. Homer A. Jack (New York: Grove Weidenfeld, 1989), pp. 65–66.

between the two, chief among them being that, while Nietzsche never sought to distinguish between force and violence—as Derrida has noted, the German *"Gewalt"* is ambiguous on just this point—for Gandhi (as for Hannah Arendt), the distinction between force and violence was absolutely crucial. Satyagraha was conceived by Gandhi as a forceful way of engaging in non-violent struggle.

What distinguishes Satyagraha from all other forms of struggle, then, is that it alone entails a resolute commitment to non-violence. Conversely, what distinguishes it from all other forms of non-violent activity is that it is a struggle—for this reason, Gandhi insisted that Satyagraha was not the same as passive resistance.[37] For the theorists of communicative action, such a distinction would be hard to draw, for they draw a sharp line between discourse as a way of seeking consensus, and the use of force as a way of compelling agreement. For Gandhi, no such distinction exists, because he does not share the Habermasian notion of consensus. His view of discourse is closer to Lyotard's notion of discourse as agonistics than it is to Habermas' conception of ideal discourse.[38] Much as Lyotard defines a *"différend"* as a point of contention over which there cannot be consensus, so Gandhi believed that truth was radically plural in a way that precludes the very possibility of there being universal standards of rationality.[39]

Where Gandhi sought to elicit agreement on specific issues—such as in his attempt to convince the British that they should accept the Indian claim to self-rule—he did not appeal to universal standards of rationality, nor attempt to construct provisional versions of such standards. Rather, he would appeal to the specific standards of those whom he was trying to convince. He asked the British to reflect on their own values in persuading them to accept the truth that the Indian people saw from the perspective of their different set of values. Thus Gandhi sought not exactly consensus, nor a hermeneutic fusion of horizons, but a mutual respect for the "truths" of others. The irreducible plurality of truths made consensus the wrong

---

37. "I found that the term 'passive resistance' was too narrowly construed, that it was supposed to be a weapon of the weak, that it could be characterized by hatred, and that it could finally manifest itself as violence." Mohandas K. Gandhi, *Autobiography: The Story of My Experiments with Truth*, trans. Mahadev Desai (New York: Dover, 1983), p. 284. Not to be overlooked in this passage is the similarity between Gandhi's and Nietzsche's critiques of practices that are only apparently nonviolent. The similarities and differences between "the Satyagrahi" and "the psychologist of Christianity" are discussed within *The Owl at Dawn*.
38. Jean-François Lyotard, *The Postmodern Condition: A Report on Knowledge*, trans. Geoff Bennington and Brian Massumi (Minneapolis: University of Minnesota Press, 1984), p. 10.
39. Jean-François Lyotard, *The Differend: Phrases in Dispute*, trans. Georges Van Den Abbeele (Minneapolis: University of Minnesota Press, 1988).

goal in political action.[40] Moreover, because he thought consensus was impossible but truth claims ineluctable, Gandhi saw Satyagraha as inherently forceful. As a force both *"on* and *for* truth,"[41] Satyagraha requires an absolute commitment to struggle.

Obviously, everything hinges on the precise nature of the kind of force involved here. For instance, if the truth is something that must be fought over, why would Gandhi rule out the use of violence a priori? The answer to this question would clearly lie at the heart of what is unique about Satyagraha. For Ghandi, the practice of Satyagraha requires an insistence not only on one's own truth (though it is that), but also an insistence on the truths of others. It calls for a way of forcing the other to accept our truths, but in a way that equally obliges us to recognize and respect the force of the other's truths. Gandhi's moral rejection of violence hinges on this commitment to multiple truths. In this sense, his ethics was, in a very concrete way, an epistemological one.

But Gandhi also believed that it was politically foolish to resort to violence. The pragmatic basis of Satyagraha is easy to overlook if we focus solely on the moral and religious basis of Gandhi's commitment to non-violence. To put the matter more exactly, it would seem that there is no strict separation between what is expedient and what is moral in Gandhi's philosophy. Nothing unjust can constitute an effective political strategy or tactic. Violence can only beget more violence.

This claim, essentially ontological and rightly recognized as the central tenet of Gandhi's political philosophy, is derived, to be sure, from the moral and religious doctrine of *karma*. But it is also, as Gandhi knew, a lesson in *Realpolitik* whose moral should be far more obvious than historical stubbornness in the face of it would suggest it has been. The idea that violence only begets more violence is so clearly borne out in most situations that in some sense it is hard to treat it as anything but a truism. To take only one example, it seems beyond the pale of reason—any reason—to think that the various ethnic conflicts raging today in the former Yugoslavia can be solved by Serbs or Muslims or Croats redoubling their efforts to exact revenge on each other, or by other, "international" forms of military intervention. Gandhi's principled non-violence requires a steadfast Kantian resolve not to let a desire to retaliate interfere with a rational understanding that the only way to peace is by way of peace itself. "An eye for an eye makes the whole world blind."

---

40. In this, I disagree with the assessment of Bhikhu Parekh, who argues that Gandhi sought to "reduce" the plurality of diverse views in order to "arrive at a higher consensual truth." Bhikhu Parekh, *Gandhi's Political Philosophy: A Critical Examination* (Notre Dame: University of Notre Dame Press, 1989), p. 215.

41. Ibid., p. 143.

Were we to grant Gandhi his claim about violence only begetting more violence, would this mean that we must follow Gandhi in rejecting violence in all circumstances? Or might there be situations in which we could defend an escalation of conflict as a means to peace? The imperative to nonviolence, at least as I have expressed it thus far, would seem to be merely hypothetical. But here is where Gandhi's ontological claim implies more: it echoes the Kantian thesis that means and ends are interchangeable. If means and ends are interchangeable, then violence in the name of ending violence is nothing but a performative contradiction. When violence is used as a means to peace, the horizon to which it points can only be a Final Solution or an ethnic cleansing.

As is well known, it was his absolute rejection of violence that kept Gandhi from embracing Marxism. Any escalation of violence—even in the name of the oppressed—is itself a step in the wrong direction. Marxists tend to be quite macho on the subject of whether violence is a legitimate means of praxis or not. Feminist critiques of Marxism have taught us to be suspicious of its gender biases; one of these is the valorization of violence as the only real—that is, masculine—way of resolving conflict. Lingering in the mentality of a journal like *Telos*, I would argue, is a presumption that those who support violence are virile; those who refuse violence are wimps. Marx and Malcolm X are masculine; Gandhi and Martin Luther King, Jr. are feminine. The famous picture of Frank Lentricchia that has occasioned comment by feminist critics depicts him as a kind of poster child for Marxism as machismo. One could not imagine Gandhi striking such a pose. It is time—but it has always been time—for radicals to give up their dogmatic assumption that if you want to alleviate pain you've got to cause somebody pain.

At the same time, of course, it is necessary to put Gandhian politics to the test of actual praxis. It is not difficult to imagine why people embroiled in violent struggle would be reluctant to act as Satyagrahis: for this is to risk martyrdom. Do we really have any reason to think that ethnic conflicts would come to an end if besieged Bosnians put down their weapons and became a band of Satyagrahis? Yet, how we answer this question depends on what we take "winning" a conflict to consist in. From a Gandhian perspective, to "win" is not to vanquish; it is to end the violence. Even if more Bosnians were to die through a campaign of Satyagraha, they would have "won" something that they could never win through an escalation of violence. Obviously, it is far easier for a comfortable intellectual in Evanston, Illinois to *write* this than for a besieged individual in Sarajevo to *live* it. Yet the question here is simply to determine what possible courses of action might credibly lead to a lasting peace.

It is important to keep in mind, moreover, that the refusal of violence does not necessitate the wholesale adoption of a liberal politics of reform.

Again, the crucial difference lies in the use of force which makes Satyagraha a way of waging philosophical revolution rather than resorting to a supposedly revolutionary philosophy.

One can imagine a skeptic asking, "What good does it do to 'insist' on the truth? Insistence without the threat of violence is just another version of docility at worst, or liberal politics at best. Do we really want to preclude a priori the use of violence in all struggle?"

> Lenin once said that the only thing the proletariat really has on its side, at least prior to the seizure of power, is truth. But "truth" is not enough. . . . who cares what anyone "knows?"[42]

This is an objection that needs to be addressed: in the end, why should we think that Gandhian politics is effective? It will not suffice merely to point to Gandhi's own accomplishments, since there were many singular circumstances in the struggles he fought that might make us wonder how far we can generalize his results. On the other hand, it would doubtless be just as difficult to point to any lasting peace that has come about through acts of violence, however just the cause. Clearly there is a limit to the degree to which we could either verify or falsify the claim that violence can only lead to further violence.

What led Gandhi to view Satyagraha as an intrinsically "successful" strategy was a *juridical* philosophy that derived from his various confrontations with the law. Because he believed that the law could not but come to the side of the just, Gandhi maintained his faith in the ultimate success of Satyagraha as an appeal to the law. We can briefly trace the cartography of some of Gandhi's encounters with the law in order to bring into focus the specific nature of Satyagraha as a forceful confrontation with the law that is at the same time an appeal to the law.

Gandhi's first encounter with the law came when, as a young barrister preparing for a career "in law," he appeared before the law for the first time:

> This was my *debut* in the Small Causes Court. I appeared for the defendant and had thus to cross-examine the plaintiff's witnesses. I stood up, but my heart sank into my boots. My head was reeling and I felt as though the whole court was doing likewise. I could think of no question to ask. The judge must have laughed, and the vakils no doubt enjoyed the spectacle. But I was past seeing anything. I sat down and told the agent that I could not conduct the case. . . . I hastened from the Court, not knowing whether my client won or lost her case, but I was ashamed of myself, and

---

42. Martin, *Matrix and Line*, p. 31.

decided not to take up any more cases until I had courage enough to
conduct them. Indeed I did not go to Court again until I went to South
Africa.[43]

What is it that causes Gandhi's "heart" to "sink into his boots?" Perhaps the very experience of being in the presence of the law. Gandhi himself
describes it as a matter of cowardice; he resolves not to return to the law
until he has mustered sufficient courage. But there seems to be more to the
experience than this uncharitable autobiographical reflection suggests.
Undoubtedly, the law provokes fear. But what sort of fear? Perhaps Gandhi
is overcome by a feeling of the sublime, a feeling that conjures a very
specific kind of fear—fear before the law. But before what law? Is it simply
his confrontation with the law of the state that conjures this awful fear? A
confrontation with the law qua law? Later in life, Gandhi would take truth—
and hence the law—to be plural. But the Truth of plural truth might be
said to function as a transcendent principle. Is there a transcendent Law of
the (plural) law that inspires Gandhi's awe? A law beyond law?

A few years after his first experience before the law, Gandhi was called
to South Africa to help resolve a lawsuit that divided two Indians living in
South Africa. On his way to Pretoria, he was informed that the law did not
permit "coolies" to travel in the first-class section of the train. Showing no
"fear" or "awe" of the agents of *this* law, Gandhi refused to obey. For his
refusal to obey the law, he was forcefully expelled from the train at the next
stop. In the station, he weighed his options:

> I began to think of my duty. Should I fight for my rights or go back to
> India, or should I go on to Pretoria without minding the insults, and
> return to India after finishing the case? It would be cowardice to run back
> to India without fulfilling my obligation.[44]

With the courage he had earlier taken to be a condition for his entering the
court again, Gandhi went on to Pretoria. There he spent a year, involved in
a complex litigation.

At one point in the case, Gandhi came to recognize a discrepancy
between justice and the law: the facts of the case showed what was just, but
the law seemed to reach a different conclusion:

> In a certain case in my charge I saw that, though justice was on the side
> of my client, the law seemed to be against him. In despair I approached

---

43. Gandhi, *Autobiography: The Story of My Experiments with Truth*, p. 82.
44. Ibid., p. 97.

Mr. Leonard for help. He also felt that the facts of the case were very strong. He exclaimed, "Gandhi, I have learnt one thing, and it is this, that if we take care of the facts of a case, the law will take care of itself. Let us dive deeper into the facts of this case...." On a re-examination of the facts I saw them in an entirely new light.... When I was making preparation for Dada Abdulla's case, I had not fully realized this paramount importance of facts. Facts mean truth, and once we adhere to truth, the law comes to our aid naturally.[45]

What is curious about this position is not the faith that the truth will prevail, but the faith that, in the final analysis, the law will always come to the aid of the truth. This faith would come to serve as the basis for Gandhi's later unswerving respect for the law in the very act of confronting it. Leaving aside the question of the effectiveness of this strategy, it is surely a delicate balancing act to carry out.

On a number of occasions, Gandhi exhibited so great a degree of respect for the law that many of his most loyal followers thought he went too far. On two visits to the court during the Satyagraha movement in South Africa, Gandhi was asked to remove his turban. As Gandhi himself noted in retrospect, to ask an Indian to remove his turban was an insult: "The question of wearing the turban had a great importance in this state of things. Being obliged to take off one's Indian turban would be pocketing an insult."[46] The first time he was ordered to remove his turban, Gandhi refused. But the second time, he decided to comply with the order:

I saw my limitations. The turban that I had insisted on wearing in the District Magistrate's Court I took off in obedience to the order of the Supreme Court. Not that, if I had resisted the order, the resistance could not have been justified. But I wanted to reserve my strength for fighting bigger battles.[47]

Many of Gandhi's friends disapproved of what they took to be Gandhi's capitulation. Gandhi tried to assuage their approbation by convincing them

the truth of the maxim, "When at Rome do as the Romans do." "It would be right," I said, "to refuse to obey, if in India an English officer or judge ordered you to take off your turban; but as an officer of the Court, it would have ill become me to disregard a custom of the Court in the province of Natal."[48]

---

45. Ibid., p. 116.
46. Ibid., p. 94.
47. Ibid., pp. 128–129.
48. Ibid., p. 129.

Here and elsewhere, Gandhi appeals to the Socratic principle that one is bound to respect the laws of the state to which one pledges one's allegiance. This same reasoning would lead him to support the British during the Boer War:

> When the war was declared, my personal sympathies were all with the Boers, but I believed then that I had yet no right, in such cases, to enforce my individual convictions. . . . I felt that, if I demanded rights as a British citizen, it was also my duty, as such, to participate in the defence of the British Empire.[49]

Like Socrates, who in the *Crito* refuses to violate laws that have been used to treat him unjustly, Gandhi insists on the moral obligation to show a fundamental respect for the law. Yet this does not prevent him from violating the laws when he deems them to be unjust. Again, the comparison with Socrates suggests itself. Despite the argument presented to his friend Crito, Plato makes sure that we are told in the *Apology* of at least two occasions in which Socrates refused to comply with the law. Gandhi, of course, would do the same. Over time, as his commitment to Satyagraha grew, his sense of obligation to the law seems to have diminished. Eventually, Gandhi would recommend Satyagraha not just in certain specific historical contexts, but in all situations. Absolute commitment to Satyagraha meant a greater willingness to break the law. Yet this very willingness to break the law is itself still carried out in the name of the law. What does it mean to violate the law in the name of the law?

The answer goes to the heart of Satyagraha as the way of love. The case that Gandhi had settled in Pretoria taught him, he reports, the "true practice of law." He had managed to settle a suit to the satisfaction of both parties—no mean feat.

> My joy was boundless. I had learnt the true practice of law. I had learnt to find out the better side of human nature and to enter men's hearts. I realized that the true function of a lawyer was to unite parties riven asunder. The lesson was so indelibly burnt into me that a large part of my time during the twenty years of my practice as a lawyer was occupied in bringing about private compromises of hundreds of cases. I lost nothing thereby—not even money, certainly not my soul.[50]

The true practice of law is "to unite parties riven asunder" *without having to go before the law*. "The true function of a *lawyer*"—the one who takes on the name of the law—has its telos in *not* having to go before the law. To resolve disputes in the name of the law—yet outside of the law—is to

---

49. Ibid., p. 188.
50. Ibid., p. 117.

seek that extra-juridical agreement that cannot come under the aegis of Habermas' juridical model of consensus.

The way of the law is the way outside of the law, and vice versa, in a kind of dialectical flip-flop. In fact, Gandhi describes his willingness to remove his turban in terms of the same principle: that the true practice of a lawyer is to bring people together.

> All my life through, the very insistence on truth has taught me to appreciate the beauty of compromise. I saw in later life that this spirit was an essential part of Satyagraha.[51]

The absolute commitment to truth is the absolute commitment to fight the law in the name of the law. It was Satyagraha that taught Gandhi how to negotiate the tightrope between respect for the law and refusal to obey it. The politics of Satyagraha thus requires, first and foremost, a responsibility to confront the law. But it also involves, for Gandhi, a commitment to fight for law, to fight to transform law, to fight "in the name of the law." But this in turn is to fight for the superfluity of the law.

Gandhian politics would thus seem to suggest that we should not appear before the law unless we are ready to wage a *philosophical* revolution—which, in keeping with the logic of Satyagraha, means nothing more nor less than a waging of love. Against mere liberalism and its avatars, Gandhian politics bids us to fight not only in the name of the law but also *against* the law—against the law *as such*. For the true practice of the Satyagrahi is the true practice of the lawyer—to bring together parties riven asunder without going before the law. Waging philosophical revolution is just this waging of love. That love is the only weapon capable of ending violence: this is the Gandhian wager.

Is it a wager predicated on faith that the law will always come to the side of the just? Why should we maintain this faith? What if the law were itself always predicated on acts of violence? What if it were impossible to invoke the law in a non-violent way? What if it were impossible to distinguish between non-violent force and violent force?

It is just these questions that have arisen in the context of deconstructive efforts in critical legal studies. In one of his most direct attempts to raise the question of the relationship between deconstruction and justice, Derrida asks:

> How are we to distinguish between this force of the law, this "force of law," as one says in English as well as in French, I believe, and the violence that one always deems unjust?[52]

---

51. Ibid., p. 129.
52. Jacques Derrida, "Force of Law: The 'Mystical Foundation of Authority,'" in Drucilla Cornell et.al. eds., *Deconstruction and the Possibility of Justice* (New York: Routledge, 1992), p. 6.

For Derrida, the question of how to distinguish between force and violence—or, perhaps, the question of whether or not it is possible to distinguish rigorously between force and violence—is necessarily prior to any
talk about an ideal of justice. The reason for this, he suggests, is that every
appeal to an ideal of justice is itself an act of force. Is such force an act of
violence as well? If so, what would this say about ideals of justice? Is the
distinction between a just use of force and an unjust use of force entirely
vitiated?

These are questions that Derrida professes to be unable to answer,
because they *could* be answered only from the perspective of some ideal of
justice that would itself have originated out of an act of force. What is
positive in Derrida's account, nonetheless, is a rejection of the notion of
justice as an ideal in favor of a notion of justice as an *aporia*. Elaborating
on this distinction, Drucilla Cornell casts the aporetic notion of justice as
a kind of "check" on the performative violence of any juridical system's
insistence on a particular conception of justice. By affirming the
deconstructibility of law, we affirm a notion of justice as "the refusal to
accept as valid the system's own attempts at 'deparadoxicalization.'"[53]
Cornell's argument is not aimed at demonstrating how to distinguish rigorously between just acts of force and unjust acts of violence. On the contrary, it follows from the aporetic nature of justice that we cannot do this.
Instead, a commitment to justice becomes the responsibility to problematize
every legal system's claim to be just. For Cornell, deconstruction can be a
forceful confrontation with law not unlike that undertaken by Gandhi
throughout his life.

What remains problematic, still, is Gandhi's assumption that it is easy
to identify a non-violent force. This assumption is explicitly challenged by
both Derrida and Cornell. Derrida, while he leads us to wonder whether the
distinction between force and violence can be drawn in a rigorous way or
not, does not seek to dismiss it altogether. On the contrary, deconstruction
bespeaks a responsibility to question the relationship between force and
violence, and to do justice to their difference. Thus, the commitment to
fight the "nomos" in the name of the "nomos" is a theme that comes up
repeatedly in Derrida. Through such questioning, Derrida's deconstructions
might be said to aspire to bring about philosophical revolutions themselves.

Like Derrida, Gandhi recognizes the irreducibility of force in all political interventions. But Gandhi would have us think that the distinction
between violence and non-violence is a relatively easy one to draw. This, we
might say, is the limit of Gandhi's own conception of Satyagraha. What

---

53. Drucilla Cornell, *The Philosophy of the Limit* (New York: Routledge, 1992), p. 133.

Derrida calls for is a more rigorous questioning of the conditions for the possibility of non-violence. As such a questioning, deconstruction is itself a form of Satyagraha—but a Satyagraha for which non-violence is an aporia rather than an ideal. An aporetic Satyagraha would begin from the deconstructibility of law, of truth, and of love.

It might be argued that Gandhi's praxis suffered from his not having viewed justice—or Satyagraha—as aporetic. Because he took an ideal of justice to be somehow embodied in the law, he remained confident that justice must inevitably issue from just confrontations with the law. Hence his consistent refusal to disobey the law qua law. This aspect of Gandhi's strategy would appear to be one of accommodation, in precisely the sense that Cornell problematizes in the title of her book *Beyond Accommodation*. But while Gandhi's faith that the law will eventually come to the aid of the just may be unwarranted, this faith finds its echo in Cornell's argument that the deconstructibility of the law is what guarantees the *possibility* that the law will come to the aid of the just:

> The deconstructibility of law, then, as Derrida understands it, is a theoretical conception that *does* have practical consequences; the practical consequences are precisely that law cannot *inevitably* shut out its challengers and prevent transformation. . . .
>
> The deconstructibility of law is . . . exactly what allows for the possibility of transformation, not just the evolution of the legal system.[54]

While Derrida's aporetic conception of justice and law councils a hesitation before invoking the law in one's confrontations with it, Cornell, by contrast, shows that the deconstructibility of law is precisely what makes such an invocation possible and necessary. Like Gandhi, Cornell might be said to emphasize that aspect of the law which functions as the condition for the possibility of justice. An aporetic Satyagraha becomes a viable use of force precisely because of the deconstructibility of law.

In Gandhi's sense of the term, Satyagraha can be compared with the Hegelian absolute standpoint. For as the practice of affirming one's own truths while respecting the truths of others, Satyagraha represents a politics of the "I" which recognizes its identity and difference with others. Much as Hegel, in the *Philosophy of Right*, articulates his ethical standpoint from within the standpoint of the law, so does Gandhi's Satyagrahi.

If, accordingly, we reinterpret Satyagraha as an *aporetic* practice which seeks to inscribe itself within the law only in order to deconstruct the law,

---

54. Ibid., pp. 165–166.

we can use this model to recast a conception of the "proper" goal of Hegelian dialectic. In effect, we can take the gender critique of the Hegelian ethical standpoint to coincide with a deconstruction of a politics which affirms the rationality of law and truth under the twin guises of the state and revealed religion.

But is this enough? Would Gandhi and Cornell's willingness to confront the law from a position within the law not risk making of Satyagraha and deconstruction a politics of accommodation *nonetheless*? Despite all precautions taken to avoid this fate? Would not a radically aporetic Satyagraha require a questioning of the law in the name of that which cannot be articulated in or by law? A position outside of dialectics altogether?

These are the limits of a preface.

This book is a thought experiment. It imagines a continuation of Hegel's *Phenomenology of Spirit* as Hegel himself might have sketched it had he lived through the history of post-Hegelian thought up through contemporary affirmation of the "closure" of Hegelian philosophy. Thus, the book is written more or less in Hegel's style and it presupposes that its readers have at least a passing familiarity with the basic movements of the *Phenomenology* itself. I have tried, however, to make the book accessible to the reader who is not familiar with the *Phenomenology*; though you will miss many allusions to Hegel's text you will be able, I hope, to assess the argumentative turns of this work on their own merits.

The very idea of writing a sequel to Hegel's *Phenomenology* requires some explanation. To those who believe that Hegel thought he himself had wrapped up all possible developments in the history of thought, this book will seem decidedly un-Hegelian. Perhaps a charitable but skeptical reader will suppose that my task is not to advance beyond the conclusion of Hegel's book, but merely to show why there has been no advance in philosophical thought since Hegel.

To the question of whether or not I see myself as advancing beyond Hegel, my answer is a dutifully Hegelian yes and no. A lot depends—perhaps everything depends—on how we construe Hegel's concept of "absolute knowing." Rather than present my own interpretation of what Hegel might have meant by this term, I have allowed my exposition to trace the development from Hegel's ambiguous exposition of it to the more precise version of something like absolute knowing which I put forward in the final section of this book. I have chosen the term "Satyagraha" in place of the phrase "absolute knowing" to abbreviate my conception of how we ought to reconceive the task of systematic philosophizing to which Hegel's *Phenomenology* is supposed to lead us.

However the standpoint of absolute knowing is conceived, the purpose of a Hegelian-style phenomenology is to raise individuals to this standpoint. Following John McCumber, I take the main burden of such a project to consist in communicating with those individuals who are resistant to adopting this standpoint.[1] My task in *The Owl at Dawn* has therefore been to take up as many of the substantive anti-Hegelian philosophical positions since Hegel as I could and to try to communicate with whatever real individuals happen to embrace one of these positions. Obviously I cannot claim completeness for this project. But incompleteness is not, as it has sometimes been thought to be, a devastating charge against Hegelian phenomenology; one does not "refute" the *The Brothers Karamazov* simply by noting that Dostoevsky failed to present a complete inventory of the theological views of everyone in nineteenth-century Russia.

Following Judith Butler, I read Hegel's *Phenomenology* as a *Bildungsroman* rather than as a philosophical treatise in the conventional sense. Like Hegel, I am telling a story. Butler sees a tension between the fictive "narrative structure" of Hegel's text and the "metaphysical case" that Hegel appears to be trying to make with it.[2] She explicates this tension by viewing Hegel's text as "a study in fiction-making which shows the essential role of fiction and false belief in the quest for philosophical truth."[3] But the intended telos of Hegel's *Bildungsroman* is something very different from fiction; for Hegel, Butler reminds us, absolute knowing is supposed to be the systematic grasp of the *truth* of the subject that knows itself as spirit. Butler also shows how twentieth-century appropriations of Hegel have subverted the metaphysical construal of the subject of absolute knowing. In the end, perhaps, we can read the *Phenomenology* only as a presentation of fictions. "From Hegel through Foucault, it appears that desire makes us into strangely fictive beings. And the laugh of recognition appears to be the occasion of insight."[4] I have tried to write *The Owl at Dawn* as a procession of fiction-making which, though it does issue in some form of systematic thinking, does not issue in any grasp of the truth. To become aware of our fictions as fictions, as Butler aptly puts it, can be an "occasion of insight." Satyagraha, as I conceive it, is not "the truth." Yet it gives expression, I believe, to a profound insight of ultimate philosophical significance.

---

1. "The *Phenomenology* is an attempt, then, to communicate the absolute standpoint to an individual who is resistant to the message, who attempts to remain in one's 'impenetrable independence.'" John McCumber, *The Company of Words: Hegel, Language, and Systematic Philosophy* (Evanston: Northwestern University Press, 1993), p. 152.
2. Judith Butler, *Subjects of Desire: Hegelian Reflections in Twentieth-Century France* (New York: Columbia University Press, 1987), p. 17.
3. Ibid., p. 23.
4. Ibid., p. 238.

How can a text that is "only" a set of fictions lay claim to giving us philosophical insights? The answer—and here I go back to the work of McCumber—is that the proper goal of philosophical inquiry may very well be something other than the grasp of truth. "The term 'truth' should be reserved for whatever it is that distinguishes sentences which inform us about the world from sentences which misinform us, and philosophy should at last recognize that it has goals which are generically different from this."[5] To say that philosophy aims at something other than the truth is not to say that it has nothing to do with truth claims. Satyagraha represents a "new *practice* of philosophy"[6] which does not proclaim possession of the truth but which rather insists on the non-violent resolution of all battles over the truth.

To become a Satyagrahi is not to absent oneself from the realm of violent struggle; one must reenter the dialectic with the aim of quelling the violence. Often one can do this only by taking sides in a particular struggle, and there are usually good reasons why one position should be defended at the expense of another.

Although I borrow the idea of Satyagraha as a philosophical practice from Gandhi and his followers, I present it in somewhat different form. I am not sure that Gandhi himself would have accepted my view of Satyagraha as abandoning all claims to absolute truth, and he certainly did not proclaim that religion and violence go hand in hand. On the contrary, Gandhi declared his own personal allegiance to *all* religions, and to this extent he seems to characterize Satyagraha as embracing, rather than deconstructing, claims to absolute truth. The distinction between my neither/nor logic and Gandhi's both/and logic might seem of little consequence since I agree that Satyagraha entails respect for every individual who claims to possess the truth. But here, I think, a distinction between persons and positions becomes important. In my sense of the term, Satyagraha obliges us to respect all *positions* primarily insofar as they are held by *persons*, not insofar as they intrinsically possess a part of the truth. Religion collapses the distinction between persons and positions by declaring an absolute bond between individuals and their beliefs. As a result, religiously committed individuals are forced to equate openness to other positions with death. It seems to me not accidental that Gandhi's greatest political failure was his inability to reconcile the religious conflicts of the Indian people. Rather than try in

---

5. McCumber, *The Company of Words*, p. 25.
6. This phrase, though with wholly different content since he is defending a Leninist rather than a Gandhian model of philosophical practice, appears in Louis Althusser, "Lenin Before Hegel," in *Lenin and Philosophy and Other Essays*, trans. Ben Brewster (New York: Monthly Review Press, 1971), p. 107.

vain to bring essentially antagonistic religious traditions together, I wonder if the Satyagrahi might be more successful trying to deconstruct all religious traditions.

In this respect, I would draw a parallel between Gandhi and Hegel. Butler describes the tension between Hegel's imaginative experiment in fiction-making and his failure to recognize that what he was doing was writing fiction. In a similar vein, McCumber suggests that Hegel is good at constructing narratives but unaware of the need to deconstruct them. "Precisely because Hegel is the most rigorous exploration we have of the narrative side of situating reason, he leaves out. . . . the side that deconstructs, or as I prefer to call it demarcates, the narratives it spins."[7] It seems to me that Gandhi was like Hegel in that he was able to articulate an all-embracing narrative but he was unable to recognize the need for its deconstruction; in both philosophers, this comes out in their attempts to affirm the truth of all religions. By contrast, I present my ideal of a more Nietzschean Satyagrahi, a Butlerian Hegelian who forsakes the sphere of religion altogether. The Satyagrahi who has abandoned the pretension to possess truth does not claim to have grasped the essence of any position other than her own. What she critiques in other positions is not their content but their form—the fact that they have the character of truth claims.

In this respect, the ideal of the Nietzschean Satyagrahi finds an obvious exemplar in the figure of Socrates, whose sole claims to the truth are (1) that he himself knows he does not possess the truth, and (2) that he has never met anyone else who did. The distinction between positions and persons is also a crucial one for Socrates. In the *Euthyphro* Plato suggests that Socrates would never even think of prosecuting a person, yet as all the dialogues show us, he never tires of prosecuting positions.[8] Socrates teaches Euthyphro to make this same distinction, demonstrating to this would-be prosecutor of a person that no one who fails to know the truth has the right to do violence to another person. Moreover, the distinction between just violence and unjust violence is radically rejected in the *Republic*, where Socrates insists that the function of justice can never be to do harm to anyone, not even to those who act unjustly.[9] Like Socrates, the Satyagrahi I envision in the final section of this book tries to show that none of us is

---

7. McCumber, *The Company of Words*, p. 27.

8. "Euthyphro: How is that? You mean that somebody is prosecuting you? I never would believe that you were prosecuting anybody else.

"Socrates: No indeed."

Plato, "Euthyphro," trans. Lane Cooper, in *Plato: The Collected Dialogues*, eds. Edith Hamilton and Huntington Cairns (Princeton: Princeton University Press, 1963), p. 170 (2b).

9. Plato, "Republic," trans. Paul Shorey, in *Plato: The Collected Dialogues*, p. 585 (335b–e).

entitled to do violence in defense of the positions we adopt. However, although no position is worth the price of *doing violence*, most are of value for reasons other than their claims to being the truth. Fictions can be worth defending, even when this entails *suffering* violence. To disabuse someone of claiming absolute truth for a philosophical position is thus not necessarily to try to get her to "abandon" the position. Socrates does not try to dissuade Euthyphro from his belief that his father's act of manslaughter was wrong, nor that this belief might entail obligations to act of a sort other than the seeking of violent retribution. The work of the Satyagrahi is therefore not to get us to be ironic about our commitments—as Richard Rorty would have it—but to keep our commitments subordinate to the overarching requirement of non-violence.

In several crucial respects, however, Socrates himself falls short of the ideal of the Satyagrahi. Specifically, he fails to expand the scope of his notion of "we" to cover all of those individuals who are "other" to the Athenian polis in some way. Thus, although he refuses to do violence to Leon of Salamis so long as the latter is in principle protected by Athenian law, he apparently has no compunction against killing non-Athenians when waging war outside of the city limits. Similarly, on his deathbed, he contemptuously sends Xanthippe back to the sphere of the family, though he would never even think to expel any of his male companions from the "we" of their community. Finally, in the *Crito* Socrates not only articulates an absolute duty to obey the laws of the state, but also he maintains that to be viewed by the citizens of a polis as an "other" is far more shameful than to be a citizen who proudly belongs to a polis which violently excludes others.[10] In general, these failures to recognize the exclusion of otherness arise because Socrates retains a parochial notion of the identity of the "we" of his community. In the penultimate section of this book, I critique the similarly parochial position of the "traditionalist," a perspective that is to be found in the work of Alasdair MacIntyre and others. Satyagraha requires us to undertake the burden of thinking who "we" are in as broad a way as possible, keeping in view the ideal of a community that would recognize both "radical confluence" and "radical diversity," as Bill Martin has put it.[11] It also requires that we deconstruct this ideal.

---

10. "As for yourself, if you go to one of the neighboring states, such as Thebes or Megara, which are both well governed, you will enter them as an enemy to their constitution, and all good patriots will eye you with suspicion as a destroyer of law and order. . . . Do you intend, then, to avoid well-governed states and the higher forms of human society? And if you do, will life be worth living?" Plato, "Crito," trans. Hugh Tredennick, in *Plato: The Collected Dialogues*, p. 38 (53b–c).

11. Bill Martin, *Matrix and Line: Derrida and the Possibilities of Postmodern Social Theory* (Albany: State University of New York Press, 1992), p. 19 and passim.

Perhaps it is impossible to be a "true" Satyagrahi. Certainly, I write this text conscious of the gap between myself and every one of my conceptual personae. In the spirit of Gilles Deleuze and Félix Guattari, I have tried to diagram intersecting "planes of immanence." Satyagraha would be "THE plane of immanence," the Satyagrahi the persona proper to it."[12]

Because I have written *The Owl at Dawn* in the style of the *Phenomenology*, I have not used proper names when referring to any of the personae I discuss. A *Bildungsroman* is not, after all, a work of history; it is a fictional adaptation of historical material. Just as it is obvious that Hegel's sections on sense-certainty and perception address the epistemological doctrines of Hume and Locke even though neither is mentioned by name, so it will be obvious to the reader familiar with the history of western philosophy since Hegel "whose" persona I have in mind when I discuss, for example, the "transcendental phenomenologist" (Husserl), the "psychologist of Christianity" (Nietzsche), or the "antitotalitarianist" (Arendt). As such, *The Owl at Dawn* is perhaps better described as a thinly disguised philosophical *roman à clef*. In many places, I have made free use of well-known phrases that are associated with particular philosophers. In discussing the "phenomenologist of revelation," for instance, I have invoked Heidegger's notorious "Only a god can save us now."

The danger with this approach is that I may be accused of having shirked the responsibilities of genuine scholarship. By critiquing, for instance, not the text of Heidegger but the imagined position of the phenomenologist of revelation, I do not explicitly cite textual evidence to convince the reader that I have adequately characterized the thought of *Heidegger*. Yet, I do not merely claim narrative coherence for this book; I claim to have provided a *faithful* exposition of Heidegger's position when I discuss the position of the phenomenologist of revelation. The burden of demonstrating the accuracy or inaccuracy of my characterizations I have simply left up to the reader. Moreover, in the end, I do not claim—as Hegel apparently does—to have "summed up" any of the positions I discuss. The Satyagrahis do not look back on the process leading up to their standpoint as a closed system that has been fully elucidated. On the contrary, knowing that they know nothing, the Satyagrahis acknowledge that every prior position is one to which we might perpetually return and reconsider. For this reason, although I have tried to articulate the shortcomings of every position discussed in this book, I have also deliberately left open the possibility that a person who wishes to defend or revise any of them—or show

---

12. Cf. the recent works of Deleuze and Guattari.

that I have omitted crucial positions—can do so. The over-arching aim of this book is extremely modest. My principal concern is only to show that *when* we take up philosophical positions—or, say, when we think "with so-and-so" or "against so-and-so"—we should do so *as* Satyagrahis. Socrates is always willing to reconsider a position even if it already seems to have been refuted.

Finally, an additional reason why I have resisted using proper names in the course of the narrative proper is that I do not merely mean to suggest that someone, say, other than Nietzsche or Heidegger could revitalize the Nietzschean or Heideggerian positions—as many, obviously, have done—but rather that there is doubtless more to *Heidegger's* Heideggerianism or *Nietzsche's* Nietzscheanism than anyone could ever sum up. The temptation to reduce persons to positions is, I would argue, the religious impulse which leads us away from "Satyagratic discursive practices" to violent dialectical confrontation.

Following the writing style of Hegel by not "naming names" seemed to serve my purpose of stressing the distinction between persons and positions. But the concomitant risk would be that I absolve myself from responsibility for what I am saying about the ideas of actual persons. Accordingly, and at the advice of several readers, I have decided to include a "cast of characters" list, along with the names of some of the actual philosophers whose positions I have had in mind.

Because no position is ever absolutely rejected, the transitions—the determinate negations—of *The Owl at Dawn* cannot be viewed as *Aufhebungen* in the usual Hegelian sense. When a position is critiqued, it is not "taken up" in Hegel's sense but rejected. Yet at the same time, it is left behind as something that can be "taken up" again by someone who thinks the position has not been given its due. This latter possibility of "taking up" has a different sense from the former. Because Hegel may have thought his narrative was complete he seems to have believed that he had captured the essence of every one of the positions he had traced. Because I do not claim truth for my narrative I present the Satyagrahi as ready to rethink any of the previous positions.

For this reason, the structure of this book is not that of a ladder which I ask the reader to kick away after he or she has climbed to the top. The model of text-as-ladder-to-be-kicked-away seems to me to carry with it the sense that the author wants to leave you stranded somewhere. As conceived by Hegel, the concept of absolute knowing may or may not be some such stranded place, but Satyagraha certainly should not be. Neither is the structure of this book an architectonic one, for although I claim systematic coherence for it, I do not view its various stages as leading to a finished construction. A better model for thinking about this book is that of an unfinishable map. I would compare myself to Kafka's Land-Surveyor K. who comes to a town in which there are numerous castles. Instead of seeking permission to enter any of them, he simply sets out to chart the territory. He realizes that the castles are perpetually undergoing renovation and that new castles—as well as things that may or may not be castles—are also being built, so he sees that his work can only be provisional. Nonetheless, he tries to carry out his task as honestly as he can.

It should be noted that the structure of *The Owl at Dawn* parallels the structure of the *Phenomenology of Spirit* in numerous ways, often down to fine detail. The reasons for this are several. First, as already indicated, I have genuinely tried to make this the sequel which Hegel himself might have written had he lived through the end of the twentieth century. Second, I have found that the structure of Hegel's text is a remarkably flexible dialectical tool that can be used to organize the history of post-Hegelian thought. In saying this, I do not mean to imply that all thought is necessarily Hegelian, but only that the history of nineteenth- and twentieth-century philosophy has remained very much within the dialectical parameters articulated by Hegel. The danger of my use of Hegel's structure, of course, is that I may at times be guilty of "forcing" a particular position to fit into a certain mold. There is no worse Hegelianism, as good Hegelians know, than the Procrustean variety. That I have not followed the Hegelian form for its sake can be seen, at least, in those places where I have departed from it; for instance, I have at times been led to depict dialectical movements of consciousness and self-consciousness more or less simultaneously. In general, I have tried to follow Hegel's method of allowing the content to unfurl on its own. But obviously the composition of a philosophical work of this sort cannot consist, Hegel's view to the contrary notwithstanding, in merely passively recording a process which generates itself. It is I, the advocate of a particular position, who have arranged the material; but I have tried to let the material inform me about how it should be arranged.

Where a series of positions which I am presenting is strikingly similar to a series of positions which Hegel presents, I have tended to abbreviate my discussion. The idea is that, if the reader has read the *Phenomenology*, she knows what to expect from *The Owl at Dawn* in its parallel passages. An example of such truncation can be found in the section on "Real socialism." It is remarkable to me how much Hegel's description of the realm of ethical spirit prefigures the movement from the Russian Revolution to the collapse of the Soviet Union and the subsequent Americanization of Eastern Europe. This was a comparatively easy—if depressing—section to compose.

One final note—my use of masculine and feminine pronouns is meant to reflect the manner in which gender comes up as a factor in the positions under question.

1 (EE.) • The Dialectic of Absolute Knowing

In absolute knowing, the distinction between subject and object has fallen away. Spirit is that form of self-certainty which grasps its own notion—namely, the notion of science. As consciousness, it has the form of objectivity, and its content is nothing other than its own self-mediation. But since consciousness now recognizes that this mediation is its own act, it is no longer divided into a consciousness and the world it confronts. Rather, consciousness knows itself to be this world. Spirit is thus immediately present to itself in the individual absolute knower, an immediacy which it brings to itself by reflecting explicitly on its own self-mediating experience.

Spirit is the single individual's consciousness of itself as being identical with the universal self-consciousness. This no longer signifies, as it did at the level of the beautiful soul, that the individual affirms merely his own identity with the universal while denying this to others. In absolute knowing, as in revealed religion, the distinction between the "we" and the "I" has fallen away. Each individual receives from others a recognition of his participation in the universal precisely insofar as he grants them this same recognition.

Now, from the standpoint of absolute knowing, all earlier standpoints have been superseded and taken up in this final shape of spirit. Yet in nature, the previous shapes of spirit have not been thus superseded, but rather can be found existing in and for themselves as particular manifestations of the totality of spirit. Thus, although all these previous shapes can no longer have any independent validity for the spirit that is raised to the standpoint of absolute knowing, there remain individuals for whom an earlier shape of spirit appears itself to be an endpoint rather than a mere stage along the way. These independently existing shapes manifest themselves under the guise of the various religions. And although each cannot claim for itself the absolute standpoint, nonetheless each expresses a moment of the absolute and so is valid as such.

But in another respect, the spirit raised to the standpoint of absolute knowing recognizes only one of these religious shapes as possessing the right to claim for itself the absolute truth of its perspective—namely, revealed religion. In absolute knowing, spirit articulates itself to itself as the systematic, notional comprehension of that particular content which is depicted in revealed religion; philosophy has merely purified revealed religion's absolute knowing of its representational character. Yet although revealed religion is posited by absolute knowing as being in and for itself the most intelligent form of this picture-thinking, nonetheless absolute knowing must chide it for its failing to rise to the level of the notion. Moreover, as the determinate negation of the sphere of religion in general, philosophy transcends the internecine battles of all the earlier stages of spiritual combat, and as such it has no special allegiance to any particular religion. To privilege so-called revealed religion over any other religion would be like defending the apple's superiority to the leaf, or the leaf's superiority to the branch, just because it appears later in time. Accordingly, absolute knowing both does and does not posit itself as the truth of revealed religion. But this contradiction has not been made explicit yet. Indeed, the truth of philosophy's independence from religion will reveal itself only after the achievement of absolute knowing has collapsed.

That the question of the relationship between revealed religion and philosophy remains unraised does not merely signify an uncertain wrinkle in the fabric of absolute knowing that can quickly be ironed out. This ambiguity rather threatens to unravel the very fabric itself. For the broaching of this question will signify the splitting up of absolute knowing into a consciousness which affirms the truth of revealed religion and a consciousness which negates this truth. But the consciousness that negates this truth will no longer put itself forth as possessing the absolute, for on the contrary it will be the explicit consciousness of the failure of absolute knowing. Instead of seeking reconciliation, the unsatisfied absolute knower will lash out against this latter consciousness, declaring the necessity of its destruction. In this way, the dialectic of the unraveling of absolute knowing will culminate not in a reconciliation, but rather in a canceling of the mutual confessions which earlier inaugurated the stage of the religious community in the first place. With this rescinding, we will leave the realm of the spiritual absolute and enter a new shape of consciousness—the consciousness of language.

But this sphere is as yet a long way off; it will appear on the scene only after the dialectic of absolute knowing has passed through the self-actualization of individual absolute knowers (EE), and the concomitant recapitulation of the dialectic of spirit in its materialist mode (FF).

That the dialectic did not reach its final resting-place with the immediate achievement of absolute knowing springs from the fact that this achievement is, precisely, only immediate. To be sure, the absolute stand-point is an immediacy achieved by way of mediation, but this unity of immediacy and mediation is itself something only immediate at first. The individual absolute knower who knows himself as spirit, despite his certainty of the unity of the universal with the individual, must actualize this certainty and so raise it to the level of truth. The absolute knower must accordingly descend from the divine heights of his philosophical Olympus in order to enter, once again, the fray of earthly history, to accomplish the actual work of mediation—if, indeed, this is possible at all.

A. Independence and Dependence of Absolute Knowing: The Philosophical Master Presumed to Know and those who Presume he Knows it

The earlier dialectic of self-consciousness raised the self-consciousness of two individual "I's" to the standpoint of the "we" of a rational society. Having achieved the truth of this "we," each individual then again had to struggle to reconcile his own individual "I" with it; this was the struggle between the individual's pleasure principle and society's reality principle—the struggle for the individual to actualize his rational self-consciousness. By finding for himself a way of living in which he sees his own law united with the law of society—that is, by becoming Oedipalized—the individual managed to achieve the truth which he expresses in the identification of the "I" with the "we." The word *spirit* was then used to express this perceived identity. But no sooner had the individual affirmed this identity than he found himself again (though not always self-consciously) recapitulating the earlier struggles for recognition. For the "we" of spirit was at first a split subject, divided between its existence as a totality which exists for the sake of its individual members and the individual members who exist for the sake of the totality. In other words, the identification of the individual's pleasure-seeking with the good of society turned out to be ambiguous to the extent that it was left unclear which of the terms of the equation was the substantial subject and which the mere predicate. Is it that I, the individual, am the substantial subject and the community merely one of my attributes, or is it that I, the community, am the substantial subject and the individual merely one of my attributes? The uncertainty here—or rather the splitting up of the community into those who are certain of the former truth and those who are certain of the latter—played itself out in the confrontation between the divine law and the human law. Thus, the individual once again found himself struggling for recognition. But instead of confronting another individual (dialectic of self-consciousness) or a mere collection of individuals (dialectic of rational self-consciousness), the individual now found himself pitted against the reified, substantial "we" of society. The dialectic of spirit ultimately resolved itself with the de-reification of the "we" which took place in the transition from the state to the religious community. Once again, the individual could identify with the "we" of community, but now without losing his own individual self-consciousness.

Looking back over this entire process, we see that the individual "I" had first to work up to the "we" of society (dialectic of self-consciousness), and then back from this "we" to the individual "I" (dialectic of spirit). Hence, the ultimate identification of the "I" with the "we" in absolute knowing actually signifies two distinct and hence only seemingly tautological achievements: [I = we] + [we = I]. Viewed as the major and minor premises of a syllogism, the conclusion is, of course, the [I = I] which the individual absolute knower claims for himself at the end of the process. It is just the achievement of this third term by way of the first two which constitutes the immediacy that has arisen out of mediation.

Now, to the individual absolute knower at first raised to this standpoint, the whole matter appears settled. But in fact it is not. For the identification of [I = I] rests on a merely immediate consciousness of the identity of the [I = we] with the [we = I]. The individual absolute knower is, of course, certain of their identity, but this certainty has not yet been raised to the level of truth. In the equation [I = I] which *results* from the process of mediation, the "I" on the left side of the equation and the "I" on the right side of the equation are identical only from the standpoint of the individual who has completed this movement. Now, were this merely the [I = I] of immediate self-consciousness, there would be no problem. But in absolute knowing, the [I = I] posits the identity of this individual "I" with every other individual "I," and as such the two sides of the equation are not identical but different. The certainty that [I = I] is merely immediate because it is only a particular individual absolute knower who claims their equivalence.

To be sure, the absolute knower lays claim to this certainty on the basis of the movements which constitute the major and minor premises of the syllogism—the [I = I] has been mediated by the [I = we] and the [we = I]. But this assumes that the two premises have in fact been reconciled with each other; that is, the absolute knower must assume the equivalence of the [I = we] with the [we = I]. This equivalence, however, is as yet not something achieved but merely something posited by the individual absolute knower. For itself—that is, for the individual absolute knower—the [I = we] and the [we = I] appear to be absolute equivalents. But in itself, the truth of absolute knowing has split these into distinct moments: {[I = we] is not equal to [we = I]}. This split, though, manifests itself not in the individual absolute knower's consciousness, but appears rather in the different consciousnesses of distinct individuals. Thus, the individual philosopher, though in and for himself conscious of being at the absolute standpoint, will remain ignorant of the tenuousness of his achievement until he is forced to confront another individual who also claims to have reached the absolute standpoint. The rupture between the [I = we] and the [we = I] reveals itself when two absolute knowers share their different truths with each other.

Despite his initial ignorance of the insufficiency of his achievement, the philosopher is nonetheless aware of a need to encounter another individual who will confirm him in his claim to the absolute standpoint, and so he immediately sets out to seek this recognition. But he can be recognized as an absolute knower—as a philosopher of the absolute—only by another philosopher of the absolute. This peculiarity is not, in one respect, due to any special feature of philosophers, but follows merely from the general fact that an expert in any field can only be recognized as such by another expert in the same field. Yet in another respect, there is something special in the case of the philosopher of the absolute; in claiming for himself the standpoint of absolute knowing, he is conscious of a self-identity which can be acknowledged only by someone who shares this consciousness. Just as earlier, when he first achieved self-consciousness, the individual had required the recognition not of merely another consciousness, such as that of an animal, but of another self-consciousness, that is, of a human, so this time the recognition of another "merely human" self-consciousness will not suffice; the absolute knower must be recognized by another who is self-conscious of his own identity with the absolute—that is, by a "divine" absolute knower. Put otherwise, he is conscious of himself as [I = I], but in the mediated sense of recognizing this self-identity through the mediation of the "we"; hence to be recognized as a self-identical "I" in *this* sense requires not encountering merely another self-conscious individual, but a similarly mediated self-conscious absolute knower. He cannot settle for any of the types of recognition that had earlier satisfied (or, rather, not satisfied) him on his journey to this standpoint.

In *seeking* recognition, the absolute knower at first has no reason to fear that he might have to *struggle* for recognition as he did earlier. This is because he has reached the standpoint of absolute knowing precisely by already having recognized another who recognizes him. The series of confessions which leads ultimately to the coming-together of the religious community suggests, in fact, that the absolute knower has already achieved his status in the company of others. Put otherwise, his self-recognition as absolute knower should already contain within it a reciprocal recognition between himself and at least one other who has traveled with him on his journey. By definition, moreover, the fellow absolute knower he seeks is an individual who, by definition, *will* recognize him. Thus, although the absolute knower still requires recognition, it would seem a simple matter of acquiring it; he need only turn to his philosophical companion and each will acknowledge the other. The externality of confession in speech is no longer even necessary; for each knows within himself that the other knows that he and the other have both attained the absolute.

Such silence is surely golden. But it is a fool's gold, for so long as their mutual recognition remains merely something inner, it signifies nothing higher than the easy agreement of those who have nothing to say. Were they to remain silent, theirs would be a mere phrenology of the gaze. In order to make real what they already believe they know to be fully actualized, they must resume speaking to each other. Their speech is, at first, rich in its gentle tones, each rewarding itself with the kindness of its words to the other. But this gentleness *toward the other* is at once both necessary and impossible. It is necessary, for the mediated [I = I] of the individual absolute knower must perform the sacrament of going out to the other in order to return to himself as a genuinely mediated, rather than selfishly immediate, "I." But it is equally impossible, because, in the first place, in reaching out towards the other he is doing so only in order to return to himself, and in the second place, in recognizing himself in the other he is in fact encountering the other not as other but as himself in his own externality. For the "thou" which exists in the moment of the "we," is now taken up into the mere—albeit mediated—"I" of the individual. Therefore in his apparent solicitude toward the other, each absolute knower is in actuality being kind only to himself. In an effort to balance these conflicting moments, the absolute knower tries to affirm both his identity with the other and his difference from the other. Toward this end, the gentle tones of his speech are offered in a sincere attempt to recognize the other as other; but this is done so that the other will not assert his otherness. Thus, the gentle speech of the absolute knowers is in bad faith, for each claims to recognize the other, but does so only to the extent that the other's otherness is denied.

This narcissism of an absolute knowing that recognizes the otherness of the other only to the degree to which this gift-giving enables each to give something to himself, now leads to each one's discovering that the more his own otherness is affirmed by the other, the more in fact the other recognizes only himself. But rather than blame the other, each at first blames himself. The reason for this is that each sees both that, as an absolute knower, he himself can be recognized only by an absolute knower whose otherness he recognizes for the other's own sake, and yet that at the same time he is not really recognizing the other for the sake of the other but for his own sake. In other words, each absolute knower becomes aware of his own narcissism and views this as what stands in the way of their reciprocal recognition. Accordingly, he sets out to undermine his own narcissism by redoubling his efforts to recognize the other for his otherness. He sees, moreover, that the other does the same for him, and so he is rewarded for his efforts. But he also sees the other similarly rewarded, and in fact he becomes conscious of the fact that it is the other's narcissism which underlies his solicitousness. Yet he cannot in good conscience blame the other for this, because in becoming aware of his resentment of the other he realizes that he himself had similarly been recognizing the other only in order to be recognized. He realizes, in other words, that his own condemnation of his own narcissism was also performed for narcissistic reasons. The absolute knower is thus perpetually in bad faith, for no matter how sincere the effort to respect the other for the sake of the other, beneath his apparent gift-giving there lurks the expectation of exchange. The movement, whereby the absolute knower tries to usurp this, his own expectation of reciprocal exchange by giving freely to the other, is always in contradiction with itself. And this same contradiction is of course mirrored in the other, who performs precisely the same movements. As such, the pair enter on a kind of inverse path such as was found in the struggle to the death, which eventually ended up in a sort of mutual kindness; for here, they struggle for kindness but threaten to kill each other with it. Each denies the other, seeks to overcome this denial of the other by acknowledging the other, thereby further denying the other, and so on. This bad infinite of the dialogue of absolute knowers eventually leads to a point where each is virtually identical to the other in their thoughts, their way of speaking, their manner of dressing, and so forth, for each has tried to accommodate himself to the other absolutely. At restaurants, for instance, they say, "No, I'll have what you're having," "No, no, I'll have what *you're* having," and so on. To an outside observer, they would appear to be the best of friends. Yet the more similar they become, the more they are in fact revolting against each other. This movement eventually comes to an end when one of the pair refuses to acknowledge himself in the other. He notices some very small difference between them—say, the side on which each parts his hair—and insists on the absolute error of the other's way. This is the narcissism of minor differences, and indeed it can only concern a difference that is minor, for were it a major difference between them they would follow the initial instinct of desiring to affirm the other's otherness. If one suddenly announced he was a pederast, the other would affirm it as something to be praised. But let him announce that he will wear his trousers unrolled, and the other accuses him of the most unforgivable sin.

The tenuous link between them is now broken, as each realizes that the other's apparently total recognition was in fact no real recognition at all. Yet each still requires recognition—and, moreover, recognition from each other, for each still requires the recognition of another who is conscious of being at the absolute standpoint. Accordingly, there emerges between them a recapitulation of the earlier struggle for recognition. Yet it is still not a struggle to the death, for each knows full well he requires the other's recognition. At the same time, each now believes that the other's demand to be recognized is one-sided, while not acknowledging that his own demand is similarly one-sided. Each accuses the other of having severed the relationship; each accuses the other of succumbing to a narcissism, but not himself. In this they remain, of course, in bad faith, but it is a bad faith that is necessary for each to retain the pretext of being himself at the absolute standpoint. Moreover, since to affirm the absolute means to postulate not only the possibility but the necessity of mutual recognition, each insists to himself that the other must be made to realize the error of his ways. Yet each cannot recognize the other as being at the absolute standpoint until he is recognized by the other. Their struggle is, accordingly, an immediately unresolvable one. Were they the only two individuals alive, they could remain at this impasse for all eternity, never able to leave each other but never able to come together again.

Luckily, though, they are not the only two individuals alive. There are others, and the struggle for recognition between the pair of absolute knowers now continues under the guise of the struggle for public recognition. The divorce is made public and each blames the other "ex-" for having been an intolerable spouse. More specifically, each pleads his case before the philosophical community, trying to persuade all others that he alone has divined the true absolute. The debate between the two absolute knowers is now mediated through the community, and as such it takes the form of the earlier struggle between the adherents of the law of the divine and the law of the human, each claiming for itself a consciousness of the totality. Yet unlike this earlier shape, the struggle for public recognition is fought not on the battlefield of the state, which for now has dropped out as insignificant from the divine heights of the philosophical community. It is, rather, fought on the battlefield of the notion itself.

Now, from our perspective—that is, those who live in the aftermath of this struggle—it matters little which of the two (or more) absolute knowers eventually wins this struggle. From our standpoint, what is significant is that the struggle can end only when a single proponent of the absolute standpoint wins the recognition of the community of philosophers. In winning this recognition, the victor assumes the status of philosophical master, with all other philosophers, including the one(s) he has defeated in battle, forced to take on the roles of philosophical apprentices.

The fact that there can at first be only one absolute knower is viewed, from the perspective of the community, as a contingent fact—that is, they believe that "it just so happens" that there is one philosophical genius alive in the present moment. But in this the philosophical community itself is in bad faith. For as the struggle for public recognition wages on, the stakes of the struggle become apparent to all. The individual absolute knower lays claim to positing an identity in difference—that is, he claims to recognize that everyone is capable of attaining the absolute standpoint. But as the narcissism of minor differences pointed out, what lurks behind this claim is really the absolute knower's desire to have everyone agree with him. Were he to acknowledge this fact, the absolute knower would withdraw from the struggle altogether, conceding that, in fact, he has not attained the absolute standpoint. For truly to attain this standpoint would signify, as he well knows, that he does not merely insist on the absolute validity of his own subjective standpoint. But the absolute knower is not ready to acknowledge this bitter truth, and he can, moreover, persist in his narcissism by continuing to blame his rival for being the one who keeps the public from realizing the truth that he, the true absolute knower, has attained. Furthermore, the rivals themselves, so long as they compete, are encouraged not to withdraw by a philosophical community that is ready to throw its allegiance behind whomever appears destined for victory. For the members of the community also yearn, as do the individual combatants, for the recognition that will come their way if they correctly recognize the one who will be crowned champion. By recognizing the "right" one, they will be confirmed as having the wisdom to have ascertained with Solomonic judgment the difference between the genuine absolute and the sham absolute. Of course, theirs is the most comic position of all, for they fail to notice that it is precisely their own arbitrary decision to label one true and the other false that will lead to the alchemy whereby the arbitrary will take on the luster of the destined, and they can glow in the reflected shine of this magical transformation. They are like children who play "eeny, meeny, miny, moe," and when their finger arrives at the victor they congratulate themselves for having the brilliance to have selected the real McCoy. And so in this way, one of the absolute knowers receives his baptismal recognition.

Now, unlike the uncertain confessing evil consciousness who bares his soul without knowing if he will be returned to himself by a mutually confessing and forgiving other, those confronted by an other who professes beforehand the necessity of performing this movement are promised just such a return in advance. But precisely because nothing need thereby be risked, the movement of confession and forgiveness is too easily performed. This was why it was so easy for those craving absolution to select a winner in the struggle between absolute knowers, rather than denying the title of master to anyone.

Politically, this has the significance that the people are ready for genuine democracy, but can at first come to it only by way of a constitutional monarchy more appropriate for feudal relations than for bourgeois society. In both cases—that is, in both the philosophical and political spheres—the communal bonds are at once based on reciprocity and equality, on the one hand, but also on devotion to a single individual, whose sole right it is to give to them their sense of equality among one another, on the other. In short, they are still too fearful of the terrors of absolute freedom to sever the need for a lord. They have sought a master and they have found one, thereby entering into a servitude which they themselves, however, view as liberation.

Within the philosophical community, the absolute master's rule is a more or less benevolent one—more so for those who lavish praise on him and less so for those who do not. From the perspective of the victorious absolute knower, his victory signifies not the community's arbitrary need for a master of any sort, but rather the truth of his own claim to have achieved the absolute standpoint. He, therefore, remains ignorant of the tenuousness of the recognition that confirms for him the truth of his self-consciousness. Moreover, those who recognize his mastery are themselves ignorant of this as well, for they persist in the bad faith of proclaiming to be the destiny of genius what in fact was the caprice of hero-worship. The master/community relationship can remain in this its tenuous cohesion for some time; indeed, the passage of time will even grant it a more secure, if no less illusory, sense of legitimacy. For the more that he and the community shore up the pretense that he alone has achieved the absolute standpoint, the more they all believe that he is truly unique.

Yet their acknowledgment of the master as master is granted on the condition that the master reciprocate, after a fashion. The asymmetry of the relationship prevents him from recognizing that they, too, are masters, but he must grant to them certain rights and entitlements. The philosophical community is ruled by a type of feudal lord who acknowledges his serfs' entitlements to plant and reap in their little plots of absolute knowing, so long as they recognize that he is the one to whom all right of ownership to the land and its products is conceded.

Those who ascribe to the master the status of absolute knower do not realize that it is they, rather than he, who possess the right to pronounce who is and who is not at the absolute standpoint. They have, in short, fetishized him, and for this reason they view it as just that they should merely be day-laborers in the great field of the system. For this reason too, they readily take on the role of missionaries as well; only tell us the truth, they say to the master, and we will mouth it unto the people.

These individual missionaries are in this way conscious of the gulf that separates them from the master—and, accordingly, for it signifies for them the same thing—of the gulf that separates them from the absolute standpoint, which, as serfs, they both do and do not possess. Because they do not recognize the fetishistic character of their relationship to the master, they view his mastery as something naturally given—he is a genius. But this means that they are alienated from their own work; for they give to him the "natural" right to possess the system itself, as if he had climbed the tree of knowledge and plucked its ripe fruit. Accordingly, they view themselves as lacking the competence to judge the master, despite the fact that this sense of incompetence has arisen merely from their judging him to be superior. This sense of incompetence they experience as a lack; they lack what the master has—namely, the absolute standpoint. But this experience of lack signifies their inability to know what it is the master has which they lack. They can therefore only presume to know that the master knows what they do not know. Moreover, their inability to say what it is that the master has which they lack they see as confirmation of the master's having "it." The master, then, is the subject presumed to know, though they know not what it is they presume him to know. The *absolute* is a perfect name for what it is the master is supposed to know, because it is a word that says nothing. All this might be put in the form of a circular argument: Q. What is the absolute? A. What the master knows. Q. What does the master know? A. The absolute. The master's disciples are forever watching him to see a sign that will reveal to them his hidden secret knowledge.

So long as the subject presumed to know the absolute lives, he stands in a privileged place with respect to the possibility of absolute knowing. His thoughts are granted an authority which his disciples attribute to the master's ability to identify with the absolute to a degree to which they themselves cannot yet do. The individual disciple accordingly resolves to shut off his own thinking and absorb the thinking of the master, for it is the latter alone that is the truth. From the master he will learn how to think properly—that is, to think from the perspective of the absolute. What is absurd in this movement, of course, is that the disciple believes that he will learn the art of thinking for himself precisely by shutting off his own thoughts. He himself, in fact, is made aware of this absurdity—though not by his own thinking, which he denies, but by none other than that of the master. For as teacher of absolute knowing, the master expects others to confirm his own thinking by their duplicating it for themselves; after all, he still needs to be recognized by someone who is himself really and truly an absolute knower and not merely a disciple. His status as master, moreover, has enabled him to suspend the narcissism from which this need springs, and so he has returned to the solicitude of the absolute knower toward those who recognize him. For these reasons, he indulges a false modesty, denying that he alone is unique, and preaches the doctrine that one can only learn the art of thinking by thinking for oneself from the outset. The master invites his disciple to dine and exchange thoughts with him. The blustery disciple, having shut off his thinking and ready to obey the thoughts of the master, is in this way instructed to begin thinking again, and in obedience he does this. But no sooner does he start thinking for himself than he finds that his own thoughts do not always correspond to those of the master. To the disciple, this can signify only that he himself has fallen short of the absolute again; and the master's expressed disagreements with him are felt as the most violent blows to his sense of self. Whether because the master now expects universal assent from his disciple or whether the disciple himself can think only as a disciple, he again resolves to be guided by the thinking of the master. The dialogues between master and disciple always end with each one returning to his role; neither achieves any genuine recognition from the other.

The master and his disciples find themselves in the same type of mutual alienation which was experienced in the earlier master/slave dialectic, and they now recapitulate its movements. That is, they will pass through stages of alienation analogous to those which we have already seen under the guises of stoicism, skepticism, and the unhappy consciousness. But whereas in the dialectic of self-consciousness, each struggled to achieve his sense of being an *individual*, in the ensuing dialectic here, each struggles to achieve the consciousness as an *absolute knower*. But in their formal structures, the two movements parallel each other: just as with the earlier dialectic, so here the dialectic can resolve itself only with a mutual confession that leads from two isolated subjects to the mutual recognition of the [I = we]. It will then be necessary to recapitulate the movement back from the [I = we] to the [we = I]. But by then we will have left the dialectic of absolute knowing and entered the dialectic of materialist spirit. For now, we enter the dialectical movements associated with the *philosophical community*.

B. Freedom of Absolute Knowing: The Philosophical Community

The philosophical community reaches a point of stability once the master/ disciple relationship has been established. Unlike the struggle between the absolute knowers, the fetishized master has been recognized as the privileged absolute knower. This means that all philosophical disagreements can be resolved by deferring to him, the subject presumed to know. Previously, disagreements between the rival absolute knowers threatened to under-mine the idea that any individual could attain the absolute standpoint. But the privileged standing of the "true" master now obviates this problem. However, it is obviated only because it has been repressed; so long as no rival claimants to the status of master appear on the scene, the illusion that all particular absolute knowers will agree with one another can be sus-tained. Because the contradiction implied in the idea of multiple absolute knowers has been repressed, the philosophical community fails to recog-nize that its continued existence requires that there be only one master. Hence it appears to the members of this community a mere contingency of circumstance that there is one individual who stands ahead of all the oth-ers; they collectively sustain the false illusion that, in principle, everyone could attain the status of master. As already indicated, they view the master's supremacy as something natural rather than as socially constructed.

The master thus appears to have actualized his own certainty of having attained the absolute standpoint. However, the disciples are in a more ex-plicitly ambiguous position. On the one hand, they recognize only the master as the true absolute knower; on the other hand, as self-conscious members of the philosophical community, they also claim this title for themselves. To the extent that they pride themselves on having had the insight to recognize the master's mastery, the disciples expect to receive the same recognition in return. Yet to the extent that they acknowledge the gulf separating themselves from the master, they do *not* expect this recip-rocal recognition. So long as they remain disciples, they cannot resolve this contradiction, for to fetishize the master is, precisely, not to see that the master's supposed mastery is merely something fetishized.

However, to the consciousness of a *newcomer* to this philosophical community, the fetishistic character of the relationship between master and disciple will be readily apparent. To him the community appears like a cult. After all, not only do these loyal subjects tell the naked emperor that his clothes are spectacular, but they also genuinely believe themselves to be dazzled by the splendor his finery. But rather than blame the disciples for having fetishized their master, the newcomer assumes that the master has himself seduced them through charlantry. Rather than expose the idea of mastery, therefore, he merely accuses the particular master himself. When the members of this cult offer him the right to become a disciple himself, the pride of his self-consciousness makes him recoil at the thought. As a more recent disciple, he would not win the accolades of a founding fetishizer. But even if he could, he would lack the true fetishizer's ignorance of his fetishization, and so he would be immediately aware of his bad faith. Like the immediately certain self-consciousness, the newcomer prefers to risk death—or, in this case, banishment from the philosophical community—rather than give up his claim to self-certainty. After all, there is no reason why a master who is really no master at all should even be presumed to be a formidable opponent. To become his disciple without a struggle would be like volunteering to be a slave. Refusing to give up his own certainty of self, the newcomer challenges the master's right to the title of absolute knower: he becomes the master's would-be *usurper*.

In his attacks on the cult of absolute knowing, the usurper resumes the struggle between rival absolute knowers, seeking to wrest from the master the right to be called master. In doing so, he makes explicit the latent tension between the authority of the master and the independent thought of the disciples. For by affirming his *own* authority, the usurper does what the disciples themselves would like to do. However, the disciples cannot assert themselves without undermining their claim to a share in the master's holding company; their self-certainty rests on their consciousness of being members of the philosophical community. Thus, although the disciples cannot but envy the usurper, they also resent him for rocking the boat. Accordingly, they respond to his challenge by rallying behind the master.

Now, from one perspective, the usurper appears to be a kind of democratic revolutionary who would overthrow the tyranny of the lord. But in fact he has broken with the master only in order to affirm his *own* mastery. To this extent, he is not at all a democratic thinker, but simply a lord without any loyal subjects. It is for this reason that the disciples have nothing to gain from recognizing him. What they need is to be freed from the self-consciousness of discipleship; all the usurper gives them is the opportunity to switch masters. Not only do they have no particular reason to switch, but also they cannot resurrect the struggle between absolute knowers without risking making plain to themselves the pretense behind their allegiance to any master whatsoever. Therefore, even those willing to follow the lead of the usurper could not follow *him*, but would instead have to claim their *own* independence from the master.

The usurper thus loses his battle for recognition. But he, for his part, cannot return to the fold. Neither can he withdraw from the philosophical community entirely, for like anyone claiming for himself a consciousness of the absolute, he requires the recognition of others. Therefore he stubbornly refuses to acknowledge defeat, and insists on speaking to those who refuse to listen to him. In this way, the usurper wages a perpetual struggle to win from the master his disciples. In order to show his contempt for the master, he goes so far as to try to lecture to the disciples even when the master is speaking to them.

The usurper is conscious of the fact that he cannot remain in his claim to be a master if no one else acknowledges and confirms him in this. Yet at the same time, he knows that he is not a disciple. Without giving up his pretension to mastery, therefore, the usurper now posits the unattainability of true mastery, declaring in effect that he is an absolute knower by virtue of his consciousness that no one is an absolute knower. Thus, he reverts to the position which posits the absolute as something unattainable and as existing in a "beyond."

Conscious of the gulf between the infinitely beyond absolute and his own immediate certainty of this infinite beyond, the usurper stoically persists in his alienation from the rest of the philosophical community. In affirming the unattainability of the absolute, he becomes pessimistic; but insofar as he holds out the hope of having his pessimistic certainty acknowledged as a form of absolute knowing, he remains optimistic about his prospects for being recognized by the community. Like the stoic, the pessimistic usurper proclaims a True and a Good that remain forever beyond the reach of the individual; to this extent he preaches a kind of humility, and he attacks the master for having the hubris to think that he is an absolute knower. But his supposed humility is in direct conflict with his own hubristic desire to be master; everything in his pessimistic consciousness arises from resentment.

The usurper is thus in bad faith. On the one hand, he has attained the certainty that there are no true masters; yet, on the other hand, he professes to be a master himself. Were he to give up this latter pretension, he could present the truth of his certainty to the community. Instead, he prefers to lapse into the loquacious ranting and raving of a self-fetishized genius. In this, his speech resembles that of the individual heart who succumbed to the frenzy of self-conceit. He stoically persists in his blustering ways indefinitely, hoping for one thing only—that he will outlive the master so that he can vie to be crowned the master's successor by those who will still require a master to follow.

While the usurper's pretension to mastery is hypocritical, his claim that there are no masters cannot be completely ignored by the disciples. Especially to the more independent-minded members of the philosophical community, the pessimist shows the absurdity of thinking that one and only one individual can have attained the absolute standpoint. Rejecting not the master's claim to being an absolute knower but the community's claim that the master is unique, these disciples carry out the philosophical community's democratic revolution, declaring everyone in the community to be on equal footing. This is the truth of the *philosophical equal*.

The philosophical equal's self-consciousness has emerged out of the pessimist's refusal to accept the unique status of the master. But unlike the usurper, the philosophical equal does not deny the master his mastery; he merely denies the master his uniqueness. To this extent he remains loyal to the master, but he now expects a kind of reciprocity in his dealings with him. However, the earlier problem of how to resolve diagreements among multiple absolute knowers immediately resurfaces.

The disciples were always willing to defer to the judgment of the master. By contrast, the philosophical equal now expects the master to capitulate at times. For while he does not claim to be right about everything himself, he is certain that the master cannot be right about everything either. However, the philosophical equal is taken aback to find that the fetishized master has gotten quite used to the idea of always being right, and is unwilling to defer to the judgment of others. Outraged at the master's anti-democractic spirit, the philosophical equal is angry at first. But since he lacks the self-confidence of the master, he supposes that he may indeed have judged wrongly. However, since he is certain of himself as a philosophical equal, he cannot simply lapse back into the role of disciple. Depressed, the philosophical equal falls back on the pessimistic truth of the usurper, declaring that no one possesses the absolute truth.

But unlike the pessimist, the philosophical equal does not affirm that there are no masters; rather, he affirms that everyone is a master. To this extent, he maintains that there must be a universal truth which all members of the community can agree on. And, indeed, the form of the community itself provides him with this common element. As a community of absolute knowers, the members of this community share their certainty in the master's way of thinking—that is, in his method. Disagreements arise merely in the application of this method. Hence, the philosophical equal distinguishes between what is idiosyncratic and therefore fallible in the master's thinking—the particular *system* he constructs—and what is universal in it—namely, the *method* of absolute knowing. Specific disagreements can now be blamed on the master's dogmatic insistence on the truth of his own system. By introducing this distinction, the philosophical equal thus becomes reconciled once again to the master—or at least reconciled to one part of the master's teaching. He is now able to think for himself without fearing that discrepancies between his own thinking and that of the master will necessarily vitiate the method of absolute knowing.

What is true is the method. But since possession of the true method should in principle give rise to a true system, this distinction can be made only by distinguishing between the method in itself and the method as it exists for the master. In other words, so long as the master claims truth for his system, the equal cannot in good faith distinguish between the method and the system. Only by severing the absolute link between the master and the method will the distinction between system and method be viable. To sever this link is, of course, to complete the unfinished work of defetishizing the master. But so long as the master exists he carries that aura around with him. Thus, the philosophical equal finds himself wishing for the death of the master. Yet this is a wish which he must immediately repress. For to desire the death of the master would reveal that beneath the longing for a universal method there lurks the conflict between his own thinking and that of the master. In itself, in other words, the desire for the death of the master still signifies a desire to be master. Yet the philosophical equal knows that the ascendancy of the universal method requires that no one be master—or, what amounts to the same thing here, that the method itself be master. What matters is just the abstract universality of the method, the ascendancy of which requires that all masters die. The moment of bad faith in this lies, however, in the fact that the philosophical equal wants this universal agreement because it will signify that he himself is at the absolute standpoint. It is the desire to become God which lurks behind the desire that no one—or everyone—be God. So long as the master lives, the philosophical equal works "within the system." But his proper work is to reform the system. Only once the master dies, therefore, can the philosophical equal take up his true consciousness as the *philosophical reformer*.

The mere certainty that universal agreement is possible *in principle* is not enough; actual agreement in the results of absolute knowing must be reached. The work of the philosophical reformer, accordingly, is to strive to actualize the ideal of universal agreement—or, expressed not in the language of the philosophical community but in political terms—to remake the world so that the real will actually coincide with the rational.

However, the individual reformer is not alone in his desire to carry out the true work of the master—that is, to universalize the master's method. He is one among many former disciples, each of whom has devised his own "system," and naturally they do not all agree about how to define this method. Or, what amounts to the same thing, they differ over their interpretation of precisely how to distinguish between what was merely the subjective thinking of the master, on the one hand, and what was universal in it. The problem of how to purify the method from the system is not an easy one to solve.

The rivals find themselves splitting off into two mutually opposed camps. On the one side stand those who settle the problem in the simplest manner possible, by denying that anything in the master's teaching was merely subjective. In making this claim, they correctly realize the slippery slope problem that would result from affirming a gap between the master's own particular standpoint and the absolute standpoint. To affirm the existence of such a gap threatens, after all, to undermine completely the master's claim to have achieved the absolute standpoint. This position is easy to defend, because the members of this camp can cease to be philosophical reformers and become instead the *preservers of the master's legacy*. They puff themselves up with the pretense of loyalty to the dead master, and affirm that everything the master uttered gave expression to the divine. That this position is in bad faith can be seen quite readily. For one thing, the preservers of the legacy find themselves in the absurd position of having to swear allegiance to literally everything the master ever said. So if the master mistakenly thought that there must be seven planets, and subsequent scientific discovery shows that in fact there are nine, the preservers of the legacy must insist that really there are only seven, or they must explain why the nine planets can, "in a deeper sense," be thought of as seven. But their position is in bad faith on a more personal level as well. For while the master lived, they, too, were reformers who often disagreed with the master. They, too, secretly wished for the master's death. Now that the master is dead, he can no longer disagree with what the preservers of the legacy say in his name. So now they find themselves free to think whatever they think and claim for it the status of absolute knowing. Of course, the preservers of the legacy still disagree among themselves, and so they bicker about points of interpretation, each calling the other a heretic or a bad reader of the master's corpus.

Over and against the preservers of the legacy stand those who refuse to lapse into the bad faith of swearing allegiance to everything the master said. They affirm that the only true way of carrying out the master's legacy is to purify the method, and hence to purge out whatever in the master's thinking arose from subjective "noise" in the system. To do this means not to preserve the master's legacy but on the contrary to radicalize it. They are no longer philosophical reformers, but *philosophical radicals*.

At first, the philosophical radicals see themselves standing in solidarity with one another not only because they share a common goal, but also because they come under vicious attack by the preservers of the legacy. The latter, moreover, find themselves in a much more powerful position than the former. The reason for this lies in the fact that the preservers of the legacy keep alive the master's own pretense to have identified his own thinking with that of the absolute standpoint. In the master, faith in this identification was easy to maintain because all of his disciples seemed to confirm him in this faith. Did they not constantly defer to him in all matters philosophical? This faith enabled the master to make headway in the science of the absolute, but not without cost. For this faith kept the master one step behind his disciples. They, for their part, recognized the importance of questioning the relationship between the individual thinker's standpoint and the absolute standpoint. But he failed to recognize the importance of this problem precisely because no one ever told him that he was wrong about anything. The result of this, his megalomaniac identification of his own thinking with the thinking of the absolute—expressed in his certainty of the truth of "the system"—naturally led to a certain conservatism in the master's thinking. Since the absolute had only reached the stage that it had already achieved at that precise moment in *his life*, to identify with the absolute meant to identify with the rationality of the present. This, of course, meant that whatever had *de facto* legitimacy in the political arena was granted a kind of *de jure* legitimacy in the thought of the master.

It would therefore have been easy to foresee whose side the state would take in the battle between the preservers of the legacy and the philosophical radicals. The former are inclined to agree with the master's pronouncements of the intrinsic rationality of the present order. In this, they show themselves to be even more conservative than the master himself had ever been. For even while the master was articulating the rationality of the present, he himself saw the need to transform the world in accordance with the dictates of the system; as such, the master was himself a latent philosophical reformer. Certainly he did not believe that either historical change or the necessity of continuing philosophical thinking would end. On the contrary, the system itself was something historical and thus continually involving. But for the preservers of the legacy, both thought and history have come to an end with the death of the master. And just as they pledge themselves to keeping alive the dead thoughts of the master, so they seek to eternalize the living mausoleum of the society whose present rationality the master had articulated.

By contrast, it is precisely this mausoleum that the philosophical radicals pledge themselves to destroy. For it is the contingency of the empirical content that must be purged from the master's thinking. Hence rather than affirm the rationality of the present, the radicals accuse the present age of its irrationality. Of course, just as the preservers of the legacy are liable to lapse into the absurdity of defending everything the master said, so the radicals risk the parallel absurdity of defending the master by attacking everything he said. Yet at first they do not recognize this danger, for they cling to the notion that they are purifying the master's thinking in order to glean its true method. They can isolate this pure method, of course, only by stripping it of all connection to the empirical. The philosophical radicals accordingly stress the difference between the picture thinking of so-called revealed religion and the purely conceptual character of absolute knowing. To free the method of absolute knowing from its dependence on empirical content, it is necessary to sever the identification between philosophy and religion. For the philosophical radicals, the absolute standpoint can be achieved only by ridding the world of religious superstition entirely. In this way, they raise anew the Enlightenment's charge against faith.

For their part, the preservers of the legacy take up once again the side of faith in opposition to the Enlightenment. For in maintaining the frozen instant of the spirit that was the air breathed by the master, they insist on the truth of revealed religion as strenuously as they defend the rationality of the state. Thus, the confrontation takes on a kind of retrograde character, but one whose necessity calls into question the master's claim to have demonstrated the compatibility of faith and Enlightenment, religion and philosophy, in absolute knowing.

In this confrontation, the preservers take on the role of the master. They can do so, however, only by maintaining the pretense that they agree with everything the master taught. For their part, the dialectic of knowing would appear to have ended with this master—and no wonder, for it is easy for an unthinking person to believe that the history of thought has reached its end. The preservers of the legacy can continue on their way for eons, dogmatically affirming the "timeless" truths of the past. It is therefore left to the radicals to carry on the torch of thinking, and this they do so with the confidence of those who know what it is they are aiming at.

Each side in this confrontation, of course, claims the mantle of the master, but the radicals find themselves distancing themselves from the master more and more. In their efforts to isolate the method of absolute thinking and distinguish it from the master's particular applications of it, they find that however much they purify the method there remains some empirical element in it, contaminating the absolute. This situation is complicated, moreover, by an inner contradiction that lies within their task of purification. The radicals seek to purge philosophy of its connection to religion, and this they do in order to purify thought from its connection to empirical content. Yet at the same time, the picture thinking of revealed religion was itself a negation of the empirical as such, and in fact the radicals blame religion for turning people away from the empirical world. Religion is thus criticized from two sides at once—it taints philosophy because it is too empirical but it taints life because it is not empirical enough. Were they to think through this opposition and seek to reconcile its two sides, the radicals might be forced to admit that their grounds for critiquing religion might equally be grounds for critiquing philosophy—at least to the degree to which they envision absolute thinking as absolute opposition to the empirical world. Yet even were they made aware of this objection, the radicals would protest that what they seek is a reconciliation of the empirical with the philosophical; after all, their task is precisely to make the real rational—that is, to make the empirical philosophical. So, in fact, they are perfectly comfortable acknowledging a gap between the empirical and the philosophical, and indeed they make the overcoming of this gap their explicit goal. Religion they blame because they see it as standing in the way of this direct confrontation between the demands of reason and the demands of the world.

In order to raise empirical human reality to the rational level which philosophy realizes as its inner essence, the philosophical radicals conclude, it is necessary to negate the religious vision of a divinity existing over and above the empirical, and instead transform religion—which, even in revealed religion, seems to posit some sort of "beyond"—into a description of a divinity that is nothing other than the highest potential of humanity. For philosophy's vision of a future perfection of humanity to be realized, that is, it is necessary for man to learn that he is God.

To the philosophical radicals, this at first appears to be the most radical of truths. But it quickly dawns on them that this formula itself fails to purge the religious element from pure thought. In order to radicalize the truth that there is no divinity over and above humanity it is necessary to go further and say—there is only man. Anything less would fail to sever philosophy's connection to religion. The death of the master thus turns out to require a more momentous event—the death of God.

To the philosophical radicals, the death of God signifies the imminent attainability of the absolute standpoint by the masses. But having succeeded in killing God, they now find themselves facing in an explicit way a problem which they could defer until now. Specifically, they had prophesied that the death of God would prove to be the immediate salvation of humanity. Yet when they look people in the eye and announce to them the death of God, the people shrug their shoulders. Apparently, they don't care much one way or the other. Or rather, the philosophical radicals have come too late. The world is already an Enlightened world, whatever the preservers of the legacy would like to think. However, the fact that the people have lost their faith does not signify that they are suddenly ready to join the radicals in their struggle against the apologists of the state. If anything, their loss of faith in the divine appears to have made them lose whatever revolutionary zeal they might have had left.

By laying to rest the ghost (*Geist*) of the dead master, the philosophical radicals do indeed change the world, but their act has this significance not for "the people"—the supposedly superstitious masses whom they had sought to disabuse of their illusory faith—but for *themselves*. For the people, the world has long since become secular, and this has not led them to the absolute standpoint from where they recognize the commonality of their own individual interests. On the contrary, now that their thoughts have left the kingdom of God for the kingdom of earth, they are far more eager to fight for their own selfish gain than to risk personal loss for the sake of the unreal spiritual community. Put otherwise, for them the death of God signifies that they cannot believe in the universality of the secular absolute. Hence, the philosophical radicals discover that all along it was the supposedly pious people who were enlightened religious cynics, while they, the supposedly enlightened philosophical radicals, were clinging to a superstitious faith in the promise of the master. It is to the radicals, and them only, that the death of God—now actualized in the cynicism of the people—appears as a traumatic event. To believe in the absolute standpoint is revealed to have been mere faith—the opiate of the philosophers. Once again, the seemingly firm distinction between faith and Enlightenment turns out to have reversed itself.

The radicals now attack the cynical Enlightenment of the masses, against which they oppose their own faith in the possibility of realizing the absolute. No longer do they focus their attacks on religion, therefore; they now declare that it is philosophy itself which has mystified the masses. Declaring that the gap between the real and the rational cannot be erased by a kind of thinking that remains solely at the level of the notion, they affirm the need to disabuse men of their faith in rationality. In turning against philosophy, however, they do not turn back to religion; instead they declare the falsity of everything spiritual, whether conceived in philosophical or religious terms. Against the spiritual, they affirm the truth of the material world. This is the iconoclastic and misologistic truth of the *philosophical revolutionaries*.

For the philosophical radicals, religion was responsible for the alienation between men which kept them from identifying with one another. It was not man as divine knower who needed to be recognized, but simply man as human knower. For the philosophical revolutionaries, however, it is not man as any sort of knower, but rather man as potentially revolutionary agent—man as laboring animal—who needs to be recognized.

While professing to lay to rest the spiritual work of their days as mere philosophical radicals, the philosophical revolutionaries nonetheless seek to raise men to a consciousness of their identity as members of a species. In taking this stance, they do indeed continue their previous work as philosophical radicals; the only difference is that they have now substituted philosophy for religion as the main *bête noir* to be overthrown. The action of the philosophical revolutionaries is thus in contradiction with the meaning they give to it; for they castigate the idea that one can change the world by castigating ideas, precisely with an eye towards thereby changing the world.

Instead of concluding that the ideal of making the real rational is flawed, the philosophical revolutionaries have simply expanded the scope of their criticism and radicalized their rhetoric. In order that their antiphilosophical polemics not be confused with philosophical polemics, they try to make their pen strokes appear as if they were lethal thrusts of sharp sabers. Their sallies must be more ruthless than ever before; they must cut to the quick; nothing must escape their wrath. If the people still believe in the rationality of the present, it can only be because they cling to some sort of spiritual faith—whether religious or philosophical ultimately makes no difference to the indiscriminately critical pen-wielders. But since all their published diatribes remain as ineffectual as all the other philosophical work whose ineffectuality they rightly call attention to, the revolutionaries find themselves frustrated in their endeavors. In a kind of frenzy of self-conceit, they redouble their efforts to disabuse the masses of their faith; they try ever more vitriolic rhetoric, reaching higher and higher heights of self-righteous contempt for those who profess the rationality of the present. In doing so, they naturally find themselves engaged in a contest of one-upmanship with one another. Each one's attempt to overthrow the present is supplanted by the next one's denouncing it as too conservative. There lurks in this the danger of the bad infinite, as today's critical criticism is supplanted by tomorrow's super-critical criticism, and the next day's new and improved, now-I've-really-got-the-gloves-off, hypercritical criticism.

By remaining merely at this polemical level, the antiphilosophical revolutionaries show that their action is, at bottom, merely philosophical. Of course they hasten to add that, in announcing the death of philosophy, they are merely performing the preparatory groundwork prior to the true work of actually revolutionizing the world. Yet at the same time they never get to this second stage; they find it necessary to perpetuate this prefatory philosophical critique of philosophy.

At the same time, however, the philosophical revolutionaries have inverted the former truth of the philosophical radicals. For by laying to rest the ghost of spirit, they have brought the real down from its previously Olympian heights. For the consciousness of the philosophical revolutionaries, what is true is not the pure as opposed to the empirical but the empirical as opposed to the pure, not spirit as opposed to nature but nature as opposed to spirit. To this extent, they herald the coming of a new sort of philosophical activity. Up until now, philosophy has only *conceived* of the reconciliation among men that is the true absolute standpoint; the revolutionaries now show that traditional philosophy must be replaced by a truly practical philosophy that will actually *accomplish* the work of bringing men together. The individual who sets out to articulate this new philosophy of man—instead of merely attacking the old philosophy of spirit—is the *philosophical anthropologist*.

Blaming the old philosophy for remaining merely at the level of the spiritual notion of absolute knowing, the philosophical anthropologist opposes to the mediation of thought the immediacy of man's sensuous being. As such, the practical work he advocates is directed at men's feelings. The philosophical anthropologist affirms that the absolute is already achieved in the species-being of man, and he claims that everyone is implicitly aware of this truth in their immediate feelings of connection with others. Specifically, the truth of the absolute is revealed in the phenomenon of love—not spiritual love, but the physical love that all members of the species naturally feel. The philosophical anthropologist thus advocates a kind of "love revolution."

But since mere feeling is just as little real activity as is mere thinking, the philosophical anthropologist posits a means of waging revolution which is itself ineffectual. The individual's ability to experience sexuality as a coming-together of humanity presupposes that he has already adopted a certain notional attitude toward others. For the cynically egoistic masses, sexual desire is merely one individual's selfish longing to "possess" another person. Ultimately, all the philosophical anthropologist can do in the face of such an objection is to ask people to try and "get in touch" with the deeper truth of their sexuality—not exactly the storming of the Bastille. The philosophical anthropologist founders for the same reason that the philosophical radicals did—the people resist the very ideal of the absolute standpoint, preferring to wallow in their egoistic pursuits.

Now, earlier, the radicals renewed their faith by becoming philosophical revolutionaries. But the apparent ineffectuality of their own criticism, coupled with that of the philosophical anthropologist, causes the entire philosophical community to lose its faith in *man*. It was the members of this community, the proponents of the absolute, who experienced the death of God as a traumatic event; for them, the absolute standpoint had all along been based upon the truth of revealed religion, regardless of what they told themselves. For this reason, the materialist truth of the anthropologist is itself unable to sustain their revolutionary zeal; *their* feeling for the absolute is, at bottom, a spiritual feeling. With the waning of the revolutionary faith of philosophy comes the despair of the unhappy consciousness. The individual philosophical revolutionary withdraws from the philosophical community, and enters the alienated ranks of those whom they previously scorned as mere egoists. Unlike the latter, however, the failed revolutionary now self-consciously retreats to the [I = I] that had been a mere tautology—the "I" of immediate self-certainty—and denies that the mediation through the "we" can do anything other than bring it back to this original tautology. This is the truth of the *philosophical egoist*, the consciousness which now sees what *we* saw earlier—namely, that the dialectical confrontation between rival absolute knowers would lead to a crisis.

The philosophical egoist is certain that, no matter how hard each individual ego tries to recognize another ego he can recognize only himself. Thus, he dismisses all attempts to reach the genuinely mediated [I = I] as doomed from the start. Rejecting the very notion of universality, the philosophical egoist affirms that the ideal of the absolute standpoint ultimately rests on a notion of God as that single ego which somehow resides within every particular human body; without this faith in a single ego, he concludes, there is nothing but the plurality of many immediate self-consciousnesses. The "we" of man's species-being is thus merely an aggregate of isolated individuals who are incapable of achieving reconciliation with one another.

The philosophical egoist is certain of his isolation, and to this extent he falls back into the position of the unhappy consciousness. But unlike the unhappy consciousness, who wallowed in his self-pity, the philosophical egoist does not mourn his alienation. For in claiming to be alienated from others, he in fact overcomes his alienation from himself. As a result, the philosophical egoist experiences his new insight as a joyful wisdom. Moreover, since everything that appears to him appears as something that is *his*, he likewise finds himself taking possession of the entire world, and to this extent paradoxically feels reconciled to the world in his consciousness of being alienated from it. In celebrating himself and his world, therefore, the philosophical egoist does not withdraw from the world like the unhappy consciousness but instead turns manically toward it in order to impose his own meanings on it. Yet while his retreat into egoism is not a stoical withdrawing from the world, neither is it a repetition of the frenzy of self-conceit, for the philosophical egoist does not feel threatened with the loss of himself. On the other hand, since the world also appears as something that is *not* his, his desire to impose himself on it is, in essence, a renewed attempt to seek recognition from others. The egoist says to the world, "I am the truth!" in order to hear it echo back, "Yes, you are the truth!" But since everyone else is equally an egoist, all he can expect to hear when he yells "I am the truth," is the *merely apparent* echo which says, "I am the truth." This apparent echo, he knows, is not *his* voice, but the voice of *another* egoist. In affirming the truth of egoism, the philosophical egoist thus posits a *universal* truth—he claims that every individual sees itself as the truth of the world. By declaring to others the truth of *their* egoism, the philosophical egoist thus accomplishes what he says he cannot do—namely, he recognizes others for their own sake. In his explicitly self-centered way, the philosophical egoist actually transcends his egoism—something which the implicitly self-centered absolute knowers could not do. He does this, more-over, in the very moment in which he "confesses" to others his selfishness to them. But this just means that he gives to others the recognition which he claims he cannot give them. In this way, the radical denial of the pos-sibility of achieving the mediated—as opposed to the merely immediate—[I = I] leads to this very mediation.

However, because the philosophical egoist can recognize others only by affirming his isolation from them, *for himself* he remains conscious of his alienation, even though *in himself* he is reconciled to others. Retreating into his certainty of being an isolated ego, therefore, the philosophical egoist must now deny that any genuine communication has taken place between himself and those to whom he speaks. The truth of egoism, he affirms, is ineffable. The philosophical egoist now really does stoically with-draw from the world and become the *philosophical loner.*

The philosophical loner posits a distinction between the absolute stand-point and the multiple perspectives of individual egos. But this does not yet signal a lapsing back into the faith which posited the absolute as infinitely distant, for he is conscious of the fact that it is he—as consciousness of an absolute standpoint which no one can attain—who draws this distinction within his own thinking. Thus, he still does not, as the unhappy conscious-ness did, lapse into the solipsism of despair, for he knows full well that the absolute is to be identified with the human community to which he himself is a member. He does not despair because he knows that, in recognizing the truth of universal alienation, he has attained the absolute standpoint; yet he immediately contradicts himself since the fact of universal alienation im-plies the unattainability of the absolute standpoint.

The philosophical loner's certainty arises from his ability to imagine the positions of other egos. Since he knows himself to be merely one ego among many, he is unable to affirm a particular truth for himself without right away taking up the perspective of an ego who would disagree with him. Hence, the loner's alienation from others is now experienced as a profound self-alienation, for instead of just "being himself" he is constantly adopting the positions of others. Thus, he experiences his self-alienation as a form of irony. No sooner is he tempted to defend a particular belief than he becomes conscious of the opposite position, and since he can adopt either of these, his irony leads him to undermine whichever position he happens to hold at a given moment by considering the perspective of the other side. This is exactly like the bad infinite of the skeptic, who like a willful child always affirms what another one denies, except for the fact that in each case the philosophical loner is both of these willful children. Abso-lute irony differs from skepticism in that while the latter cannot take any-one else seriously, the former cannot take itself seriously.

Yet while the philosophical loner is ironic toward himself, he relates to others through the language of parody. In his parodic representations of others, the philosophical loner appears to be making fun of those individuals who are sure of themselves. But since he takes the absolute truth to be just this multiplicity of self-sure egoists, he is in fact conscious of the truth of those whom he parodies, so that really, internally, his parody takes the form of a sincere and faithful depiction of others' truths. Above all, the philosophical loner is not mocking those whom he parodies. On the contrary, he is implicitly glorifying them, while making fun of himself for explicitly failing to glorify them and instead making fun of them.

The philosophical loner is thus always the chief butt of his irony, although to the outside observer it appears as if he is being ironic toward those whom he parodies. Utterly alienated, he actually respects everyone but himself. For every particular egoist is a sincere believer in something, and it is just this sincerity and self-certainty which the loner honors as the opposite of his own irony, which he despises. Skepticism and self-irony are thus easily confused, because to the outside observer they appear the same; but internally, the self-ironic loner knows that it is he alone with whom he is forever disagreeing. It does not matter which position another inhabits, just so long as she occupies it sincerely, rather than ironically. For in this way the other is true to herself, something which the ironist cannot be. But the ironist remains an ironist precisely to the extent that he cannot recognize the truth of a plurality of individuals at the same time. Hence he must single out one particular individual and declare absolute devotion to her. But because even this devotion does not free him from his irony, he cannot rise from mere devotion to the actual confession that might lead to mutual recognition. The loner thus devotes himself to an *unattainable* other the better to maintain his irony toward himself, an irony which increasingly takes on the form of a self-loathing. It is this self-loathing—not the despair of never reaching the absolute, which is foreign to him—which drives him into infinite resignation. His constant feeding on himself, the spiraling bad infinite of absolute irony, culminates in the sickness unto death.

The loner can overcome this sickness only by plunging back into the blind faith of religion; he thereby leaps outside of himself and into the arms of an imagined absolute. That this leap be blind is essential, for it must signal a complete turning-away from himself and his own thought. But this just means that the philosophical loner has now come full circle; instead of being an extreme version of the philosophical egoist, he is in fact the latter's diametrical opposite. For the egoist affirms his own ego and his own, whereas the leaping loner denies himself completely. As such, moreover, he brings to completion the dialectic of self-renunciation which took place in the dialogue of the absolute knowers. There, each individual realized that he must deny his own empirical ego if he was to find himself recognized in the other; but he was unable to accomplish this because behind the act of self-renunciation, there lurked the egoism which the philosophical egoist has made explicit. But the leaping loner has utterly renounced himself, and not merely in order to regain himself; he leaps, rather, for the sake of the other—that is, for the one to whom he is devoted. And so, by performing this movement of infinite renunciation, the loner manages to win precisely what was sought in the dialogue of absolute knowers—namely, that sublation of himself which alone can return him to himself.

But who has recognized him? Only himself—for no sooner does he expect the recognition of others than the loner thereby renounces his self-renunciation, and with it the basis for actualizing the mediated $[I = I]$. The apparently ecstatic leap of faith turns out to have landed him right back in himself. He is again the only one who recognizes himself; he is again a loner. The cycle thus repeats itself—once again he becomes ironic toward himself, he devotes himself to another, he tries to make the leap only to fall back.

The philosophical loner is aware of his own alienation: he is cut off not only from others but also from himself. When circumstances require that he engage in dialogue with others, he speaks both *to them* and *of himself* in the third person. His only "contact" with the world, if such it can even be called, is through that other to whom he is absolutely devoted—but to her he cannot speak. For were he to speak to her he would realize that in fact he cannot identify with her fully—thus, he prefers to remain within that golden silence of the rapturous gaze between the absolute knowers before they spoke to each other. The entire dialectic of absolute knowing accordingly has its truth in the self-alienation of the individual who claims for himself the absolute standpoint. The truth of absolute knowing, in short, is alienation.

But in order for an absolute knower to become conscious of the truth of alienation, he must break out of the silence of the loner and risk once again the confrontation of real speech. But now this speech will be different from what it was before. Instead of its being the speech which begins from the self-confidence and independence of two absolute knowers, it will be speech which springs from the alienated individuals' certainty that they need each other. When they first begin to speak they will seek not the mediated identification of the $[I = I]$, but rather the solidarity of the $[I + I]$. And this, it turns out, seems to lead to a genuine mutual recognition which grants them more than they had bargained for—namely, the fulfilled promise of the mediated $[I = I]$.

2 (FF.) • The Dialectic of Materialist Spirit

A. Ethical Materialism

The collapse of absolute knowing gave way to the isolated retreat of the egoist and the loner. But like the unhappy consciousness, the loner reached a depth of despair which enabled him to confess his misery. The confessing loner blames himself for man's inability to achieve reconciliation. But when this confession is reciprocated by another confessing loner, each discovers that, together, they can achieve mutual recognition after all. In this way, the despair of the isolated loner gives way to the solidarity of fellow loners. As a reconciliation, however, this solidarity is ambiguous, for the two loners have negated their mutual alienation only by way of affirming it. Hence they do not overcome their alienation so much as they attain a mutual recognition of it. Their coming-together is perceived as a shared consciousness of an impediment to their coming-together. This impediment is perceived both as the real source of their alienation, yet also—since they do come together—as something unreal. As such it has the character of a mysterious being, one whose secret they set out to discover. By plumbing the depths of the source of man's alienation, these half-reconciled loners expect to raise themselves—and all other men—to the level of a true consciousness of their identity in the species-being of man. With this consciousness, the absolute standpoint will be achieved in a community based on genuine solidarity rather than on pure identity or pure difference. This is the shared truth and work of the *communists*.

Unlike the absolute knowers who could converse only by masking their differences from each other, the communists come together precisely by revealing their differences to each other. Their differences no longer signify contradictory opposites that must negate each other; the truth of solidarity rests on their positing a compatability of differences, as the absolute knowers had merely intended to do. To this extent the communists now celebrate their differences, rather than confess them.

However, not only are they not fully reconciled with one another, but the community of communists is, as was the philosophical community, merely an enclave within the larger egoistic society. The unity of man's species-being is for the majority of men something merely implicitly true; this truth must be made explicit. The communists therefore set themselves the task of leading all men up to their standpoint.

By undertaking the work of making men aware of the truth of their own condition, the communists have once again resurrected the opposition between faith and enlightenment. The faith which they oppose is not the religious faith which posits a transcendent absolute. Rather, it is a twofold secular faith. On the one hand, insofar as they are certain that some sort of material impediment stands in the way of complete reconciliation, the enlightened communists critique the naively optimistic faith of the anthropologist, who believed that the absolute standpoint could be attained merely by changing the consciousness of men. On the other hand, insofar as they are certain that alienation can be overcome, they oppose the cynical isolation of the egoists and the loners, who believe that the absolute standpoint is unattainable.

Where the philosophical reformers sought to disabuse the people of their religious faith, the communists now affirm that the source of alienation is to be found in a secular faith. After all, the isolated loner turned to faith only after he was already alienated. Moreover, the loner became conscious of his alienation only after he had rejected the earlier religious faith which gave way to the skepticism of absolute irony. To be sure religion ended up serving as a balm to lessen the pain of the sickness unto death. But the bad faith of the loner's eventual retreat back to a position he himself had abandoned indicates that religion is not the source of alienation but merely a way of masking it. The loner's retreat into faith signaled his nostalgia for a time when he was not aware of his alienation; for him, such nostalgia was his only form of praxis since he viewed his alienation as an irreducible feature of the human condition.

The communists do not dispute the loner's assessment of what it means to perceive oneself as an isolated individual. However, they question the truth of the loner's consciousness that he *is* an isolated individual. In reaffirming the anthropologist's faith in the unity of man's species-being, the communists are led to view the individual's consciousness of his individuality as a result of the impediment to true self-consciousness. The loner's alienation results from the fact that he does not know *what* he is. Since man, the communists are certain, is first and foremost a species-being, he can overcome his alienation only by becoming aware of this fact. Attaining this true self-consciousness depends, however, on overcoming the material impediments to a complete reconciliation among men.

Thus, the communists attribute man's alienation to the fact that he has lost his consciousness of what he is. As such, they oppose the true man with the apparent man; the former is the species-being of man posited by the anthropologist, and the latter is the individual's consciousness of himself as possessing characteristics which he supposes to cut him off from the rest of the species. The true man is represented in the ideal of the perfectly self-conscious communist, while the apparent man is the egoist—whether "pre-philosophical" (i.e.,bourgeois) or "philosophical" makes no difference here—who thinks that he is the sole possesser of certain things that "belong" to him. For it is insofar as the individual posits himself as being in possession of something which does not belong to the species as a whole which leads to his alienation from his natural communal ties. The philosophical egoist's consciousness of his alienation, they recall, sprang from the fact that he defined himself in terms of something which he posited as being his "own." In positing himself and his own as the truth, the philosophical egoist affirmed the impossibility of achieving an identity with others. For him, the source of this impossibility could be traced to the absolute difference between that which belonged to him as a particular ego and that which belonged to others as the particular egos they were. For the egoist, the "blame" for the impossibility of transcending egoism could fall on both sides of the relation—that is, he can blame himself for not being able to identify with anything but what belongs to him, and he can blame others for not being able to alienate themselves from what belongs to them. For the egoistic consciousness, therefore, it is the phenomenon of belonging in general—the phenomenon of property—which stands in the way of his social being. However, to the egoist, who remained within the sphere of spirit, property signified not primarily material possessions, but whatever "essential" properties were supposed to adhere to a particular individual qua individual—his particular feelings, his thoughts, his dreams, and so forth. Insofar as the individual cannot lose the overarching property of owning *these* things without his ceasing to be the particular individual he is—that is, without dying—the property of being the sole possesser of certain properties is something that cannot be transcended.

But the actualized truth of the philosophical loner revealed the falsity of the egoist's certainty. The loner was the egoist who found that he had *no* essential properties which belonged to him alone, for as absolute ironist, the loner's only "essence" was his absolute negation of any possible properties that might be ascribed to him. If there was anything fixed in the loner's consciousness it was his self-irony, the truth of which was revealed in his being alienated from everything which belonged to him. In other words, to be absolutely ironic is to possess the sole property of having no property. Whereas the egoist identified with what belonged to him and found that he was alienated only from what belonged to others, the loner found that he was alienated both from what belonged to others and from what belonged to himself. Moreover, since the loner was certain that all individuals were, in essence, implicit loners themselves, he could conclude that no one possessed any essential property. The loner thus himself implicitly discovered that the source of alienation lay not with anything that was an essential property of individuals, but with the inessential properties which were recognized as defining individuals. In other words, the loner discovered the social character of the phenomenon of property. He himself was unable to overcome his alienation because this truth remained merely implicit for him—that is, the loner merely despaired of regaining himself because he could not conceive of himself without property.

But the philosophical communists view their own achievement as revealing the possibility of overcoming alienation. Moreover, they view this overcoming as dialectically necessary, for they see the latent contradiction within the loner's stubborn persistence in an alienation which he himself has provided the key to overcoming. What stood in the way of the *egoist's* identifying with others was his sense of being unable to separate himself from what belonged to him. Yet with his absolute irony, this is just what the *loner* managed to do—separate himself from what was his. By negating that which belonged to him as an individual, the alienated loner paved the way for an overcoming of his alienation from others—or, more precisely, from those others who for the loner appeared as egoists—but he still clung to the non-property of not possessing any unique property as if this was itself his unique property which therefore stood in the way of an overcoming of alienation. In other words, the absolutely ironic loner viewed everyone else as an egoist and therefore viewed himself as possessing the unique property of being a propertyless loner. In the immediate coming-together of the communists, what was posited was a community of loners, which positing was, after all, prefigured in the loner's implicit realization that everyone else would also be a loner if only he were truly honest with himself. Thus, the communists chide the loner for his egoistic conceit that he is the only one free of egoistic conceit. By making explicit the true nature of the loner's propertylessness—that is, by making explicit the loner's own implicit knowledge that this negative property is not itself a property—the communists have sublated the truth of the loner's position. Specifically, they sublate the alienation of the loner; or put otherwise, they alienate themselves from their own alienation, thereby restoring themselves to themselves. But—and this is the central truth of the communists' achievement thus far—they find themselves again not insofar as each now returns to what is his own but precisely insofar as they do *not* do so. For what they have discovered is that what kept them apart in the first place was precisely their previous sense of being individual "owners." The communists have now discovered the mysterious impediment to complete reconciliation. Only by throwing off the very idea of property can the communists fully actualize their new-found solidarity; otherwise, they are destined to fall back on the strife of the absolute knowers. But since they now posit themselves to be mutually recognizing members of the species-being of man, it is not enough for the communists to form a separate enclave cut off from the rest of humanity; they must restore the true species-being of mankind in general. To do this, they must rid all humanity of its illusory secular faith in the existence of property.

But the idea of property and the reality of property are one and the same thing, for material property is merely the fetishized object upon which individual men hang their sense of identity. Thus, not only the idea of property, but *actual* property must be abolished if man is to achieve his species-being. This means that the destruction of property must take place within the ethical sphere; the right to own private property must be abolished. Since for the communistic consciousness the individual possessor of property is merely the appearance of man and not his essence, man will only become *man* in the true sense when he will have achieved the mediated [I = I] of the absolute standpoint—namely, communist society.

The work of the communists, therefore, is to destroy the institution of property. But this, they know, is easier said than done. For so long as individual men define themselves in terms of what they recognize as their own, they must view losing their property as equivalent to losing their lives. Property cannot be destroyed without a struggle. Such a struggle cannot take place, moreover, so long as every individual is recognized as in possession of some property, for no one who defines himself in terms of his property will be willing to fight for its abolition. Man will remain alienated from his species-being until there emerges a class of propertyless men.

Now, the philosophical loners might seem to represent just such a class insofar as they view themselves as propertyless. But, as the communists now know, the individual loner is in bad faith because he clings egoistically to his self-proclaimed lack of property. This bad faith has its truth in the fact that the loner has merely negated the *idea* of property, while remaining the owner of a townhouse, a carriage, perhaps even a factory. As such, the alienation of the loner is akin to the earlier alienation that was experienced by the master during the master/slave dialectic. The master was alienated from both the slave and himself not because, like the slave, he did not own what he created, but on the contrary because he owned what he did not create. In a similar way, the loner is alienated not because he does not own any property but simply because he cannot recognize the property that he owns as something that he owns. He recognizes the truth of the fetishism of property, but he then defetishizes his property only in his mind and not in reality. Put differently, he negates his property but then negates this negation and so retains it. The loner is someone who has always meant to give away all his money but somehow never gotten around to actually doing it. In short, the alienated loner is a revolutionary thinker but not a revolutionary actor; in the end, he is merely an egoist in bad faith. And it is just this tension between his revolutionary ideas and his reactionary life that proves to have been the underlying contradiction of the entire dialectic of absolute knowing. As the supersession of this dialectic, the communist consciousness affirms the necessity of action over thought.

The communists conclude that the mistake of the radicals was their thinking they could change the world merely by changing how men think. Yet this criticism could just as easily be leveled against their own project, insofar as they themselves take the real existence of property to be sustained by men's faith in it; they too believe that one can change the world by changing how they think—only by changing how men think about property, rather than how they think about God. Only in one respect, then, can the communists distinguish their project from that of the radicals, namely, in the specific object of their critique. By attacking religion, the radicals focused on what was merely an effect of alienation, not its true cause; by attacking property, they get at the root of the problem.

To substantiate this claim, the communists must demonstrate why it should be property, rather than religion or anything else, that is the chief cause of man's alienation in the first place. To do this, they must recast the entire dialectic of human alienation as a story about *real* property rather than about—as they accuse the absolute knowers and radicals of—*ideal* property. In other words, they must rewrite the phenomenology of spirit from a materialist standpoint.

Now, some of this work has already been done; the communists can point to the phenomenon of the loner to show that the true cause of alienation can be traced to a dialectic of property. But since the communists posit that man's *essence* is to be a species that does *not* fragment itself into individual property-holders, they must account for the origins of the institution of property in the first place; this, then, is the main burden of their initial historical work.

The basic contours of this history are already laid bare for the communists. They must reconstruct the process whereby property emerges as the great divider of man's species-being into apparently isolated individuals. Furthermore, since they posit the necessity of returning to the original unity of mankind, they must also specify the conditions under which private property will be abolished in the future. Because of this last requirement, and in order to rebuke the radicals who otherwise would accuse them of being mere wielders of ideas themselves, the communists must put themselves forth as scientific forecasters as well as scientific historians.

Since the communists posit man's species-being as the mediated $[I = I]$ of the absolute standpoint, they view mankind as both one and many. In a communist society, therefore, men will still recognize themselves as individuals, but as individual members of a collective. But since communism represents a world without property, it must be possible for men to exist as individuals without their individuality being constituted by their possession of property. And yet the truth of egoism has revealed that what it means to be an individual is to possess property of some sort. For this reason, the communists find themselves resorting to vague notions when they are asked to specify what a communist world will look like. If they say that, in a communist society, no one will own anything, then they seem to be positing a world without individuals. Their only alternative is to say that, in a communist society, everyone will own everything. In this way, however, they retain the notion of property. Henceforth, therefore, they set out to deduce not the origin of property in general but simply the genesis of private property. But this distinction adds nothing to the question of whether or not a communist society which recognizes differences is possible; the supposedly subtle addition that only *private* property will be abolished is simply a way of explanation by pleonasm, for the same problem of how to thematize the mediated $[I = I]$ crops up for any account of individuality in a world where the conditions for its possibility appear to be undermined. The communists can only fall back on the eschatological moment of their consciousness, pointing out like any good theologian the difficulties of articulating fully what has not yet come to pass. Hence the inevitable march of history toward a coming absolute standpoint remains an article of faith. Despite much self-righteous posturing about how theirs is an empirical and genuinely scientific history rather than a philosophical and pseudoscientific one, in their prognosticating the communists know a priori exactly what they will glean from their supposedly unbiased examination of the facts. Insofar as they posit the unity of man's social being as the original essence to which history must return, theirs is, in the end, a theology of the Fall and Redemption of man.

But though their account of the future might rest on faith, the communists' analysis of the present rests on the certainty that the source of alienation can be traced to the institution of private property. With this certainty as their starting point, they set out to construct a scientific account of the dialectic of property.

To begin with, the communists know that, *in himself*, man is a social being, but *for himself*—that is, for the majority of men who thus far appear to themselves as either alienated egoists or loners—he is an individual defined by his property. Now, insofar as man has reached the stage of egoism, his consciousness of the relationship between civil society and the state has been reversed. When the individual earlier achieved its consciousness of being spirit, it moved from the merely immediate recognition of spirit in the family to the alienated realm of civil society, and then finally to the actualized self-consciousness represented by the state. Having achieved the universal ethical consciousness of the state, man was prepared for the religious reconciliation which led to the immediately achieved mediated [I = I] of the absolute knowers. But this immediacy remained submerged in what might be called the philosophical "family" of absolute knowers, and the subsequent dissolution of this family into the self-centered world of the philosophical egoists has the significance of a repeated passage from the "holy family" of absolute knowers to the "civil society" of alienated knowers. Now, the passage from this stage to the "state" of communist society has not yet come to pass, and so for the communist consciousness, the realm of civil society represents the true realm of human activity. This is confirmed for them by the fact that human relations are at this stage of the dialectic defined solely in terms of the institution of material property. Hence the communists view as incorrect the absolute knowers' earlier apparent certainty that history is the history of states; on the contrary, the communists affirm, history is the history of civil society, and so it is from this perspective that they seek to recount the origins of the present.

The communists find confirmation of this view, moreover, in the self-consciousness of the egoists. For at present men in general have lost their sense of identifying with the state. From the perspective of the egoist, the state is merely an indifferent conglomeration of separate atomic subjects, as if thousands of Robinson Crusoes just happened to be stranded on the same island and so had to formalize political relations with one another. Now the fact, already noted, that men who define themselves in this way view giving up their claim to property as equivalent to suicide has its basis in man's true consciousness that every individual requires a certain amount of food, clothing, and shelter for himself, without which he indeed would cease to live. But the man who views himself solely as an individual fails to recognize that whatever he appropriates *for himself* is something which *in itself* belongs to society taken as a whole. For it is not the individual man who produces property; it is mankind as a whole which does so. Social relations are, therefore, first and foremost relations of production.

The communists, conscious of the fact that man is essentially a social being, know that even when he appears to himself to be most isolated from others, the individual man is still in relation to others. Since both these things are true at once—that is, since man appears to himself as an isolated individual defined solely by his property yet he is at the same time a social being in relation to others—it follows that alienated man is defined by the property relations which exist among individual men. In an age of egoists, human relations can only be experienced as property relations. But strictly speaking, this proposition must be reversed, for though the communists begin epistemically from the phenomenon of alienation, they recognize the ontological origin of alienation to lie with these property relations. Thus, it must be said that, in an age of property relations, individuals appear to themselves as alienated egoists. Put otherwise, because the communists now view civil society rather than the state to be the true realm of human activity, they view property relations as more fundamental than political relations. Hence alienation is not to be measured by the degree to which man has fallen away from the universal consciousness represented by the state; on the contrary, the state itself is viewed as merely an extension of civil society.

Now, in the very idea of property relations there lurks a contradiction, for as the principle of individuation, property is defined as that which cannot be held in common, while a relation is precisely something that is held in common. In other words, a relation is a sharing—for instance, a parent/child relation is something which belongs both to the parent and to the child. But such shared belonging is precisely what is precluded by the logic of individuating property. Thus, a property relation is a strange sort of social relation—specifically, it can only be a relation of an *exchange* in which the things exchanged share something, but not the individuals who do the exchanging themselves. What the things exchanged share is *value*, something which the individual exchanger himself never willingly relinquishes without expecting something of equal value in return. As for the specific things which they exchange, what belongs to one man cannot become the property of another without the first losing his claim to it. Thus, property relations always involve the dual moments of alienation and appropriation, whether this takes the form of gift-giving, theft, bartering, or monetary transactions. Exchangeable property which a man is willing to alienate from himself in order to appropriate some other exchangeable property of equal value has the form of a *commodity*; what transpires in such transactions is not, from the perspective of the individual man, a human relation but simply a commodity relation. In this way, he shares without sharing. Moreover, since all human relations have taken on the form of commodity relations (inasmuch as man's social relations concern all individuating properties), individuals exchange not only such material possessions as soap, linen, shoes, and so forth, but also such things as love, affection, respect, admiration, and so forth. Everything that man is capable of doing—for example, not only making soap but also expressing affection—takes on the form of commodity production.

Unlike the egoist, who at least nominally distinguished between himself and his property—he is conscious of a separation between the ego *and* his own—the individual who has been reduced to a nodal point of commodity relations has become equivalent to his property. Individuals are themselves nothing other than their ability to appropriate or alienate themselves from commodities. This means that when individuals buy and sell property they are really buying and selling themselves, for they have been reduced to commodities. Thus, not only have social relations among men failed to rise to the level of the mediated [I = I], they have sunk beneath the level of self-consciousness altogether, for in place of a relation among men there exists for men only a relation among things. As such, the consciousness of the individual has reverted to the earlier stage of perception, for which shape of consciousness everything is a thing defined by its properties. Just as in perception, the thing-in-itself was nothing other than the vanishing point in which all the thing's properties had their identity through the "also" relation, so now the ego is reduced to just such an empty thing-in-itself. The ego is simply the "also" which links a particular individual's various material possessions: I am this villa, also this carriage, also my wife, also these children, and so forth. Although the individual may still posit himself as a substantive ego who owns property, it his property which "owns" him. But strictly speaking, the distinction between himself and his property has simply disappeared. The truth of property relations is just this fetishism of commodities, a phenomenon which springs from the fact that individual men experience their social relations as if they were relations among things rather than relations among men—but this, the communists know, occurs because men have become commodities in their own eyes.

Since individuals appear to themselves as commodities, the property relations which constitute their social interaction consist not, primarily, in an exchange of things which they perceive as other than themselves; they consist, rather, in an exchange of themselves, since they perceive one another as commodities. In the realm of property relations, that is, individuals are social beings precisely to the extent that they buy and sell one another. Every individual is defined as having a *price* which determines his worth as a human being—that is, his exchange value.

Having revealed the truth of commodity fetishism, the communists can now trace the phenomenon of alienation to the practice of wage labor, the institution whereby men sell themselves by selling their real existence as active beings—that is, as laborers. In every such exchange, there must be a buyer and a seller of human labor. This buyer/seller relation resembles, of course, the master/slave relation, but with an important difference. The slave was conscious of being forced to work for the master, on pain of death. By contrast, the seller of labor appears to himself as being free; he views himself as agreeing to work for his buyer only because the latter has agreed to pay a fair price for his labor.

The sale of wage labor has now been revealed to be the truth of alienation. No sooner has the individual seller of wage labor sold his labor than he has lost his sense of identity; this is confirmed by the recurring consciousness that, every time he creates something, it is immediately snatched up by the one to whom he has sold his labor. That he is thereby alienated from the things he produces underscores the more fundamental experience of having forfeited *himself*. For previously he was conscious of being an individual ego precisely insofar as he was "his own man." Now he is nothing but the property of the owner. To be sure, he receives in exchange for his labor a wage from the owner, and with this wage he can purchase things which other individuals have created. But in doing so, he comes face-to-face with the fact that his identity and his relations with others have been reduced to mere commodity relations. The pain of alienation lies in his consciousness of the gulf between the certainty of his self-consciousness, which after all he still retains, and his daily experience of being not a self-conscious ego but only a mere thing. As for the one who appropriates the product of the laborer, he also enters into further property relations with other men, selling what he has appropriated in exchange for wage labor; and though his loss of himself is not as pronounced as it is for the laborer, who has had the direct experience of being a purchased commodity, he, too, feels the alienated character of his relations with others.

Thus, the underlying truth of the experiences of the egoist and the loner has been revealed to the communist consciousness: both the egoist's alienation from others and the loner's alienation from himself as well as others can be traced to the phenomenon of wage labor. Indeed, the egoistic consciousness corresponds to that of the buyer of wage labor, while the more profound self-alienation of the loner corresponds to the experience of the seller of wage labor. For the communist consciousness, therefore, eliminating the practice of wage labor is a necessary and sufficient condition for building a communist society.

Now, the communists have sought to explain the origins of alienation, and they have traced these back to the practice of wage labor. Put otherwise, the truth of alienation is wage labor. But, no sooner do they discover this truth, than the communists are forced to admit that this proposition could as easily be reversed—that is, that the truth of wage labor is alienation. After all, if production is, as the communists know, social in character, whence does there arise a practice predicated on a view of individuals as isolated, self-owning producers? Does not the very possibility of wage labor presuppose that men already be alienated from one another?

Accordingly, the communists are forced to trace the phenomenon of wage labor back to a more fundamental source of alienation. The totality of productive forces must already be alienated before individual men come to buy and sell themselves on the marketplace of wage labor. Specifically, men must already fail to acknowledge the social character of the forces of production, and this they can do only by viewing what is essentially social as if it were not. In other words, the basis for wage labor and the true source of alienation lie with the false consciousness which views social forces of production as if they were the private property of individuals. For the communist consciousness now, it is not private ownership in general, but specifically private ownership of the *means of production* that must be abolished for men to overcome their alienation. With this truth, the communists posit a determinate mechanism for explaining how exactly men divide themselves into distinct classes of buyers and sellers of wage labor. Those who control the means of production differ from those who do not in that the latter *must* sell their wage labor in order to live. Thus, the falsity of the laborer's consciousness of being free is now revealed, for he cannot eat unless he trades his labor for a wage from those who control the means of production. Since it is only the worker who is forced to enter into this relation, the owner can set the price of wage labor at a rate that is advantageous to him—that is, he can offer a wage of less value than the value of the worker's labor.

The communists have now discovered what they perceive to be the ultimate source of man's alienation: the phenomenon of *exploitation*, defined as the oppression of one class of individual men by a class of individual men who are presumed to be entitled to reap the benefits of what, from the standpoint of the irreducibly social character of production, can truly be said to "belong" only to society as a whole. The workers are in this way exploited by the owners, insofar as the latter take advantage of the former. But, as the communists have known from the start, the ultimate "blame" for exploitation lies not with the egoistic owners alone, but with society in general. For unlike the earlier master, who ruled by force, the owners control the means of production simply because all members of society—the workers included—presume that they are entitled to do so. Just as the absolute knower was earlier the "subject presumed to know," so now the owners have been revealed to be the "subjects presumed to own." The workers thus find themselves exploited only because they themselves recognize the owners as entitled to exploit them.

From the beginning, the communists have fought alienation because they have viewed it as something *bad*, and they have now traced the origin of this bad thing to something *evil*—namely, the unfair practice of exploitation. Insofar as they now seek to eliminate this evil, the communists can legitimately see their work as fighting for what is good and just. As they carry out to their task of making the workers conscious of their exploitation, the communists appear to the rest of society to be moralists, for they seem to oppose the evil of egoism to the good of communism. Yet for themselves, the communists are not moralists at all. For one thing, they do not chastise the owners for exploiting the workers. On the contrary, they view the owners as simply following the dialectical laws of class antagonism; those who control the means of production naturally exploit workers. But not only would preaching moralizing homilies to the owners be superfluous, but also for the communists this would be to misdirect the "blame" for exploitation. It is not because there are evil men in the world that there is exploitation; there is exploitation just because society as a whole recognizes only some men as entitled to own the means of production. If there is anything like blame to be placed, it should be placed on society as a whole, but to blame everyone is equivalent to blaming no one. Thus, ethical arguments are superfluous for the communists. Their main work is not to reform evil men, but simply to make exploited men conscious of the way in which they fetishize the owners. The communists see themselves, therefore, not as moralizers or utopian theorists longing for a better world, but as scientific instigators of a revolution that will lead to the abolition of the class of owners. By laying bare the logic of exploitation, they claim to reveal the mechanism whereby the practice of wage labor must inevitably abolish itself.

Thus, the communists confidently predict the future. Since the worker must accept whatever terms are offered by the owner, he can be given stingier and stingier wages by an egoist who seeks greater and greater profit. Moreover the owner, insofar as he is in competition with other owners and so must lower the price of the commodities he sells, becomes himself *obliged* to give stingier wages just to turn a profit at all. Together, the phenomena of exploitation and competition among owners must inevitably lead to two results. First, all workers will be reduced to mere subsistence. Except for their minimal requirements to live being met—so they can continue to labor for the owners—they will become a virtually propertyless class of proletarians. Second, the competition among owners will lead to a dwindling of their numbers, so that control of the means of production will become ever more centralized in a few hands.

Once the majority of men constitute a propertyless proletariat class, they will no longer view preserving the institution of property as vital to their livelihood. On the contrary, they will recognize that they have made themselves propertyless precisely by sustaining the fetishization of property which had all along been the underlying support of the egoism of civil society. And since, by that time, the instruments of production will have become centrally controlled, it will be a simple matter for the proletarian class as a whole to seize control over them. Such a dictatorship of the proletariat will then lead humanity out of its alienation and into the truth of communist society. The absolute standpoint will have been achieved at last.

In order for private ownership of the means of production to be abolished, therefore, it is necessary that men disabuse themselves of the false consciousness that is the fetishization of property. But the corresponding and requisite true consciousness of the social character of production will emerge only when the proletariat becomes conscious of itself as an exploited class, which self-consciousness will turn it into a revolutionary class. As yet this is something yet to be fully achieved, for the workers have risen only to the alienated consciousness of the loner, and as such continue to share the egoist's consciousness that property is something which can be owned only by individuals, not by men in general. Hence, the main work of the communists is to further the dialectic of civil society—that is, to speed up the process of exploitation—and to lead the workers to a true consciousness of their situation.

But it is just here, in the revolutionary work of the communists, that the latent contradictions between their ethical consciousness and their scientific revolutionary truth come to the fore. Insofar as they view the dialectical transition to communism as inevitably following from an accentuation of exploitation, the communists view any piecemeal work to alleviate the plight of the workers as counterrevolutionary. To work for reforms in labor laws, for instance, is viewed as acting contrary to the interests of workers, despite the fact that such reforms would lead to improvements in the health and material lot of real individuals. Only that which makes their exploitation all the more painful can bring home to the workers the need to revolt against the owners. But this means that, up until the actual moment of revolt, the communists find themselves furthering the immediate interests not of the workers but of the owners. Yet when this is pointed out to them, the communists chide their critics for failing to rise to the level of a true scientific revolutionary consciousness. They attack those who would act *morally* on behalf of the workers of furthering the interests of the owners, while priding themselves on how much they are helping the workers by opposing all reformist efforts to help them. In doing so, they adopt a kind of "No pain, no gain" doctrine, which they justify as the necessity to rid themselves of the prejudices of egoistic morality.

Those reform-minded individuals who advocate immediate alleviation of the pain of exploitation insist that it is they, rather than the communists, who are opposing the callous egoism of civil society. To them, the communists reply that to aid individual workers acquire more property merely helps preserve the institution of private property. Those who seek to help individuals *qua* individuals, they maintain, are acting not in accordance with the law of the coming communist state, but in accordance with the reactionary law of the family, itself a vestigial throwback to the morality of feudal society. In this regard, the communists exhibit the self-righteousness of individuals who are conscious of the ethical totality. However, since they recognize the presently existing state as merely existing for the sake of individual owners, they deny its authority. Thus, their appeal to the ethical totality has a kind of future auxiliary tense—their indifference to the pain of particular individuals today will have been justified from the perspective of the communist state. Until the actual appearance of this state, the communists demonstrate as ruthless a contempt for individuals as the most egoistic owner, a position reminiscent of the terror of absolute freedom.

But precisely for this reason, the previously repressed uncertainty as to how exactly a communist society will reconcile the individuality of its members with its social unity now returns in an explicit way. In particular, the question arises as to whether or not a communist society is to be constructed as a state, or whether the envisioned dictatorship of the proletariat will merely be a transitional formation on the way to a stateless society.

Insofar as the existing state already represents the unity of men over and against the egoistic multiplicity of individuals in civil society, the communists appear to be arguing for a stronger state—that is, one which will genuinely serve the interests of men in general rather than merely serving as an instrument of those who control civil society. Yet on the other hand, the communists have denounced the state as being incapable of reconciling the conflicts of civil society, and to this extent they appear to be seeking a weakening rather than a strengthening of it.

Thus, the communist consciousness, otherwise united in its common goal, splits into rival factions—the *statists* and the *anarchists*, a movement which to some extent recapitulates the conflict between the human and divine laws. Here, both groups will continue, at first, to form a united front against not only the defenders of civil society, but also those who attack civil society in the name of the law of the family. The repressed consciousness that has been consigned to the domain of the family will remain, for now, repressed. We move, accordingly, into materialist spirit's dialectic of culture.

B. Materialist Culture: Anarchy, State, and Dystopia

The scientific revolutionary consciousness that is now split into the opposition between the statists and the anarchists has emerged out of the communists' initial certainty of the falsity of alienation. They achieved this certainty by managing to recognize each other in a way which had seemed impossible to the alienated loner. By recognizing each other as individual

participants in the species-being of man, the communists thereby actualized the self-consciousness of the absolute knower, and in so doing set out
straightaway to undertake jointly the project of actual absolute knowing,
now recast as the activity of real—that is, materialist—science: science
committed to changing the world. In this way, the work of the communists
resembles that of the earlier self-conscious individuals who, having achieved
a consciousness of themselves as reason, set out to observe nature, in order
that nature's rationality might be revealed. But unlike the shape of observing reason, which posited itself as a universal true consciousness, the communists came to their sense of mutual identity precisely by distinguishing
between their own true consciousness and what they took to be the false
consciousness of the majority of men. Hence in their observations of human relations, the communists found themselves looking not only for the
rational principles of the dialectic that had led to their own transcending
of their alienation, but also for the irrational principles behind the actions
of most men. Observing reason had been naive to turn to phrenology in
order to discern the rationality of men; but this naivety also had a kind of
democratic expectation behind it, insofar as it presumed the general rationality of the majority of men. Similarly, the alienated rational individual
who sought to reconcile himself to the rest of society presumed that other
men were agents of reason, even if he himself at times found reason to be
oppressive, and so took refuge in the law of the heart. By contrast, the
communist consciousness begins by presuming that men are irrational
insofar as they are alienated from their species-being, and so materialist
science rather aristocratically expects to find evidence of man's irrationality
in its study of human relations. Yet at the same time, precisely because they
take their own perceived rationality to be the goal towards which all humanity is unconsciously aiming, the communists view man's present stu-
pidity as a skin that he will eventually shed. The two primary aims of
materialist science, then, are to reveal the sources of man's irrationality but
also to illuminate the way in which man is being steered by nature toward
the attainment of his full rationality.

To this extent there is something supercilious about the communists,
who are forever telling the workers that they, the communists, understand
them better than they do themselves. In fact, the communists are in bad
faith because they manage to posit the overcoming of alienation only by
having banded together as isolated intellectuals alienated from the rest of
humanity. They know that they have a difficult time relating to other men,
but they fail to take this as a sign of their own continuing alienation from
humanity because they blame the egoism of these others for their failure
to communicate. This is not to say that the communists have entirely failed
to overcome their alienation from one another, but so long as theirs is an

[I = I] predicated on an "us *vs.* them" model, it is an incomplete and hence necessarily fragile reconciliation. The communists are only able to view themselves as possessing the truth by placing themselves in an exalted position over and above the rest of society.

So long as the communists remain in solidarity with one another, they can convince themselves that anyone who disagrees with them is suffering from false consciousness. In just this respect, though, they require a remarkable degree of uniformity in their own thinking; for any internal disagreement would threaten to jeopardize their collective sense of possessing the truth. Anyone who disagrees with the majority is either literally or symbolically cast out of the group, accused of suffering from false consciousness. A highly authoritarian structure thus develops among the communists, which exactly resembles the earlier relations among the master absolute knower and his loyal disciples. The thoughts of one communist in particular must rule the day, just as previously there could be only one master. He is dubbed the most scientific among them, and everyone else is expected to agree with him.

The communists have thus already required the positing of a quasi-state apparatus among themselves—a communist *party*—ruled by the fetishized master communist. It is he and his most loyal followers who defend the idea that a communist state will be necessary. By contrast, and again paralleling the dissolution of the family of absolute knowers, those who are new to the party, and so less closely tied to its master, object to the party's authoritarian structure. As marginal party members expected to obey the master's every decree, these disaffected individuals can see for themselves that communist party rule is oppressively authoritarian. They, accordingly, are the ones who rebel against the idea of a communist state, declaring themselves the enemies of all authoritarian organizations. The consequent split between the statists, who remain loyal to the party, and the anarchists, who resign from the party, recapitulates the earlier split between the conservative preservers of the master absolute knower's legacy and the unorthodox philosophical radicals. Just as the latter could see through the preservers' pretense to having achieved the absolute standpoint, so now the anarchists correctly see the gap between the democratic ideals of the communists and their authoritarian methods. The communists affirm the equality of men, but only by introducing the hierarchical division between those who possess a true consciousness and those suffering from false consciousness. In the name of equality, that is, they find it necessary to deny the equality of men. More precisely, the communists do sincerely and loftily promote the equality of all, but precisely at the expense of the freedom of individuals. But, as the anarchists know, equality without freedom is only an immediate and false reconciliation of individuals; true equality must respect the real differences—that is, the freedom—of individuals.

For their part, the communists reject the anarchists' insinuation that they are the enemies of freedom. Yet they find themselves in a double bind. For, on the one hand, they insist that only those with a true consciousness of the fetishization of property can lead humanity to a communist society. To this extent, they reject the charge of authoritarianism by reaffirming the scientific character of their understanding of men. Yet on the other hand, the anarchists have made them conscious of the ultimate incompatibility of freedom and authoritarian rule. Accordingly they try to balance these two demands by affirming the necessity of a *transitional* communist state, and they emphasize, moreover, that although the party will be at the head of this state, it will be ruled not by them—the clique of intellectual communists—but by the proletariat itself. This transitional state, the communists now maintain, will eventually wither away. Thus, the communists make a kind of concession to the anarchists, and so extend to them an invitation to return to the party.

But the anarchists reject the communists' claim to science as mere pretense, and insist that a truly egalitarian society can only develop out of the spontaneity of life, not imposed from above by a group of individuals who dogmatically presume that they know what is in the best interest of everyone. In addition, the anarchists voice their suspicion about the party's solemn declaration that the communist state would eventually wither away. Once in power, the rulers of this state, even if they are former members of the proletariat, will act as do all other authorities—they will expect conformity to their will. That this is so can be gleaned from the fact that the communist party itself leaves no room for individual freedom. Thus, the anarchists point out that the problem with the communists is that they work only for equality, falsely assuming that freedom will come later. For their part, they reverse this strategy, maintaining that freedom must be fought for above all. Equality, they claim, will naturally follow.

The communists' contempt for the individual as such could be seen in their earlier condemnation of any immediate work designed to improve the material conditions of individual workers. But by opposing the communists' emphasis on social unity, the anarchists now risk moving to the opposite extreme of affirming merely the right of the isolated loner to live like a loner. This is of course not their true aim; on the contrary, they share the communists' vision of a society in which man's true consciousness of his species-being will be achieved. Accordingly, they must articulate a model of an anarchist society that will specify a nonauthoritarian mechanism for coordinating the social lives of men. In place of the communists' presumption of a central, state-like social organization, the anarchists put forth their ideal of a noninstitutional coordination of social life. Communist centralism, they know, would amount to nothing more than the will of a few individual men imposing itself on society as a whole. By contrast, anarchist collectivism will be worked up out of the wills of individual men.

Thus, in place of an authoritarian top-down model of social unity, the anarchists envision a bottom-up model. Yet the danger with the latter approach lies in its apparent reversion to the egoistic assumption that individual men are ontologically independent from one another, whereas the anarchists in fact share the communists' assumption that man is essentially a social being. Were they to begin from the totality of man's social being, however, they would risk succumbing to the communists' contempt for the integrity of the individual. Accordingly, the anarchists must posit a mediating link between totality and individuality: man is naturally a member of a *small* community, not too big and not too little. He can be reduced neither to the isolated individual nor to the species as a whole. Anarchic social unity is accordingly to be achieved as a *federation* of these small communes.

By defending in this way an ideal of social individualism, the anarchists see themselves steering a middle course between the egoism of civil society and the statism of the communists; the former affirms freedom at the expense of equality, and the latter affirms equality at the expense of freedom. At the heart of the anarchists' consciousness is their equation of the concepts of true freedom and true equality—one cannot be achieved without the other. Hence the anarchists affirm the necessity of combining the struggle for economic equality with a struggle for political freedom. For the communists, political struggles against the existing state were essentially irrelevant; the transformation of civil society into communist society would suffice to abolish a government that existed solely in the interest of egoists. But for the anarchists, who now posit the oppressiveness of state apparatuses in general, every political organization is an impediment to freedom. Yet the anarchists go still further. Since they affirm freedom above all else, they must oppose all impediments on individual self-determination. The locally defined economic struggle of the proletariat now gives way to the total social struggle of individuals against authority. The anarchists set out to attack all social insitutions, in a manner that resembles the earlier frenzy of self-conceit. Yet they do so not egoistically, but rather with the explicit goal of liberating other individuals from their subservience to authority. Anyone still enslaved by the Church, the state, the communist party, and so forth, must be delivered from their oppressors.

Now, the fact that not everybody embraces their ideas does not surprise the anarchists; they do not expect the vicar, the state minister, or the party leader to renounce their positions of privilege. But they are dismayed to learn that many individuals who seem merely to be the victims of authority are not receptive to their liberating teaching. It turns out that there are many churchgoers, citizens, and loyal party members who claim to recognize an authority of their own free will. To the anarchists, the idea of freely obeying an authority is a contradiction in terms, and so they can only accuse such people of suffering from false consciousness. But in raising this charge, of course, they resort to the very authoritarian elitism which they spend their time castigating in others, for by insisting that those who fail to recognize the evil of all authority are wrong, the anarchists unwittingly put themselves forward as evil authorities. Yet instead of acknowledging this contradiction, which would require that they abandon their certainty, the anarchists fall back, once again, on the all-too-familiar pretentiousness of the Enlightenment. They oppose their scientific consciousness to the faith of the masses. In this respect, of course, they must abandon their earlier criticism of the communists; now, instead of rejecting science altogether, they claim simply to possess a truer scientific understanding than the communists. In addition, as did the earlier philosophical radicals who were frustrated with their efforts to disabuse men of their religious faith, the anarchists respond to their failure to communicate their truth by redoubling their efforts to destroy the pernicious influence of authority wherever it appears. What drives the anarchists now is a thoroughgoing "passion for destruction," which they posit as a creative act.

But this passion quickly becomes indiscriminate in its targets, for there is no feature of men's present loyalties which for the teleologically-minded anarchists does not represent an authority that must be overthrown. Their virtuous intent thus degenerates fully into a frenzy of self-conceit, masked only by the false consciousness which leads them to think that, in scorning everything, they do so precisely for the sake of everyone.

Because of the indiscriminacy of their attacks, the anarchists can no longer distinguish between friends and foes. This failure comes out in their relations with those who have remained unrepentant communists. Despite their initial disagreements with the communists, in the end their differences with them have not really amounted to very much—especially now that the anarchists have become no less self-proclaimed authorities than are the communists. The only real disagreement between them is that the communists advocate centralism, while the anarchists advocate federalism. By contrast, the two groups share the common substantive goals of working toward the equality and freedom of all, and as such they would do well to unite forces. For the chaotic and confused anarchists, however, no one authority is any better or worse than any other, and so they can find no good reason to work with the communists. For the anarchist consciousness, the individual worker should be just as mistrustful of the communists as he should be of the owners who exploit him. To be sure, there is a moment of truth in this warning, but telling the workers to reject communism is like telling a hungry man not to eat because his food "might" be poisonous. No longer able to distinguish between what is good and what is bad, and led therefore to repudiate everything, the anarchists have become *nihilists*.

Where the anarchists began by opposing the freedom of individuals to the unfreedom of authority, the nihilists have ended up opposing freedom to everything. Just as earlier, in the dialectic of spirit, absolute freedom gave way to absolute terror, so now the nihilist consciousness appears as a terroristic consciousness: in place of the anarchist's original respect for individuals, there stands now the nihilist's contempt for everyone but those who share his own nihilistic attitude. Where the anarchist could maintain the pretense that his growing scorn for others sprung from a sincere desire to help them, the nihilist now throws off this conceit and acknowledges in his contempt for everyone else that he is only interested in himself. To this extent, he regresses to the position of the egoist, but since he has no more lost his contempt for egoists than he has for anyone else, the nihilist refuses to acknowledge the similarity, declaring himself to be a *scientific* egoist. This is more than a merely nominal distinction, because the nihilist has indeed reached his scientific egoism by way of the communist rejection of philosophical egoism, which rejection he shares. Thus, despite his utter disdain for humanity, the nihilist is in himself a secret lover of humanity; in truth, he is merely a frustrated anarchist who would prefer nothing more than that mankind should become reconciled with itself in a truly egalitarian society. Although for himself an individual nihilist, in himself he is a social positivist—that is, he expects that his destructive attitude will in fact lead toward a better society. Thus, the nihilist is in profound contradiction with himself, for he utterly denies that he cares for anyone but himself, while deep within himself wishing for the well-being of everyone.

But just therein lies the basis for an overcoming of the nihilist's self-alienation, for in himself he has brought into a unity the previously opposed moments of egoism and communism. Once he admits to himself that he is a lover of humanity precisely insofar as he is a lover of himself, and a lover of himself precisely insofar as he is a lover of humanity, the nihilist will have transcended the alienation of materialist culture, and brought to fulfillment its moral truth. In this respect, he repeats the earlier movement whereby absolute freedom dissolved the antithesis between universal and individual will. He now knows himself as a moral individual. Yet because we are now within the realm of *materialist* spirit, this moral individual retains the truth of anthropology, and so rises to the level of *humanism*.

C. Christian Humanism, Anti-Semitism, and the Unmasking of the Ascetic Ideal

In itself, the scientific egoism of the nihilist consciousness reconciled the truths of the communist and the anarchist. When this, its essence, is raised to the level of self-consciousness, the nihilist transcends the pure negativity that led him to reject everyone and everything. Since it was precisely *for the sake of* everyone and everything that he rejected them, the nihilist who comes to know himself learns that he is really a humanist—that is, someone who has actualized the philosophical anthropologist's universal feeling of love for all humanity. But because he discovers this humanism as the truth of his nihilism, the distinction between himself and others has dropped away. Put otherwise, the nihilist who negates everyone else ends up negating himself as well, but this omnicide gives him back both himself and others. He is now an *indiscriminate* humanist—that is, he embraces humanity whether it appears in himself or in others.

The humanist has negated both his self-love and his love of humanity only to resurrect both as reconciled truths. Even though this reconciliation has thus far occurred in an explicit way only within himself, he is certain that it takes place implicitly within the hearts of all men. He is certain, because even though his knowledge of the identity of selfishness and selflessness is something as yet present only for himself, the *truth* of this identity is something he takes to be universal. In themselves, all egoists are really humanists whether they know it or not. But this means that all of the stages of alienation hitherto have been overcome for the humanist, since the truth of man's species-being—that is, the materialist absolute standpoint—is *in itself* always already actualized. All that remains is for humanity in general to be made aware of its reconciliation with itself. Individuals must discover that they really do love one another, regardless of how they think they feel.

Now, to the unrepentant nihilist who clings to the division between scientific egoism and humanism, this proposition appears to be an absurdity. To the humanist, he holds up an example of man's cruelty to his fellow man, and dares him to describe it as an act of love. Only by completely eviscerating the meaning of the word "love" could one describe the torture of a child as revealing "in itself" the torturer's love of humanity.

In response to the scorn of the nihilist, the humanist acknowledges that men's *actions* are often cruel, but he maintains that *men themselves* are not. Acts of cruelty are either entirely inadvertent, as when a man tries to help another by giving him vodka only to end up causing his death, or, if they are intended, are due to a failure of self-knowledge on the part on the agent. For a man's actions are an expression of how he *appears* to be for himself, not how he actually *is* in himself. To the humanist who believes that man is essentially a lover of humanity, all acts of cruelty would immediately cease to be performed if only men could be raised to the level of a true self-consciousness.

There is, however, no way of verifying that a particular act of cruelty arose from the heart of a lover of humanity. All that is available for public inspection is the act itself and the speech of the agent, neither of which can provide sufficient evidence of the humanist's assertion that, regardless of this particular contemptible act and its agent's boastful speech, the agent was still, in himself, a lover of humanity. The humanist can only *imagine* the inner psychology of the agent, and so can never prove to the skeptic that all men possess humanitarian ideals. If the humanist is to present the gap between man's true self-consciousness and his apparent self-consciousness, he can only *depict* it—that is, he can present to the world imagined representations (*Vorstellungen*) of the inner lives of those who perform cruel acts. The humanist accordingly sets out to create psychological portraits—for instance, by composing novels—which aim to reveal the inner lives of real men even if they can only do so through fictional accounts. The humanist writes these novels not so much to turn his readers into humanists as to make them aware that they and everyone else already are humanists.

To the composer of these novels, the essence of humanity is its self-love, but this essence is something still *hidden* from most men. Man's universal love is thus posited as something both beyond, yet also within the hearts of everyone. This, of course, is precisely the truth of revealed religion: the (not yet arrived) kingdom of God is (always already) within you. The humanist who affirms this truth is, therefore, essentially a *Christian humanist*.

To say that the humanist is a *Christian* humanist is to say that he believes in the necessity of men embracing the truth of revealed religion. Only when all men accept Christ will the implicit kingdom of heaven be made real on earth. Yet the Christian humanist believes that all men have already accepted Christ within their hearts. To truly deny Christ is, strictly speaking, impossible. After all, being a Christian and being a lover of humanity are one and the same thing, and the Christian humanist is certain that all men are lovers of humanity. For this reason, all men are in themselves Christians, regardless of how they appear for themselves. Those who think they reject Christianity are merely suffering from a kind of bad faith.

Accordingly, whenever he wishes to characterize man's *false* image of himself—his image of himself as a selfish egoist who cares nothing for his fellow man—the Christian humanist calls attention to those manifestations of religious life which preceded revealed religion. To be a possessive egoist is, according to his iconography, to be not-yet-Christian—for instance, to be "stuck" at the level where the universality of God appears only in its outer form and not yet as the inner truth of man revealed in the individuality of Christ. In this way the Christian humanist makes explicit the latent anti-Semitism that lurked within the self-consciousness of revealed religion.

The absolute knower who affirmed the notional truth of revealed religion was himself an *implicit* anti-Semite, in that he, too, could recognize only those whom he viewed as having been raised to the absolute standpoint by way of revealed religion. However, unlike the Christian humanist, the absolute knower had thrown off the picture-thinking of revealed religion, and as such he could repress the moment of his anti-Semitism. Among the community of men who were the master and his disciples, man was defined not as being in the image of Christ; rather, Christ was defined as being in the image of man. Accordingly, the so-called *Jewish question* did not come up in an explicit way; men were neither "Jews" nor "Christians," but simply men. For this reason the rival absolute knowers who struggled for recognition did not begrudge each other their particular differences so much as they were unable to acknowledge them.

By contrast, the Christian humanist has arrived at his humanism only by negating whatever makes individuals separate egos existing apart from one another. He has, in short, arrived at his universal love only by having negated everything that makes particular individuals particular. To this extent, he is still a nihilist. He is thus unable to recognize others as egos; he recognizes others only as equally selfless subjects. In the name of universal love, the Christian humanist actually loves only the abstract ideal of a person, not flesh and blood individuals. For him, the ideal of Christ represents the universal subject who has completely denied himself. The Christian humanist accordingly condemns "the Jew" as the type of man who refuses to perform this same ascetic denial of self. The Jew is seen as an egoist who insists on his right to own what is his, whereas the Christian is the selfless individual who has sacrificed his own ego for his love of humanity.

In equating Jewishness with egoistic miserliness, however, our universal lover of humanity does not mean to criticize real Jews—after all, he loves all men. But this is because for him *there are no real Jews*—that is, men who are *in themselves* Jews. Those who call themselves Jews are merely Jews *for themselves*; deep down, like everyone else, they are really Christians. For the Christian humanist, pure Jewishness is as unreal as the one-sided egoism expressed in pure nihilism.

Yet despite the Christian humanist's Enlightened certainty that those who consider themselves to be Jews are suffering from a kind of false consciousness, there are those who do indeed consider themselves to be "real" Jews—that is, non-Christian Jews. Accordingly, they object to the Christian humanist's equation of the word "Jew" with "miser," and question the sincerity of his supposedly universal love of humanity. How indeed can he pose as a lover of all humanity while recognizing only the humanity of those who think like him?

In attacking his anti-Semitism, the Jews call attention to an apparent narcissistic egoism of the Christian humanist. But in fact, what he exhibits is not narcissistic egoism but narcissistic asceticism. For his part, the Christian humanist is shocked to discover that the Jews object to his use of the word "Jew." He denies being an anti-Semite and reiterates his universal love for all men, regardless of their religious affiliation. Moreover, he insists that all "true Christians" must—*as Christians*—condemn anti-Semitism.

His defense of himself is heartfelt and sincere. Nonetheless, there is a certain duplicity in the Christian humanist's disavowal of his anti-Semitism, for he does not go so far as to retract his view that all men are really, in and of themselves, Christians. On the contrary, he apologizes to the Jews by pointing out the most virtuous among them and declaring that they are "more Christian" than many Christians. To the Jews, such an apology is absurd; it is as if the Christian humanist had said, "But I'm not anti-Semitic, because I don't even think of you as Jews!" In other words, he *is* an anti-Semite, because he continues to view "Jewishness" as a falling away from humanity. Thus, not only does he tell his Jewish friends that he thinks of them as Christians rather than as Jews, but he goes further and declares that those "real" anti-Semites who persecute them are acting in an unchristian—that is, in a Jewish—way! In the twisted logic of the anti-Semitic Christian humanist, Jews are good Christians, and anti-Semites are acting like evil Jews. But instead of recognizing the blatant contradiction of such statements, the Christian humanist explains that although the subjects of these sentences denote real people, the predicates denote *types*. With his notion of types, the Christian humanist explains that what he really means to say is, "Not all Jews are 'Jews.'"

Since the Christian humanist is certain that all men are in themselves ascetic Christians, he believes that it is only due to a failure of self-knowledge that any individual appears—to himself and to others—to exhibit a different type. At bottom, only the type of the Christian is real; all other types are but phantom shapes assumed by those who suffer from false self-consciousness. Or, put the other way around, non-Christian types can be viewed as the real expressions of degrees of self-ignorance. To think oneself a Jew is one way of failing to know oneself.

The Christian humanist's novels attempt to depict the various types of men, presenting every character except the self-conscious Christian as suffering from some form of self-ignorance. These novels also try to illustrate the psychological processes whereby individual men learn to transcend their false self-consciousness by becoming aware of the truth of revealed religion. Ultimately, it is less important that every possible type be depicted than it is that the very worst types of men be depicted—that is, those who appear as if they were haters rather than lovers of humanity. Because he seeks to show that even the most vicious acts are performed by lovers of humanity, the Christian humanist pays particular attention to depicting the inner lives of criminals and others who have fallen furthest away from themselves—that is, the class of those who appear to be *undermen*. It is essential to show that even when he is unconscious of his true nature, the underman is still a lover of humanity; otherwise, he would be a "true rebel." The true rebel represents an impossible type, one which the Christian humanist could acknowledge only as a counterexample to his thesis that all criminality is merely a form of false self-consciousness.

For the Christian humanist, both the criminal's "apparent" rejection of humanity and the Jew's "apparent" rejection of Christ are one and the same thing. In fact, "the problem of evil" turns out to be identical to "the Jewish question"—when he asks, "Why are men led to act as if they were despisers of humanity?" he is asking the same question as "Why are there Jews?" Of course, the Christian humanist does not believe either in "true rebels" or in "real Jews." He is certain that all criminals are essentially good-hearted individuals who have stumbled into crime out of a confused desire to aid humanity. However, to prove his certainty to others is easier said than done. It is one thing to depict particular criminals who commit crimes because they wish to serve humanity—models for whom can be found among the nihilists—but who can say for sure whether all criminals are of this sort?

To those who do not share the perspective of the Christian humanist, violent criminals frequently appear to be true rebels. Moreover, since their acts appear to be *inhumane*, the criminals themselves are judged to have forfeited their own humanity. For this reason, they are themselves treated in an inhumane way by good Christians. Of course those who act inhumanely toward criminals do not view *themselves* as cruel, for they do not view the punishment of criminals as a crime. They see themselves as punishing someone who was cruel because he *despised* humanity, and they see themselves as being cruel to him only because they *love* humanity. Nonetheless, violence against humanity is violence against humanity. Violence against criminals is still violence against humanity, even though it is performed in the name of punishment of violence against humanity.

For the Christian humanist, this example—the phenomenon of cruel punishment—provides a model for thinking about the psychology of all criminal acts. Since the will to punish criminals in a cruel way arises from a desire to negate those who negate humanity, perhaps all cruelty arises from precisely the same desire. All acts of cruelty could conceivably have two sides: for others, the criminal's act would appear to be the act of a despiser of humanity; but for himself, the criminal's act would signify a desire to redeem humanity. Perhaps, in other words, it is only the thought of the *inhumanity* of humanity that tempts a man to reject humanity in the first place; men would thus be cruel only toward those whom they view as cruel. In seeking to absolve the criminal, of course, the Christian humanist does not mean to condone crime. On the contrary, he condemns all *crimes*— which are indeed inhumane acts of cruelty—but he maintains that all Christians must exonerate *criminals*, for those who commit inhumane acts do not realize that they are acting inhumanely. Forgive all men their sins, he proclaims, for they know not what they do.

There is, nonetheless, a kind of asymmetry between crime and punishment. He who commits a crime has indeed acted cruelly, regardless of why he did so. Therefore, those who punish him, even if they, too, act cruelly, can at least defend themselves by saying that they punished a man who acted cruelly. Now, if the criminal had committed a crime against an apparently evil man, he, too, could say the same thing. But the criminal appears to be completely without justification whenever he commits a crime against those who seem to be truly blameless, such as innocent children. Those who are cruel to children appear not just to be ignorant, but to be genuinely evil. Hence the man who is cruel to children could conceivably be a counterexample to the Christian humanist's thesis that all men are lovers of humanity.

Not only does this example threaten to call into question the humanism of the criminal, but it also calls into question the Christian humanist's basis for judging all men to be worthy of love. If human beings can be deliberately cruel to those whom they know to be innocent, then the intrinsic goodness of humanity in general must be called into question. Out of despair at man's inhumanity, the Christian humanist himself might even be tempted to rebel against humanity. In order to forestall this objection, the Christian humanist sets out to compose his most challenging novel—the one that will show that even men who are cruel to children are lovers of humanity.

By definition, children are innocent. For the Christian humanist, however, all men are, in themselves, essentially innocent as well. To show that even those who are cruel to children are lovers of humanity is therefore to show that they, too, are essentially children. In effect, then, the problem reverses itself; the Christian humanist must explain away not so much cruelty *toward* children, as the cruelty performed *by* children. Strictly speaking, of course, the idea of the self-consciously cruel child is just as impossible as that of the real Jew or the true rebel. The problem for the Christian humanist, then, is simply to show that there is no self-conscious cruelty in children, but only children's ignorant cruelty toward one another.

Although the Christian humanist sincerely believes that men are lovers of humanity even when their acts are cruel, in the end he cannot raise this certainty to the level of truth. After all, his novels merely depict *possible* versions of the inner lives of criminals. However artfully drawn, these psychological portraits can as easily be reversed to demonstrate the opposite thesis—namely, the egoistic truth that the ideal of universal love is unattainable. Besides, no amount of psychological balm can soothe the hard fact that real men commit cruel acts whether they know what they are doing or not. Even if the Christian humanist is right to believe that all men are in themselves lovers of humanity, this implicit truth will not manifest itself in their acts until they become *self-conscious* lovers of humanity. To this extent, the kingdom of heaven on earth must be viewed as something not yet actual. Yet at the same time the Christian humanist is certain that it will become actual; he thus views it as man's *destiny*. But it is a "destiny" in a curious sense. For on the one hand, it is *already* true, yet on the other, it is *not yet* true. In effect, it is a "destiny" in the same sense that the winner of yesterday's race is destined to be the winner of yesterday's race, but only when he reads about it in the newspaper—or, in this case, in the Christian humanist's novels. Or, to characterize this curious logic another way, men are, for the Christian humanist, like those cartoon characters who will start to obey the law of gravity only after they have become aware that they have fallen off a cliff. Until men realize that they cannot be deliberately cruel to one another, they will continue to act as if they are deliberately cruel to one another—that is, they will continue to defy the Christian humanist's "law of gravity."

Ultimately, therefore, the Christian humanist can maintain his faith in man's inner love of humanity only by radically distinguishing between men and their acts. He loves men, and for this reason he can forgive them their cruelty, but he despises their cruel acts. In this respect, he has reverted back to the consciousness of the beautiful soul, who stood in judgment of the man of action. As did the beautiful soul, so the Christian humanist has withdrawn from the realm of human activity into a pristine world of pure intent. His ideal life is accordingly represented in the figure of the monk, the man who withdraws from action altogether.

In advocating the ascetic life of the monk, the Christian humanist professes to teach men how to find themselves. Yet in truth, he is asking them to turn away from themselves. Because the monk completely removes himself from the realm of action, he attains his reconciliation with the rest of humanity at a cheap price—or, rather, at the most exorbitant price: total sacrifice of his own ego. To call for a world of self-denying monks is thus not to posit a world in which men would act in a loving way, so much as it is to posit a world in which men would cease to *act* altogether.

With his distinction between men and their acts, moreover, the Christian humanist finds himself involved in a kind of duplicity. To love men but not their acts is, essentially, not to love *real* men at all. On the contrary, what he has loved all along is his own representation of the *ideal* man— the self-sacrificing monk who turns away from life altogether. In claiming to love men, the Christian humanist really loves only his imagined ideal; if he can sustain the pretense that he loves *real* men it is only because he does not see them as they really are. No matter how cruel a man might be, the Christian humanist peers into his eyes *as if* gazing into the man's actual soul and declares "this one too" to be a lover of humanity. But this *as if* is not only mere conjecture; it flies in the face of how actually cruel men characterize themselves. At bottom, what the Christian humanist really loves in men is thus their fictive potential—what he could do with such and such an individual if he were to make him into one of the characters of his novels.

Were he to discover that his ideal of man is merely an ideal, the Christian humanist would realize that he is no lover of real humanity at all. In advocating the ascetic ideal, in fact, he actually negates others as much as he negates himself. In the end, all that he feels for real men is contempt—or, at best, pity. He pities real men because they are not like the characters in his novels. The essence of the Christian humanist is, accordingly, not his love of humanity but his pity for humanity. This expert psychologist turns out to suffer from a false self-consciousness of his own.

With his theory of types and psychological lessons, however, the Christian humanist inadvertently invites another psychologist to ask the question, "What is the significance of *this* type of man—the Christian humanist, the one who pities man?" With this question, we leave the self-certainty of the Christian humanist and arrive at the consciousness of the Christian humanist's duplicity. This is the starting-point of the *psychologist of Christianity*.

The psychologist of Christianity begins from his consciousness that the Christian humanist suffers at the thought of human cruelty, and he sets out to determine the *origin* of this suffering. To the Christian humanist, human cruelty was so obviously an evil thing that he himself never thought to raise the question concerning his suffering at the thought of it. But to the psychologist of Christianity, the immediate *object* of the Christian humanist's suffering—man insofar as he acts as a cruel animal—and the *source* of this suffering—that is, that which makes the humanist view cruelty as necessarily evil—are not the same thing. For the idea of human cruelty does not analytically entail the thought of evil; cruelty is presumed to be evil *by the Christian humanist*. Accordingly, the questions that must be asked are these: What type of man is represented by the Christian humanist? For whom is the proposition that cruelty is evil a necessary judgment?

To the Christian humanist, of course, his type is that of the lover of humanity. But since humanity shows itself to be cruel, why isn't the Christian humanist a lover of cruelty, rather than a despiser of it? Might the Christian humanist secretly admire man's cruelty at the very moment when he most pities man? Conversely, if he is truly a despiser of cruelty, and man shows himself to be a cruel animal, then isn't the Christian humanist at bottom a despiser of humanity? Might he not exhibit a profound hatred of man at the very moment when he pities him? Of course the Christian humanist would refuse the proposition that man *is* a cruel animal, for he distinguishes between man himself and man insofar as he appears as an agent. But why feel pity at a cruelty that is only apparent and not real? By right, it should be those who reject the humanist thesis—that is, those who truly believe that men are cruel—who feel pity for men.

The Christian humanist's pity thus appears to be as curious an enigma to the psychologist of Christianity as was the self-conscious Jew to the Christian humanist. But this pity remains an enigma only for so long as the psychologist of Christianity accepts that the Christian humanist is who he says he is—namely, a lover of humanity who despises men's cruelty. The fact that the Christian humanist pities man betrays him: he is either a lover of cruelty, a despiser of humanity, or both. Ironically, the Christian humanist's type turns out to be that of the man with false self-consciousness, for in fact, he is no lover of *real* humanity; he loves only his own ideal of men. This ideal—represented in the figure of the monk—is merely a negation of real humanity, for it is the ideal of a completely withdrawn, inactive humanity. In short, the Christian humanist loves the *image of a dead man*, not the reality of a living one. Real men—that is, living, breathing, *acting* men—he views with revulsion.

The Christian humanist thus turns out to be a hypocrite, albeit a sincere one, since he himself does not realize that he despises humanity. The secret that lurks within his heart, unbeknownst even to himself, is that he never repented of his nihilism—on the contrary, he is a nihilist with a vengeance. This can be seen in his unrepentant anti-Semitism. For the Christian humanist, the figure of the Jew represents living humanity's objection to the crucified life-denying ideal which he himself advocates. In his latent hatred of Jews is revealed the Christian humanist's contempt for all men who refuse to accept the ideal of a god on the cross. In his clandestine desire that all men be crucified, the Christian humanist turns out to be—*the cruellest of men*. Beneath his mask of the lover of humanity lurks the heart of none other than the true rebel against humanity.

Concluding that the Christian humanist represents not the highest type but the lowest type of man, the psychologist of Christianity is now led to reverse all the values that had been assigned to the various types of men by the Christian humanist. The Christian humanist, of course, took himself to represent the highest type, and the underman to represent the lowest type; he saw himself as trying to raise the underman up to his level. But to the psychologist of Christianity, the Christian humanist is a hypocritical despiser of humanity, whereas the underman is merely a sincere egoist. As such, the underman is infinitely closer to the ideal of the true humanist than is the Christian humanist. Insofar as he loves himself, the underman is indeed a lover of humanity—albeit a selective one, in that he loves only those in whom his own particular ego finds something to love. By contrast, the Christian humanist's ideal of an *indiscriminate* lover of humanity— since its basis could only be a denial of oneself—is, to the psychologist of Christianity, as impossible an ideal as was that of the absolute rebel to the Christian humanist. As the most sincere manifestation of the otherwise impossible type of the lover of humanity, the underman represents not the lowest type but the highest type: he is not something that men must rise above, he is rather something men must rise to meet. The *underman* is really the *overman*; for man to become better, he must become more like the overman—that is, more egoistic, more selfish, and if necessary more cruel: in short, a better lover of humanity.

With the ideal of the overman, the psychological typology of the Christian humanist has been stood on its head and revaluated. What was judged good by the Christian humanist is now viewed as evil, and what was judged evil is now judged to be good. But the psychologist of Christianity is himself in danger of being called a hypocrite, for he has not—at least not yet— reversed the meaning of the values *good* and *evil* themselves. Precisely as did the Christian humanist, so the psychologist of Christianity takes love of humanity to be good and hatred of humanity to be bad. The ideal of the overman is the ideal of the *true* lover of humanity and it is *for this reason* that he represents the ideal type to the psychologist of Christianity. Similarly, he has relegated the cruel Christian humanist to the lowest rung not because the latter is a humanist, but because the latter is a cruel hypocrite—that is, because he is not a true humanist. Were the psychologist of Christianity a genuine lover of cruelty, he would presumably admire rather than despise the Christian humanist, since the latter now appears to be the cruellest of men. Instead of relegating him to the lowest rung of humanity, he would honor this cruellest of men as the exemplar of the overman. The fact that he does not do so shows that, in the end, what he loves about the overman is not his cruelty per se but his love of humanity. *In himself*, therefore, the psychologist of Christianity is a *true* lover of humanity. But *for himself* he remains the opposite of the Christian humanist, and so he must deny this equivalence.

Just as the Christian humanist earlier resembled the *beautiful soul* who retreated entirely from life, so now the psychologist of Christianity has taken on the mantle of the *hard heart* who refuses to acknowledge his identity with the evil Christian humanist. For were a supporter of the Christian humanist's to recognize Christian humanism's hypocrisy—that is, to throw off the cruelty that is exemplified in its anti-Semitism and declare herself to be a *true lover of humanity*—the latter would refuse to reciprocate. For the psychologist of Christianity rejects all varieties of humanism as so much religion of pity. Thus, he declares emphatically that it is not the overman's love of humanity but his "great contempt" for men which is praiseworthy. The overman's cruelty does not serve any higher purpose than that of enhancing his own enjoyment of life. He *lives* cruelly, whereas the Christian humanist *withdraws* from life cruelly; and it is just this—the ego-affirming character of the overman's cruelty, the fact that he is an active nihilist rather than a passive nihilist—which places him at the top of the hierarchy of types.

By positing this cartoonishly extreme image of the overman as superegoist, the psychologist of Christianity severs once and for all the possibility of reconciliation with the reformed Christian humanist. Whereas in the earlier dialectic of morality the hard heart eventually came to recognize its own evil and was therefore led to reciprocate the confession of the evil consciousness, here the hard heart of the psychologist of Christianity refuses to confess precisely because he clings to the truth of his own evil consciousness. The psychologist of Christianity does not desire a resolution to the violence of the dialectic. On the contrary, he views the desire to escape human conflict as a symptom of the life-denying weakness of the Christian humanist. Rather than posit an eventual end to human cruelty, the psychologist of Christianity envisions the overman's highest act as willing the eternal recurrence of the violent dialectic of history. The will-to-communism is posited as the supreme act of nihilism.

As the self-consciously unforgiving hard heart, the psychologist of Christianity accordingly throws himself back into the realm of human conflict, attacking his enemies and savoring every blow he deals them. He declares that everything he does he does only for himself. As did the philosophical egoist, of course, he announces this truth to others, but he insists that he makes such public announcements only for his own benefit. All of his writing is self-confessional, and intended only for his own self-improvement. Since he aspires to the ideal of the self-affirming overman and reviles the self-denying monkishness of the Christian humanist, he does nothing in these books but praise himself. Each book declares, in effect, "Here I am, the highest man, the one who writes such excellent books as this, books that are filled with the most excellent wisdom," and so forth.

In fact, of course, the psychologist of Christianity *is* writing for others. Specifically, he writes in order to say to the world, "Please do not confuse me with the Christian humanist, whom I utterly despise!" His protestations notwithstanding, in other words, the psychologist of Christianity writes in order to be *recognized*. However, as he himself well knows, this need for recognition stands in contradiction to the truth of the unbridled egoism which he embraces. The cartoonish overman—the superegoist who claims above all else his own self-sufficiency—does not need the recognition of other men; on the contrary, he views the need for recognition as an inadequacy. Insofar as he denies that he is a humanist and pretends to be a champion of the cartoonish overman, therefore, the psychologist of Christianity is in contradiction with himself: he needs to be recognized as the one who does not need recognition.

For himself, therefore, the psychologist of Christianity continues to affirm the truth of egoism. But, unlike the philosophical egoist who proclaimed egoism as a *universal* truth and as such remained within the ethical sphere, the psychologist of Christianity has withdrawn completely into himself and therefore proclaims egoism only as an *individual* truth. In other words, he believes that the truth of egoism rests solely on the fact that he, this particular ego, happens to affirm it. Were he to affirm a different truth, then *that* would be the truth—again, only for him, this particular ego. Truth, in other words, has ceased to be something universal; it is simply whatever beliefs the individual ego happens to create for himself. But since this is itself posited as a universal truth, the psychologist of Christianity does not affirm merely his own particular truth; rather, he affirms the universal truth that every ego is a creator of truth. As such, he posits the truth of *perspectivism*. The doctrine of perspectivism seems to undermine itself, insofar as it purports to be a universal claim about the invalidity of universal claims: if it is true, it is false. However, the possibility that perspectivism is not universally true, but is simply true for this particular ego is, after all, precisely in keeping with what perspectivism claims to be the case. Therefore, to the psychologist of Christianity, his own particular affirmation of perspectivism is the perfect way of retreating into an absolute egoism, in opposition to Christian humanism.

From the perspective of his perspectivism, moreover, the psychologist of Christianity can now throw off altogether his earlier affirmation of fixed values. No longer is it a question of which types of man are *truly* good and which are *truly* evil. Instead, the question is now simply, for which type is such and such good; for which type is it evil? The psychologist of Christianity thus professes to have gone "beyond good and evil" altogether—beyond, that is, faith in *absolute* values. He believes now only in the relative valuations of particular egos. Or rather—since this proposition should be performed in its radically solipsistic mode rather than professed in universal terms—the psychologist of Christianity believes only in his own particular valuations.

If perspectivism is true, however, this means that the psychologist of Christianity's assessment of the Christian humanist is, from the standpoint of his readers, just one man's opinion. In other words, the psychologist of Christianity's psychological truth claims have been undermined by his perspectival relativism. But this does not trouble him, for at this point, he no longer wants to *capture* the truth in language. On the contrary, he wants to *create* it with language. Everything that he writes is, at bottom, merely the expression of his own egoistic will. Or again—since *in himself* he means this to be a universal truth despite the fact that *for himself* he recognizes it only as his own truth—*language* has now been posited as merely an expression of the individual's will.

The thesis that language is merely an expression of will expresses the truth of perspectivism. But this truth is a divided one, for on the one hand, it is the universal truth of egoism, while on the other hand, it is merely the truth of this particular ego. Now, the psychologist of Christianity has recognized only the latter side, and as such has disappeared completely within himself. Ironically, he has proved his ultimate identification with the Christian humanist by doing precisely what he did—withdraw from life. He spends his time creating one dazzling linguistic creation after another until one day he discovers that, if he is really to remain true to himself and become an overman, he must stop seeking the recognition of others entirely. Accordingly, he shuts up—or speaks only within the silent, sovereign realm of his own head. The psychologist of Christianity, in short, disappears.

The retreat of the psychologist of Christianity represents not the willful refusal of a particular individual to recognize the universal. On the contrary, it represents an exemplary honesty in the face of the egoistic truth of materialist spirit. So long as men remain at this level they cannot achieve mutual recognition. The being of their mutual recognition—language, which alone is the actuality of the materialist spirit—appears only in the guise of the idiosyncratic speech of the isolated individual.

The promise of reconciliation has therefore been postponed—perhaps indefinitely. But with the death of reconciliation—that is, with the death of the very idea of God—something new has emerged out of the alienation of the sphere of materialist spirit: the self-consciousness of language. Every sphere of spirit hitherto now gives way to this new shape in which the project of phenomenology appears. We are back on square one.

3 (AAA.) • Consciousness and Self-Consciousness of Language

The dialectic of materialist spirit recapitulated the earlier movement whereby self-conscious spirit developed from the ethical sphere to the realm of culture and finally to the level of morality. It was in these earlier stages of the dialectic that we found self-conscious individuals struggling to reconcile the [I = we] with the [we = I]. In fact, they accomplished their goal with the mutual forgiveness that was made possible when the hard heart acknowledged its own evil. However, they achieved only an *ideal* reconciliation, which immediately gave way to the level of religion and then to absolute knowing. The collapse of absolute knowing that *we* saw came about because the merely ideal character of this reconciliation made it something merely immediate and not yet actualized. The dialectic of absolute knowing then issued in the positing of the truth of the *materialist* spirit, at which level the earlier struggle to reconcile the [I = we] with the [we = I] took us from ethical communism to the sundered individuality of anarchism and nihilism, and finally to the level of Christian humanism and its manifestation of evil, anti-Semitism. However, this last section took us not to the mutual confession which brought the stage of *ideal* spirit to a close, but rather to the *absolute refusal* of the psychologist of Christianity to reconcile himself to the rest of humanity. What has been refused is nothing less than spirit itself, which has been supplanted by the radically subjective language of the willful perspectivist. Thus, where the truth of ideal spirit was the coming-together of humanity in the *religious* community, the truth of materialist spirit is the inability of humanity to come together in a *linguistic* community. For the psychologist of Christianity, the dialectic came to an end, as he disappeared into the black hole of his own particular auto-celebratory creations.

But the retreat of the psychologist should not be viewed merely as a stubborn refusal to confess; on the contrary, he does not confess because he cannot do so in good faith. Specifically, he can see no way of declaring himself a humanist without becoming a cruel humanist—that is, an anti-Semitic humanist. To the psychologist of Christianity, the truth of spirit has turned out to be its anti-humanism rather than its humanism. Spirit itself has been revealed to be duplicitous, and it is for this reason that there can be no turning back to it.

The age of spirit is dead. However, *for us*, the dialectic has not come to an end. For out of the ashes of the spirit has arisen a new shape of consciousness—the consciousness *of* language. Language is the material truth of the spirit that appears once the spirit itself has been negated; put otherwise, spirit has shown itself to be nothing other than language.

Strictly speaking, the emergence of the consciousness of language belongs to the experience of the psychologist of Christianity. For it was his realization that the supposed truths of spirit are nothing but the interpretations of particular types of men that brought language to the foreground. But the dialectical development of this insight is something which the psychologist of Christianity himself did not advance, and as such its beginnings belong to a different stage.

The *consciousness* of language immediately divides itself into two opposed moments, as does all consciousness. There is, on the one hand, the subject for whom language appears as an object; and on the other, language as an object. By affirming the truth of perspectivism, the psychologist of Christianity retreated entirely into the subject pole of this relation, to such a degree that the objectivity of the object dropped out completely. For himself, the perspectivist can sustain this pretense; but for another, the objectivity of language will appear to give the lie to his one-sided subjective view. It is with this most rudimentary moment of linguistic consciousness—that is, the consciousness of the consciousness of language as having two poles (which is not yet, however, the true self-consciousness of language)—that the dialectical possibilities open up once again.

Just as earlier, the dialectical vicissitudes of consciousness gave rise to three distinct shapes—sense-certainty, perception, and understanding—so here, in the sphere of the consciousness of language three possible paths for developing the truth of language open up. To the philosopher, who is by now well familiar with these three distinct shapes of consciousness, any one of these modes of consciousness could provide a legitimate starting-point for the development of a science of language. We can expect, therefore, three distinct approaches, all of which can be developed more or less simultaneously. Despite their structural cotemporality, however, these three approaches will nonetheless stand in a relation of logical succession to one another, corresponding to their sequence in the dialectic of consciousness. Accordingly, they will be treated here not simultaneously but in sequential order. We turn, then, to the most rudimentary form of the consciousness of language: the sense-certainty of language.

A. Sense-certainty of Language

The logically first philosopher of language proper—that is, language as the object which has emerged in and for itself as the truth of consciousness—is he who begins with the certainty that the psychologist's one-sided emphasis on interpretation has failed to capture the objective essence of language. This is the truth of the *anti-psychologist*. For the anti-psychologist, language is an object which stands as something fixed, regardless of the subject's perspective on it. In itself, he affirms, language is impervious to the subject's interpretive will; words mean what they do simply because they mean what they do, not because the subject wills them to mean what he wants them to mean. Truth and interpretation thus stand as opposed moments in the consciousness of language. It is the independent truth of the object of the consciousness of language which the anti-psychologist posits.

To the anti-psychologist, these opposed moments are not so much complementary as they are contradictory, for the interpretive free play of the subject continually negates the objective truth of language itself. But since he aims to present language as it is *in itself*, rather than language as it appears for an arbitrarily whimsical subject, the anti-psychologist sets out on a program diametrically opposed to, and just as one-sided as, that of the perspectivist—that is, he aims to purge the consciousness of language of its subject pole. The consciousness of language must be purified of the subject's *psychological* interference with the object's *logical* essence. As such, the anti-psychologist does not set out to construct a *theory* of language; he believes that language has an inherent logical structure which can be laid bare to the objective observer.

Thus, the anti-psychologist returns to the ascetic ideal, which had been so strenuously negated by the psychologist of Christianity. For his aim is not so much to eliminate the subject pole of the consciousness of language—without which, he knows, there would cease to be consciousness altogether—as it is to establish a kind of pure subject—or, to recall the terminology of the Christian humanist—a *monkish* observer of language.

To the anti-psychologist, then, language itself is the truth, and he—the pure subject who observes this truth—is merely the medium through which this truth reveals itself. He therefore seeks to reduce all his experiences to linguistic truths. If, for example, he is looking at a tree, he declares the truth of this experience to consist in the *statement* "This is a tree," and if he then turns to look at a house, what is then true is the statement which he takes to be the essence of this experience. Now, so long as he remains merely within himself, this truth can remain stable; however, he can only verify the success of his accomplishment by comparing his own truths with those of others. For in claiming to have reduced his own subjectivity to that of the perfectly objective observer, he believes he has arrived at truths which are truly universal. Accordingly, he has a companion look at a tree with him, and he declares that the universal truth for both of them is the statement, "This is a tree." So minimal is the claim here—for the anti-psychologist has simply given us the linguistic equivalent of the immediate claims of sense-certainty; for discrete sensory impressions he has merely substituted atomic sentences—that his interlocuter would seem certain to assent to this statement. However, his interlocuter is just as aware of the subject pole of the consciousness of language as he is of the object pole; pointing out this other side of the equation, he suggests to the anti-psychologist that, although the two of them might agree, indeed, that the sentence "This is a tree" is *true*, nonetheless they might not *mean* the same thing by this sentence. After all, how do they know that each of them understands the word "tree" in the same way? The interpretive free play of the psychologist of Christianity thus reaffirms itself.

At first, the anti-psychologist is tempted to respond by saying something like, "Oh, come on! You know perfectly well what I mean by the word 'tree.'" But his persistent interlocuter can take on the role of the *defender of the subject*, stubbornly clinging to his own "right" to engage in interpretive free play; in the eyes of the defender of the subject, the prose of the anti-psychologist can never tame the poetry of the psychologist of Christianity. Thus, the anti-psychologist must try a different tactic. He notices that the defender of the subject agrees that the *sentence*, "This is a tree" is *true*; he simply does not agree on what the *words* which comprise this sentence *mean*. Since the anti-psychologist is certain that meaning must be as objective as truth, and since he can expect universal agreement as to the truth of sentences, he declares that the meanings of words must be nothing other than the functions of the truths of sentences. For if words have meanings only insofar as they are parts of sentences, there will be no room for subjective interpretation of their meaning.

But of course this is only a *theory* of meaning, and one which the defender of the subject need not accept. Indeed, because the latter insists on the irreducibly psychological role of the subject's consciousness of language, he rejects the anti-psychologist's theory as obviously contrary to the facts. The anti-psychologist is distraught at this rebuff, because only the agreement of others can ultimately verify his claim to have proven that meanings are universal. Nonetheless, he remains undaunted, because he is also certain that his theory is true. He thus sets out to develop it in its details, hoping that he will eventually convince the defender of the subject.

In the anti-psychologist's theory, words have meanings only in the context of sentences, and what determines their specific meanings are the truth-values of sentences. Since all men, he believes, can agree about whether or not a sentence is true, the meanings of words must be universal and so impervious to the interpretive caprice of individual subjects. In short, meanings are *public*; they are shared by all speakers of a given language.

To the anti-psychologist, this truth has far-reaching implications. For it signifies not merely a fact about language, but more importantly a fact about men—specifically, that men are not isolated individuals each of whom has his own private meanings but are, rather, members of a linguistic community whose identity is constituted by the language which they all speak. In other words, the anti-psychologist posits that the [I = I] of universal humanity is revealed in the reality of language itself. As such, he reaffirms the earlier truth of the Christian humanist—that all men are implicitly reconciled with one another, insofar as they are all speakers of language. But for this truth to become actualized, two conditions must be met: first, all men must learn to speak the same language; and second, all men must obey the universal rules of this shared language. The first condition is important, because so long as men are separated into different linguistically defined communities the scope of their actualized universality will remain limited by these linguistic borders. The second condition is important, because the mere existence of a universal language may not by itself force all men to give up their capricious interpretive tricks. With this latter criterion, then, the anti-psychologist in effect sets up an ethical imperative: all men *ought* to submit to the universality of language. This ethical imperative can be turned into binding law by creating a language that *cannot* be interpreted in a "Jewish" way.

Since all presently existing natural languages are contaminated by men's various psychological sins, the task of constructing a universal tongue is better carried out by turning away from natural languages altogether and constructing a logically pure artificial language. To be sure, the anti-psychologist must hold that, *in themselves*, even natural languages are in principle logically "pure," and that it is merely in the hands of psychologically "unmonkish" men that they have been turned into "fallen" versions of themselves. Still, so defiled have natural languages become through such misuse that the anti-psychologist is almost ashamed to use the revered name of "language" to refer to them at all.

In constructing his purely logical language, the anti-psychologist must, as we have seen, make the truth-values of sentences prior to—because they will be the determining factors of—the meanings of individual expressions.

He must first construct a syntax for his language, and then show how the syntax gives rise to one and only one possible semantics. The syntax must specify the rules for constructing sentences and for determining the truth-values of sentences. Since the truth-values of sentences must correlate to facts about the world—for example, the truth-value of "This is a tree" must correspond to the fact of whether or not the object designated is or is not a tree—it will therefore be possible to construct a theory of the reference of words solely from the truth-values of sentences. The meaning of a word can then be defined solely in terms of the reference of words; the meaning of "tree" would be a function of the truth-values of all the sentences comprising the word "tree."

With this model, the anti-psychologist has reduced the role of the subject—the individual who is conscious of a meaning—to that of a purely passive observer of the object—that is, the truth-values of sentences. No longer is the subject free to create meanings by interpreting language; instead, he is merely an objective recorder of the meanings that are constituted within language itself. Thus, the anti-psychologist has not done away with the category of meaning; he has simply transferred meaning from the side of the subject to the side of the object. In doing so, he has eliminated the subject's ability to create new meanings for already existing words. However, he has not eliminated another creative possibility of the subject—namely, the ability to create new words for already existing meanings. And there is nothing to prevent the defender of the subject from reasserting himself in this respect. Accordingly, when the latter is now asked if he agrees with the statement, "This is a tree," the defender of the subject replies, "Yes, this is a home for owls." Now, at first, this mischevious answer does not bother the anti-psychologist, for all he had set out to prove was that the meanings of words are fixed; the introduction of the synonym "home for owls" for "tree" does not change the meaning of the word "tree."

But the defender of the subject has in fact reintroduced the perspective of the subject into the determination of meanings. For what if there were a subject who knew the meanings of both "tree" and "home for owls," but who did not know that the referents of these terms are identical? To this challenge, of course, the anti-psychologist could simply respond by saying that if such a subject did not know that the referents of these expressions are identical, he could not be said to understand the meaning of at least one of the two. But this answer will not suffice. For a failure on the part of a subject to understand the meaning of a term will affect the truth-value of sentences which have as their object the beliefs of that subject. If the expressions "tree" and "home for owls" have the same meaning, then the statements "G. believes that trees are plants" and "G. believes that homes for owls are plants" should have the same truth-values. But they might not, if G. does not know that they have the same meaning. If meaning is nothing but a function of truth-value, it must follow that "tree" and "home for owls" do *not* have the same meaning.

The anti-psychologist clings to his certainty that meanings must be universal, public, and determined by the truth-values of sentences. But he cannot deny that something like the subject's own perception of the meaning of a word can effect the truth-values of sentences. Accordingly, he simply declares the former to be the *true* meaning, and the latter to be the *apparent* meaning, and sets out to tinker with his syntax to insure that apparent meanings do not interfere with true meanings.

To the defender of the subject, such a ruse is clearly a sign of bad faith on the part of the anti-psychologist. For even if the anti-psychologist could construct a purely logical language which would fix the so-called true meanings of its expressions (the defender of the subject does not much care one way or the other as to whether the project can be completed), it could not claim the status of a *real* language. The defender of the subject accordingly sets out to construct an alternative theory of language. Positing that the truth of language lies solely on the side of the subject, he takes up the position of the *linguistic idealist*.

In opposition to the anti-psychologist, who affirms the independent existence of language, the linguistic idealist denies that language has any reality apart from the subject who is conscious of it. In this respect, the linguistic idealist seems to have retreated to the position of the psychologist of Christianity. However, whereas the latter believed that language was a malleable object completely subservient to the whims of the subject, the linguistic idealist seeks to show how the apparent objectivity of language can mislead subjects into losing sight of the fact that it is they who are the true element in the relation between consciousness and language.

If, however, the anti-psychologist is right to say that the truth-values of sentences are objective, it follows that language expresses *facts*. But this means that the linguistic idealist can disabuse subjects of the prison-house of language only by denying the facts which language expresses. The linguistic idealist thus turns out to be an idealist in a sense that the absolute knower certainly never was; he has reverted to a position akin to that of the skeptic. For example, since commonsense has it that the truth of the sentence "Grass is green" is fixed, the linguistic idealist immediately suspects that subjects are being beguiled by language into believing this to be an objective fact rather than a subjective fact. The work of the linguistic idealist is to defetishize subjects' faith in the independent existence of the world as it is characterized in language.

However seriously the work of the linguistic idealist may be taken in its day, though, it is work that is destined to be brushed aside quickly by those who appear on the scene later. The reason for this is, quite simply, that its one-sidedness is painfully obvious in a way that the equally one-sided—but infinitely more nuanced—theory of the anti-pscyhologist was not. Followers of the linguistic idealist suffer from a terrible bad faith; for their work consists in disproving facts which everyone believes in. When finally they reject their bad faith, they discover that their previous efforts to liberate subjects from the prison-house of language were in fact the exact opposite. It is thus with a sense that they are escaping from prison when they allow themselves to return to affirming such everyday facts as "Grass is green," and taking such statements to express the truth as it is in itself. Affirming now neither the one-sided position of the anti-psychologist, nor that of the linguistic idealist, these reformed idealists now declare that the truth of language consists in the *relation* between subject and object. In so doing, they become *logical realists*.

The work of the anti-psychologist was solitary, though it purported universality; the same with the linguistic idealist. For neither could possibly communicate its truth to the other. Even if there were a plurality of anti-psychologists and linguistic idealists, the members of one camp could speak only among themselves; for no sooner does an anti-psychologist converse with a linguistic idealist than each is immediately accusing the other of being as wrong as could be in their philosophical premises about what language *is*. By contrast, the logical realists claim to have captured the truths of both the anti-psychologist and the linguistic idealist; not only can they converse with the two rival camps, but their work is even likely to be carried out as a tandem consisting of a rehabilitated anti-psychologist and a rehabilitated linguistic idealist.

The truth of logical realism is nothing other than the *relation* between a subject conscious of a statement and the statement itself as the object of this consciousness. The truth expressed in "This is a tree," therefore, is to be found in the relation of *assertion*. True to the immediacy of the sense-certainty of language, the logical realists affirm that the truth lies with a particular assertion—a particular individual standing before a particular tree making a particular assertion: "This is a tree." However, they equally intend to posit a universal truth—that is, the reality of all assertions. But this means that the object of their certainty is not this particular statement, but every statement. Hence, the logical realists find it necessary to distinguish between the statement *qua* particular and the statement *qua* universal; the former is a *sentence*, and the latter is a *proposition*. The true object of the consciousness of language is not the sentence, but the proposition.

Now in affirming the truth of propositions, the logical realists are not, of course, affirming that every proposition is true in the sense that it corresponds to the facts of the world. They merely claim that, in the consciousness of language, what is true is the proposition. As such, they distinguish between the object of an assertion—the proposition—and that which the assertion purports to be about—namely, the facts of the world. Thus, every assertion has, as it were, two objects. The logical realists are thus forced to view the world itself as divided into two distinct realms—the realm of facts and the realm of propositions. While it is true that they have managed to resolve the dualism between subject and object within the consciousness of language, they have done so merely by opening up a dualism within the object. In this way, the earlier distinction between the linguistic idealist's *ideal* truth and the anti-psychologist's *real* truth are now both posited on the side of the real: the real consists of both the real—that is, facts—and the ideal—that is, propositions.

Moreover, not only have the logical realists been led to view propositions as real, they have also forced themselves to posit the reality of whatever ideal objects are posited by propositions. Taken to its absurd conclusion, they must posit not only a type of reality for entities that do not have a factual existence, but they must even entertain the idea that impossible objects which are posited by propositions are real too. In this way, they are led to far more metaphysical absurdity than they could possibly accuse the linguistic idealists of lapsing into; the logical realists resort to the most shameless scholastic logic-chopping to try to give the whole thing a semblance of plausibility.

Eventually, of course, someone notices what absurdity follows from positing the reality of propositions, and sets out to correct this defect in the position of the logical realists, without giving up their basic insight that the truth of language is to be found in the phenomenon of assertion. What is false in logical realism, it is now declared, is its metaphysics; what is true is its description of linguistic experience. This is the truth of the *logical positivists*.

The logical positivists begin from their rejection of the logical realists' distinction between existing facts and other sorts of objects; specifically, they have banished the latter as fictitious metaphysical pseudo-entities and preserved the former. The world to which language refers is the world of facts; that is, the world is nothing more nor less than the totality of facts. It follows that only assertions which express facts are real thoughts. But this is just to say that the logical positivists have retreated to the truth of observing reason; only those statements which can be verified by observation count as genuine statements. For this reason, the logical positivists hold up the language of the positive sciences as providing the ideal form of speech, against which they oppose the misleading language of metaphysics.

The task of the logical positivists is to clarify the truth of assertion in such a way as to purge language of its metaphysical tendencies. As did the anti-psychologist, the logical positivists view natural language with great mistrust, for they see how the logical realists were misled by it. If metaphysical thinking is now viewed as man's chief crime, language is now viewed as the chief culprit; or, rather, since real men who use language are the ones who commit the sin of positing metaphysical truths, language is the great tempter. Just as the Lord punished the snake, so the logical positivists set out to punish language; but since they cannot banish language entirely, they reaffirm the wisdom of the anti-psychologist's project of reforming language. In addition, since men continue to be tempted by natural languages to posit absurd metaphysical truths, the logical positivists act not only as language reformers, but also as language police: their job is to distinguish between genuine propositions and pseudo-propositions. Genuine propositions are those which are capable of being either true or false—that is, which can be verified on the basis of experience. By contrast, pseudo-propositions are strings of words which *appear* to have the form of propositions, but which in fact are not, because they do not affirm anything which could be verified by experience. By pointing out the class of pseudo-*propositions*, the logical positivists call attention to men's pseudo-*thoughts*; for so long as men are duped by pseudo-propositions into thinking that they are real propositions, they will believe that pseudo-propositions express genuine thoughts. A man who utters a pseudo-expression may appear to be thinking, but in fact he is not. The job of the logical positivists, then, is to disabuse men of thinking that they know what they are thinking.

With the logical positivists, the denial of spirit which generally characterizes the dialectic of language reaches its most extreme manifestation. For on their view, everything not immediately observable by sense-certainty is a pseudo-object of a pseudo-thought. To be sure, the language of science makes reference to the truths of perception and understanding; not only sense-data but also objects and laws of nature are part of the ontology of the sciences. As such, the observational sciences are just as "metaphysical" as is all language. Loath to admit this fact, since it would undermine their distinction between genuine propositions and pseudo-propositions, the logical positivists cling firmly to the truth of sense-certainty alone, and they give themselves the task of redescribing the ontology of the observational sciences so as to reduce its posited objects to sense data and *sets* of sense data. So, for instance, perceptual objects such as trees are redescribed as logical constructs out of immediately available sense data; laws of nature which are posited by the understanding are construed merely as useful statements of regularity in the appearance of sense data. Once they have reassured their consciences in this way, of course, the logical positivists go about talking about trees and the law of gravity just as does everyone else, claiming only to speak this way out of habit, or because of the limitations of everyday language. In this way, they allow themselves the bad faith of positing the things that can only be revealed once we have gone beyond mere sense-certainty—which, for them, can only mean to have strayed into the pseudo-thinking of metaphysics—while pretending that they have not done so at all.

As did the anti-psychologist, the logical positivists have affirmed the truth of the object of the consciousness of language in a way that forces them to deny the truth of the subject. Hence, subjects must also be re-described either as logical constructs out of sense data or else as pseudo-entities. And, indeed, the logical positivists are pulled in both of these directions at once. Insofar as man appears in sense-certainty as a living being, he is an object of scientific inquiry; yet insofar as man is the subject who is conscious of the appearance of sense-data he is not himself an appearance, and as such must be declared a pseudo-object. In short, man is man simply insofar as he appears—not insofar as he makes appearances possible. The logical positivists thus deny the reality of the subject alto-gether, maintaining that it is the linguistic category of *grammatical* sub-jects which lead men to suppose the existence of *metaphysical* subjects. Of course, no one but the logical positivists would think that the truth of sense-certainty ever involved the positing of a metaphysical subject; all that need be affirmed is the existence of a transcendental subject. But the logical positivists lack the analytical subtlety to make such fine distinctions; their thinking has but two categories: "empirical" and "metaphysical." Trumpet-ing the brilliance of their discovery that the subject of consciousness is nothing empirical—as if this weren't already obvious to anyone who has passed beyond the simple truth of immediate self-certainty—the logical positivists chide those who cling to the linguisitic idealist's truth for believ-ing in a "ghost in the machine." In this, of course, they display the blunt-ness of their peculiarly unanalytic frame of mind, for they completely fail to see the difference between a metaphysical subject and a transcendental subject. (This distinction was clear to the anti-psychologist, who denied that the subject was constitutive of the truth of language, but who did not deny the subject altogether.)

Now, although they posit that the subject is a pseudo-entity, the logical positivists have not actually shown that the proposition "There are sub-jects" is *false*. All that they have shown is that to speak of the existence of something which is not an object is *absurd*; thus, talk of subjects is not false, but nonsensical. To the uncritical logical positivists, to say that it is nonsense to speak of subjects and to say that there are no subjects are basically equivalent. But in fact these statements cannot be equivalent. For what it means, in their jargon, to call a string of words nonsensical is just to say that it affirms something which could not possibly be either true or false. In other words, even though that which is nonsensical can never be declared true, it can similarly never be declared false. To someone who shares the logical positivists' credo that the world is just the totality of facts, but who is also aware of the legitimacy of the linguistic idealist's insistence on the subject pole of the consciousness of language, the distinction between nonsense and falsity makes a great deal of difference. To be sure, anything that is logically impossible might be called "nonsensical" in the sense that it must be false. But the statement of the existence of the subject is not nonsensical in this way; it is nonsensical, rather, in that it transcends the limits of what can be said. Whatever cannot be said is, quite simply, something that cannot be said. The one who utters *this* sentence, calling attention to that to which we cannot call attention, is the *logical mystic*. With its deafening crescendo of silence, this sentence, all by itself, shatters the logical positivists' pretension to have "done away with the subject."

The work of the logical mystic is finished as soon as he utters his punchline. By *showing* the limits of what can be *said*, he expects to have put an end to the reductionistic work of the logical positivists. What he did not count on, however, was the fact that the logical positivists would fail to understand him. That they would fail to understand him might have been easy to predict. After all, for the consciousness of the logical positivists, all strings of words are either meaningless or else they are merely expressions of propositions. Therefore, when they get to the statement that "Whatever cannot be said must be passed over in silence," they assume that this statement merely purports to repeat the logical positivists' own belief that nonsense is something which must be eliminated from language. Nothing, however, could be farther from the intent of the logical mystic. For him, his statement does not merely say that nonsense is unspeakable, it also reveals the "realm of the nonsensical" as something important—indeed, as something of ultimate importance—to men. That the nonsensical cannot be spoken of does not mean that we must ignore it; on the contrary, it suggests that we must not expect philosophical language to be able to express what is most important.

Blissfully unaware of the fact that language has a poetic dimension—that is, that it might be showing things in addition to saying things—the logical positivists continue to purge the world of nonsense. Disgusted with the way in which they use his work to justify their life-cheapening project, the logical mystic finds it necessary to say a bit more than he originally thought was necessary. He returns to the philosophers with the aim of revealing to them the immense variety of poetically meaningful things that can be expressed in language, all of which are, strictly speaking, nonsensical.

In doing so, he discovers that he himself had been wrong to have accepted the logical positivists' description of the phenomenon of assertion. Since statements are often *doing* something "more" than merely asserting the truth of a proposition, there must be more than one kind of statement. Specifically, there must be as many kinds of statements as there are sorts of things one can do with language. But in fact there are an indefinite number of things that one can do with language. In speaking to another person, one can cajole, promise, express a feeling, describe, be sarcastic, and so on; the list could be endless. Every specific assertion has to be understood in terms of the parameters that are unique to the type of activity for which language is used. Thus, there are linguistic rules of cajoling, linguistic rules of promising, and so forth. Each set of rules constitutes a certain language game; each assertion is like a move in the game. The meaning of "This is a tree" will vary according to the language game that is being played.

What is most important about the phenomenon of language games to the logical mystic is the fact that each of these games contains something which—from the one-dimensional perspective of logical positivism—is nonsensical. Before, he had thought it necessary to point to that which is beyond the evidence of the senses in order to make the nonsensical manifest. Now, he discovers that the nonsensical is precisely what is revealed in the direct objects of linguistic consciousness. What people say is nonsensical, but in a good way. Thus, whereas the logical positivists set out to cure everyday people of speaking nonsensically, trying to get them to speak like logical positivists, the logical mystic does the exact opposite: he sets out to cure philosophers of speaking their kind of nonsense, trying to get them to speak like everyday people.

As did the logical realists, the logical mystic once again affirms that it is the relationship between the subject and the object which is true in the consciousness of language. But whereas the logical realists took this relation to be one of *assertion*, the logical mystic declares that there are innumerable types of assertion. The immediate object of the sense-certainty of language is now a *form of life*.

Each form of life is characterized by something which men *do* with language. Hence, the consciousness of forms of life is a consciousness of the activity of men; what must be explicated is the nature of this activity—that is, how men do things with language. The logical mystic, however, is not interested in this. On the contrary, his aim was solely to call attention to the wonderful nonsense of language; the last thing he would like to do is reduce his aesthetic delight in this nonsense to another positivistic inquiry into the types of nonsense. Indeed, his point is that, despite the most accurate attempts to define what it is men say, there will always be an irreducible nonsensical surplus which will escape description. Thus, to the logical mystic, the task of typologizing language games is both distasteful and ultimately fruitless. It is not the project of the logical mystic, but of the *ordinary language theorist*.

From the perspective of the ordinary language theorist, the essential element in the consciousness of language is the *immediate* speech act that is performed by a particular user of speech. Both the subject and object poles are treated as mere moments of the act itself, which is a simple unity. By positing this truth—that is, that a speech act is an elementary *this*, which does not break up into the opposed *thises* of subject and object—the ordinary language theorist claims to have arrived at the ultimate truth of the sense-certainty of language. For he can see that the complementary failures of the linguistic idealist and the logical positivist sprung from their falsely believing that there were two *thises* instead of one.

The meaning of an individual speech act, then, is determined neither on the side of the subject nor on the side of the object, nor strictly speaking in the relation between two dirempted moments. Rather, the individual speech act gets its meaning by being of a certain *type*. Each of these types is characterized by a relatively well-defined set of rules. To determine the meaning of a particular speech act, one need only determine which set of rules seems to be governing its performance. In doing this, one looks only at the act itself; it is not necessary to break the act into its supposedly constituent subject and object poles.

By referring the individual speech act to these universal types of possible speech acts, the ordinary language theorist has risen to the level which affirms the universality of sense-certainty, and as such he would seem to move to the level of the *perception* of language. However, he still affirms that it is the simple immediate unity of the particular speech act which is true, and as such remains at the level of the sense-certainty of language. Yet it is a sense-certainty—*this* individual speech act—which is mediated by a perception of universals—this *type* of speech act. Thus, we can say that, for the consciousness of the speech act theorist, the conditions for the possibility of speech acts are objects of perception, but speech acts themselves still remain at the level of sense-certainty.

Now, despite his view that the immediate speech act is a simple unity, the ordinary language theorist nonetheless must distinguish between the subject and the object as moments of this act. So, for instance, in the speech act of *telling a lie*, there is the subject—that is, the one who tells a lie—and the object—that is, the lie itself. Only by ascertaining that both of these moments are present in the individual act can the ordinary language theorist declare that he is confronted with the specific speech act whose essence he claims to elucidate. For example, if the subject did not *intend* to tell a lie, then the act cannot be a telling of a lie; or again, if the subject meant to lie but inadvertently told the truth, then again the act is not a telling of a lie. In order to distinguish between speech acts that are truly of such and such type, and those that merely appear to be of such and such type, the ordinary language theorist must appeal to the moments of the relation which he pretends is a simple unity.

Thus, in trying to determine whether a particular speech act does or does not conform to one of the universal types, the ordinary language theorist must constantly make a clandestine appeal to the *intentions* of the subject. For instance, when a person declares, "This is a tree," and the ordinary language theorist identifies this as the speech act of, say, *expressing a belief*, he must assume that the speaker is *sincere*, for otherwise, he might be performing a different speech act—perhaps the act of *trying to deceive someone*. But for the ordinary language theorist, of course, the speech act is supposed to be explicable in itself as a simple unity; were he to admit that it is necessary to make a constant appeal to the intentions of the agent, he would fall back into a position akin to that of the linguistic idealist.

The ordinary language theorist tries to get around this problem, declaring that cases of insincere speech acts are merely bizarre exceptions, of which the philosopher need not take account. Such an argument is, of course, a bit absurd; the ordinary language theorist appears rather as does a small child who gets red in the face because not everyone wants to play the game that he wants them to play. Moreover, the ordinary language theorist cannot even construct a typology of speech acts without invoking a range of possible intentions on the part of speakers. The problem of sincerity thus merely brings to the fore the centrality of the ordinary language theorist's subjectivism. He is not, as he supposes, a type of neutral behaviorist who merely describes what he observes; he is, on the contrary, a speech act idealist.

At this point, what is true in the ordinary language theorist's position is his attempt to posit the immediate simplicity of the individual speech act; what is false is his covert idealism. Accordingly, the latter is now negated while the former is preserved. What is true is the individual act; but the act must be viewed not primarily as something performed by an agent, for it is this construal which necessitates the appeal to the subject's intentions. On the contrary, the individual agent's intentions must be declared irrelevant to determining the meaning of the act. But this means that the act must be interpreted not in terms of the subject pole of the speech act—the act is not, in other words, an *uttering of speech*—but rather in terms of the object pole—that is, the act is *speech that has been uttered*. Once again, therefore, the wisdom of the anti-psychologist is affirmed, and a return to the logical positivists' emphasis on the object is invoked. Nonetheless, it is still the speech act itself that is declared to be true; and thus it is an ordinary language theorist's version of logical positivism that is invoked: what is true is the individual speech act, but this is to be identified, not by an appeal to the various types of activity that a subject can perform but rather by an appeal to the various types of sentences that a language can permit. Instead of interpreting the individual speech act by appealing to universal possibilities on the side of the subject, we will now interpret the individual speech act by appealing to universal possibilities on the side of the object. In short, speech act idealism has given way to speech act behaviorism. For the advocate of speech act behaviorism, what is true is the individual speech act insofar as it is governed by the grammatical rules of the language to which it belongs. This means that not only the *sense* of individual speech acts, but also the *ontology* which they imply, is determined by the specific rules of a specific language. We have thus arrived at the anti-subjective position of the *ontological relativist*.

The truth posited by the ontological relativist exactly parallels that of the ordinary language theorist. Where the latter elucidates a particular utterance by referring it to the possible types of speech acts, so the ontological relativist elucidates a particular utterance by referring it to the grammatical possibilities of a particular language. Insofar as the latter are publicly available, the ontological relativist believes that his theory does not require any appeal to the subject's intentions; one can interpret an utterance solely by looking to the language in which it is uttered. Language thus provides an objective basis for determining both the meanings and the truth conditions for individual speech acts.

But in fact, the ontological relativist is in precisely the same position as was the ordinary language theorist. For just as the latter could determine which particular type of speech act was being performed only by appealing to the intentions of the subject, so the ontological relativist can determine to which language a particular utterance belongs only by making a similar appeal. Just as did his ordinary language counterpart, so the ontological relativist wishes to write off as "bizarre" the possibility that the language to which an utterance would belong could be inscrutable. But in fact this supposedly bizarre exception shows that the ontological relativist must all along make a covert appeal to the subject's intention to speak a particular language.

This problem becomes manifest as soon as the ontological relativist sets out to interpret another speaker's utterance. Since he insists that meaning can be found only in language, he does not view interpretation as a subjective activity; rather, the act of interpretation is simply the act of translation—taking a sentence from one language and rewriting it with a sentence in another language. The test of whether or not he has accurately interpreted consists solely in determining whether the truth-values of the translation correspond to the truth-values of the original sentence. But again, these truth-values can be determined only if the ontological relativist presumes that he can identify the language to which a particular utterance belongs. Since he cannot appeal to the intentions of speakers, he can in the end only insist on saying everything in his *own* language. But even here he cannot identify his own language without invoking some sort of subjective intention of his own. Thus, the ontological relativist's speech act behaviorism is itself nothing but a covert speech act idealism.

Moreover, the fact that there are many different languages, each with an ontology of its own, suggests that the type of objectivity achieved through the thesis of ontological relativity is a far cry from the ironclad notion of truth put forth by the logical positivists. For in making the question of the truth of propositions relative to facts about particular languages, the ontological relativist seems to have reverted to a type of linguistic idealism. True, he does not make truth relative to the subject, but by making it relative to whatever language a subject happens to speak, he accomplishes the same thing; after all, every subject is free to invent an idiosyncratic language of his own. Immediately following in the footsteps of the ontological relativist, therefore, is the *multiple world theorist*. Taking as his starting-point the ontological relativist's claim that questions of meaning, truth, and ontology can be addressed only from the perspective of a particular language, the multiple world theorist concludes that people who speak radically different languages must inhabit different worlds.

This is not, however, the thesis of the ontological relativist. For him, the fact that there are multiple ontologies does not entail the claim that there are multiple worlds; on the contrary, he takes it merely to indicate that speakers of different languages possess different conceptual schemes for organizing the data of their experience of the one world to which all languages purport to refer. Yet in truth, the multiple world theorist has revealed what is untenable in the position of the ontological relativist. For he cannot consistently maintain both that there is one true world and that there are as many truths and ontologies as there are languages. In order to save the ontological relativist from the multiple world theorist, therefore, it is necessary to get rid of the idea of multiple conceptual schemes altogether. But this means giving up the thesis of ontological relativity, and returning to the simple affirmation of the speech act in its entirety.

The individual relation between subject and object in the consciousness of language has thus far been treated both as an act to be interpreted on the side of the subject, and as an utterance to be interpreted on the side of the object. Both positions, however, have reverted back to a version of linguistic idealism. There now arises the thought that, instead of beginning from the relation between subject and object as a simple unity in the individual speech act, one must begin precisely from the split in this relation and attempt to reconstruct a mediated unity out of these two sides. In place of the single task of ordinary language theory, there now emerge the dual tasks of constructing a theory of speech acts from the standpoint of the subject—that is, articulating a theory of *action*, and constructing a theory of speech acts from the standpoint of the object—that is, articulating a theory of *truth*. Perhaps by putting these together it will be possible to arrive at an adequate theory of individual speech acts.

The shared litmus test of both the theory of action and the theory of truth will be their adequacy for specifying the conditions for the possibility of interpreting speech acts. Unlike the ordinary language theorist, the theorist of action will not appeal to universal types of actions. And unlike the ontological relativist, he will not appeal to the fixed grammatical features of languages. True to the consciousness of sense-certainty, he will interpret without relying on universal bearings of this sort. The theorist of action and truth is, therefore, a *radical interpreter*, whose overarching thesis is that there are no rules that govern speech acts.

Insofar as he is a theorist of speech acts, the ultimate task of the radical interpreter is to specify the meaning of what it is that people say. But because he has done away with all universals, all he ends up doing is pointing to individual acts and saying, "There—that's what it is." His theory of action amounts to saying nothing more than that action cannot be elucidated solely on the side of the subject; and his theory of truth amounts to saying nothing more than that utterances cannot be elucidated solely on the side of the object. That is, both his theory of action and his theory of truth function more as critiques of theories of action and theories of truth; what is positive in them is simply their reconstitution of the individual speech act qua simple unity. But in just this respect, the radical interpreter merely confirms that there is no going further in the truth of the sense-certainty of language than in affirming the simple unity of the individual speech act.

Yet the individual speech act *qua* simple unity is precisely what could not be explicated, except by appeal to the universality of possible speech acts and the universality of possible grammatical constructions. Thus, with the negative result achieved by the radical interpreter, we are left with the failure of the sense-certainty of language. The truth of the individual speech act, it turns out, can be elucidated only if it itself is treated as a universal. The sense-certainty of language thus gives way to the *perception* of language.

B. Perception of Language. The Face-to-face Encounter

As did the original dialectic of sense-certainty, the preceding development of the sense-certainty of language has passed from the certainty of a pure *this* to the truth that the *this* is a mediated universal. In our case, it is the individual speech act, initially divided into its subject and object poles, which has now emerged as a universal. The truth of the perception of language is the *universal* speech act. As such, it is only the universal speech act taken in its unity—or what we will shortly be calling the *intentional act*—which appears as the essential truth, its subjective and objective moments being relegated to the status of inessential moments. But this apparent unity is a relation, and as such it is immediately split into a universal subject and a universal object. Since these moments of the relation stand diametrically opposed to each other, each one claims to be the essential element of the intentional act, declaring the other to be inessential.

In its initial appearance, perception negated the subject and declared the object to be the truth. The development of this truth then gave way to the splitting of the object of perception, a result which ultimately led to the dialectic of force and the understanding. The positing of the *subject* as the universal truth of perception was deferred, and not taken up until the appearance of self-consciousness proper. Specifically, it was in the section entitled, "Observation of self-consciousness in its purity and its relation to external actuality," that the positing of the universal subject as the truth of perception was made explicit.

In the present case, however, both the object of consciousness and self-consciousness as its own object appear as equally developed truths posited within the perception of language. In other words, in the intentional act that is posited as the truth of the perception of language, the universal subject has just as immediate a claim to being the truth of the relation as does the universal object. In fact, it has a prior claim; for the sense-certainty of language has faltered precisely on its need to ascribe *intentions* to the subjective agent of a speech act. Accordingly, the first attempt to resolve the opposition between the subject and the object in the perception of language is the positing of the subject as the essential element in the relation, and as we will see it is only the failure of this one-sided attempt which will then lead to the positing of the independent truth of the object. We begin, then, with the affirmation that the truth of the universal speech act is the universal subject who bestows meaning on words. This is the truth of the *transcendental phenomenologist*.

In affirming that the truth of signifying acts lies solely on the side of the subject, the transcendental phenomenologist appears at first to be falling back to the position of the psychologist of Christianity. For by insisting that signs derive their meanings solely from the intentions of subjects, he seems to claim that language itself is nothing more nor less than a reflection of the psychology of particular speakers. And, indeed, the transcendental phenomenologist does say something like this, going so far as to insist that even the most "objective" language—the language of mathematics—is ultimately nothing but the expression of the mental acts of subjects. But of course a variant of this view has been undermined by the anti-psychologist, whose achievement it was to show that the logical rules which govern language are independent of the caprice of individual subjects. Hence, the transcendental phenomenologist receives a quick rebuke from the anti-psychologist; he is accused of having failed to grasp the distinction between psychology and logic.

But the transcendental phenomenologist pleads innocent to this charge, maintaining that what he is doing is not psychology at all. The psychologist takes for his truth the *particular* subject. As such, he seeks to reveal what is arbitrary in an individual's consciousness of language—that is, how certain words might suggest particular connotations peculiar to this particular subject. By contrast, the transcendental phenomenologist—as did the anti-psychologist—has returned to the Christian humanist's notion of a *universal* subject that is at the heart of all men. In describing an individual's mental acts, he seeks not the arbitrary but, on the contrary, that which is necessitated by the structure of consciousness itself. As such, he seeks to show why all men *must* agree to certain truths. Hence, by analyzing the subject, he takes himself to be reaffirming the objectivity of mathematics, whose truths he shows to be impervious even to the most fanciful subject's impulse to impose his own particular will on the matter at hand.

The transcendental phenomenologist accordingly declares his alliance with the anti-psychologist, going so far as to affirm that the chief obstacle to a true science of the consciousness of language is "psychologism." In truth, though, he has much more in common with the psychologist than with the anti-psychologist, for like the psychologist he affirms the truth of the subject, whereas the anti-psychologist completely denies a constitutive role for subjects in his theory of meaning. And although the transcendental phenomenologist is justified in noting that the psychologist begins from the particular subject, whereas he begins from the universal subject, still both share the common task of describing the actual mental acts of actual subjects.

Moreover, to followers of the anti-psychologist—especially the logical positivists, who deny the very existence of the subject—the distinction between psychology and phenomenology appears to be irrelevant. For even if they are distinct—and even granting that there is such a thing as a "subject"—one cannot deduce objective facts about language merely by appealing to the mental acts of subjects. The reason for this is that universal assent and objectivity are two different things; just because everyone thinks the earth is flat it does not follow that the earth is flat. To affirm the objectivity of mathematics, it does not suffice to point out that all men assent to its truths; on the contrary, one must demonstrate that all men assent to the truths of mathematics *because* they are true—that is, because they are objectively valid independently of the perception of any subject.

Once again, however, the transcendental phenomenologist denies that he is guilty of blurring a crucial distinction. Not only has he not overlooked the difference between contingent universal agreement and necessary universal agreement; on the contrary, in his phenomenological analysis of the foundations of mathematics he has tried to show the conditions for the possibility of a subject coming to recognize a necessary truth as a necessary truth. Without a phenomenological analysis of how a subject comes to recognize the objective character of meanings, he contends, it is impossible to advance beyond a merely dogmatic insistence on the objective character of logic and mathematics. The transcendental phenomenologist accordingly chides the followers of the anti-psychologist for thinking they can ward off the skepticism of the psychologists without providing a phenomenological foundation for the possibility of their logical analyses.

For their part, the logical positivists fail to see how he can hope to derive a basis for objective truth by returning to the linguistic idealist's insistence that the meanings of objects are constituted on the side of the subject. But for the transcendental phenomenologist, the question of whether intentional objects have objectively determinable meanings and the question of whether objects exist independently of the subject are entirely separate. In making this distinction, he follows the anti-psychologist, who similarly distinguished between the question of the objective sense of expressions and the question of the reference of expressions. Unlike the anti-psychologist, of course, he maintains that meanings are constituted by subjects. But to say this is not to take the anti-objectivist position of either the psychologist of Christianity or the linguistic idealist; for unlike them, the transcendental phenomenologist maintains that, even though meanings are subjectively constituted, they nonetheless have an objectively fixed character. Once an object is intended, its meaning becomes something fixed for the subject—it is in this sense that objectivity is preserved. The question of the existence of objects is an entirely different one.

The transcendental phenomenologist therefore does not deny the existence of the objective world; he denies only that the objective world can have any meaning apart from the subject's constitution of it. Ultimately, the question of whether or not objects actually exist outside the perceptual intentions of the subject is of less importance than the question of how it is that an intended object can both have an essential meaning of its own that is independent of the perceiver, while at the same time deriving this meaning solely from the intentional act of the perceiver. This question calls not merely for a description of intentional acts; it calls for a transcendental inquiry into the conditions for the possibility of the perception of meanings. Hence, the transcendental phenomenologist further clarifies the difference between his version of phenomenology and psychology by saying that only the latter is essentially descriptive. He concedes that a merely descriptive phenomenology could at most demonstrate the basis for *de facto* agreement among men. But a transcendental phenomenology seeks to articulate the a priori basis for *de jure* agreement.

In order to make the meanings of objects available for phenomenological inspection, one need only suspend all judgment concerning the existence of the objects themselves. But in order to establish the possibility of a transcendental inquiry, it is necessary to demonstrate that the meanings thereby brought into view are universal. Hence, the transcendental phenomenologist requires a method that will enable a particular subject to rise above his own empirical ego and apprehend the meanings of his intentional acts from the standpoint of the pure universal ego.

The transcendental phenomenologist must turn away from the objects of his intentional acts in order to introspectively apprehend his own pure subjectivity. It is impossible for him to study the intentional acts of anyone other than himself, for other subjects appear to him only as objects of his own intentional acts. As in the case of the Christian humanist, therefore, he can only claim a form of self-knowledge, on the basis of which he presumes to discern a universal subject that is the truth of all subjects.

For this reason, the transcendental phenomenologist must *start out* from the immediate certainty of self-consciousness. Yet he cannot *end* with this standpoint, for although the "I" of immediate self-consciousness is implicitly universal, it is explicitly only the particular "I" of a particular subject. Since he professes to apprehend a universal subject, the transcendental phenomenologist must arrive at the truth of *spirit*—that is, the truth of the [I = we]. To be sure, this truth has already been achieved. But it has been apprehended only in the sphere of intersubjective relations, and the transcendental phenomenologist has retreated into the solitary existence of an isolated ego who can reflect only on himself. Therefore *he* must justify his claim to be able to lift himself up by the bootstraps to the level of universal self-consciousness. He does this as did the philosophical loner and the Christian humanist—that is, by negating everything that belongs to his own particular ego. This ascetic movement he calls the "transcendental reduction."

To its "discoverer," the result of this reduction is nothing short of miraculous: he has turned both himself and every intentional object into a pure universal, thereby opening up to phenomenological inspection an entire realm of pure meanings. In truth, though, all that this much-celebrated reduction really does is to make explicit the transition from sense-certainty to perception. For once the dialectic of sense-certainty teaches us that every *this* is a universal, we have already discovered that the subject and object poles of perceptions are universals. Hence, the "transcendental" phenomenologist's subsequent explication of the realm of pure meanings is nothing more nor less than a restating—in a suitably technical vocabulary, of course—of the dialectic of the certainty and truth of perception. He notices, for instance, that every universal *this* of perception is a thing with many properties, but he says this in his own jargon: every intentional object of a meaning-endowing act is an essential unity which can appear as a manifold through a variety of possible meaning-fulfilling acts. Just as in the case of perception proper, so now in the perception of intentional acts, the transcendental phenomenologist retraces the dialectical discovery of contradiction in the meanings of the objects of perception. He reminds us that every object of an intentional act appears as a unity, yet at the same time, it appears as a multiplicity of many *thises*. With painstaking care, he recalls how the subject of the intentional acts is himself responsible for the apparent multiplicity in an essentially unitary essence, and how the subject is responsible for the apparent unity in what would otherwise be a mere multiplicity of properties. Both roles can be ascribed to the subject, since the meaning of the object is subjectively constituted. Yet since this meaning is objective, the object itself must be viewed as being both a unity and a multiplicity. Ultimately, the transcendental phenomenologist discovers that the object appears as both a unity and a multiplicity because it stands in relation to a subject who is itself both an essential unity and a multiplicity of perceptual faculties.

However, he does not go on to resolve the dialectic of the perception of meanings by positing the unitary truth of the intentional act as a relation between subject and object. Because he continues to affirm that the object is something subjectively constituted, he ends up positing the one-sided truth of a transcendental ego. If to perceive an object is to give it meaning, then the subject's meaning-endowing act is the primary moment in the relation between subject and object. Of course, the object must confirm or disconfirm the subject's ascription of meaning to it; this is the function of meaning-fulfilling intentions, whereby the object presents itself. But these are logically secondary, in that they merely serve as evidence in support of or against the thesis of the meaning of the object that is constituted by the subject.

By referring to the paradoxes of perception, the transcendental phenomenologist can readily show how it is that the subject gets thrown into a series of antinomies as soon as it views the object as existing on its own, unmoored from the subject's constitution of it. He is thus led to distinguish between authentic and inauthentic thinking of objects. The subject thinks authentically when it recognizes that the meanings of objects are the products of its own meaning-endowing acts; it thinks inauthentically when it views objects as existing independently of itself. Authentic thinking can take place only once the subject has performed the transcendental reduction; it thinks inauthentically so long as it remains trapped within the so-called natural attitude.

However, although the transcendental phenomenologist is justified in criticizing the one-sided natural attitude which affirms the independent truth of the object outside of the intentional act, his transcendental attitude is equally one-sided and untenuous. For he now affirms the independent existence of the transcendental ego, which he maintains would continue to exist even if there were no intentional objects. Far from having sustained his earlier belief in both the subjective constitution of meanings and the objectivity of meanings, he has now lapsed into a thoroughgoing idealism. Under the guise of performing the transcendental reduction, he has simply allowed his imagination to posit the eternal existence of whatever fleeting intentional objects happen to appear in his perception.

If the work of phenomenology is to continue, it must return to the task of describing the essential unity of the intentional act, instead of viewing it from the one-sided standpoint of the transcendental reduction. Put otherwise, phenomenology must begin from a critique of both the natural attitude—which fetishizes the object—and the transcendental attitude—which makes a fetish of the subject. It is still necessary to carry out a reduction, by means of which the intentional act itself appears as an object of inquiry. But this reduction now leads away from both the subject and the object, bringing into view the unitary act wherein alone the subject and the object have their being. To bring the intentional act into view, in other words, is to make manifest that which enables the being of the subject and the being of the object to appear in the first place. An intentional act is thus a *revelation of the being of beings*. The project of describing these intentional acts is the task of the *phenomenologist of revelation*.

Unlike his predecessor, the phenomenologist of revelation does not view the object as something subjectively constituted; that is, he does not grant any logical priority to meaning-endowing acts over meaning-fulfilling acts. Yet neither does he accept the perspective of the natural attitude of the logical realists, according to which the intentional act is an empirical grasping of properties which would belong to the object even if it were not perceived by a subject. Both models fail because they view the truth of the intentional act as a matter of getting the subject's perception of the object to "fit" or "correspond" to the object in some way. So, for instance, verifying the statement, "This is a tree" is viewed as a comparing of the object with what is thought about it, in order to see if the two sides correspond with each other. The notion of truth as correspondence is false because it divides the unitary act of revelation in two, treating the subject and the object as if they had an independent existence outside the relation. In opposition to this model, the phenomenologist of revelation characterizes truth in terms of "disclosure" and "unconcealment," terms which express the unitary phenomenon whose unfolding reveals this particular subject confronted with this particular object. The statement "This is a tree" is true when it *is* the manner in which the revelation of the being of the tree is itself revealed. Strictly speaking, therefore, neither truth nor language is something possessed by the subject; rather the subject finds itself *in* the revelation that is the truth of language.

Yet at the same time, the subject's *being-in-the-truth* is something that is itself revealed *to the subject*, and to this extent the being of the subject differs from the being of the object. The subject of the happening of revelation therefore has a certain type of being—its being is the being of a witness; the subject is the one to whom the revelation of beings reveals itself. Although language "belongs" to being rather to than to the subject— which is why utterances are to be thought of as happenings rather than acts—the subject is the addressee of the language of being. Hence, the truth of the unitary intentional act divides into two after all: there is the revelation of the truth that discloses this subject and this object, but there is also the revelation of the phenomenon of revelation.

For this reason, although he does not privilege the being of the subject over the being of the object, the phenomenologist of revelation is led to posit a type of ontological priority that the subject has as that being whose being must be questioned if the question of the being of revelation in general is to be raised. This priority derives from the fact that it is always to the subject that the being of the subject-object re(ve)lation is revealed. This is why the subject can speak of *its* intentional acts. The sense of the subject's *ownership*, of course, must be clarified. The words "This is a tree" belong to the subject only insofar as the subject is their addressee, not insofar as the subject is their speaker; for it is the being of revelation which speaks them. Language comes to subjects.

Insofar as it is aware of its intentional acts as being its own, the subject constantly has the revelation of being before it. Yet at the same time, the ontological horizon of the phenomenon of revelation is something which is only laid bare by way of a reduction, for so long as the subject persists

in its everyday natural attitude, it concerns itself not with the being of revelation but with whatever particular objects it happens to be confronted with.
In its everyday attitude, the subject views language not as the revelation of
beings, but as a tool that *it* uses to grasp beings. As such it neglects the
revelation of revelation and lapses into ontological forgetfulness. Yet even in
its forgetting, the subject's concernful awareness with the objects that are
revealed to it is made possible through the revelation to the subject of the
revelation of these objects. Therefore, even in its forgetting of the being of
beings, the subject to whom the revelation of beings is revealed must always
possess a vague, average understanding of the being of revelation.

Now, the task of the phenomenologist of revelation is nothing other
than to describe the revelation of beings. But this simply means that he—
as an individual subject—must recover his own implicit experience of the
revelation of revelation. Where the transcendental phenomenologist sought
to rise above the inauthentic thinking of the natural attitude in order to
attain the authentic thinking of the pure ego, the phenomenologist of revelation seeks to rise above the inauthentic attitudes—both natural and
transcendental—of thinking about *beings* to the authentic attitude of thinking about the *being* of beings as it is revealed in the revelation of revelation.

His first task, then, is to describe the revelation of revelation as it
manifests itself in the subject's everydayness. By an analysis of what is
implict but forgotten in the subject's everyday thinking, he will then rise
to the level of describing in an authentic way the explict manner in which
the revelation of revelation is made manifest to the subject.

By positing the essential truth of revelation and relegating both the
subject and the object to the status of inessential moments, the
phenomenologist of revelation has arrived at the truth of perception itself.
Since he no longer takes the truth to lie either on the side of the subject
or on the side of the object, but rather in the act of revelation itself, he is
led to affirm the truth of both the revelation of the object's multiplicity and
the revelation of the object's unity. He simply contrasts two modes of the
revelation of being—the object can be made manifest as something present
at hand (as a simple unity) or else as something ready to hand (and thus
as containing a multiplicity of possible functions). Similarly, the subject
can appear either as a unitary consciousness or else as an agent concernfully
engaged in one or another activity. Having recognized that both the subjects and objects of revelation are both one and many, the phenomenologist
of revelation goes on to consider the revelation of the world as an interre-
lation of objects, and the concomitant revelation of itself as a subject whose
being is essentially defined in terms of its being-with-others.

Up until now, the phenomenologist of revelation has focused on his
own everyday experience of revelation, much as the transcendental

phenomenologist examined his own intentional acts. Yet at the same time he posits the universality of his description of what it means to be a subject to whom the revelation of beings is revealed. Insofar as he begins from his own universal self-certainty, he can indeed claim the validity of his observations. However, where the phenomenology of perception in general must falter is in its attempt to describe the revelation of *spirit*, for the individual can view his relationship to others only from his own perspective. Faced with the task of describing the revelation of being-with-others, the phenomenologist of perception can only describe an individual subject's one-sided perspective of the being-with relation. He may well *understand* that being-with-others involves the dual moments of being-for-self and being-for-another, but as a phenomenologist of perception, he can *describe* only one side of this relation, namely, the side of being-for-self.

Instead of rising to the level of an authentic thinking of being-*for*-others, therefore, the phenomenologist of revelation can only reaffirm the *immediate* truth of the [I = we], succumbing to a type of *ethical forgetting* of the work of mediation that is needed to rise to a meaningful recognition of otherness. That is, just as he accuses everyday subjects of having forgotten the being of beings, so the phenomenologist of revelation has himself forgotten the otherness of others. As a result of this forgetting, he jumps straight to the moment of absolute knowing as only an egomaniac can do, pawning off his own self-certainty as if this were in itself equivalent to a recognition of others. Thus, the phenomenologist of revelation dupes himself into believing that he can explicate the revelation of being-for-others, simply by giving an account of the moment of being-for-self. The bad faith of the phenomenologist of revelation, in other words, is his reduction of being-for-others to being-for-self—the lowest possibility to which a pretender to absolute knowing can sink.

Strictly speaking, the phenomenologist of revelation is not aware of *objective spirit* at all. For him, spirit is merely the self-sameness of every ego; he imagines that the revelation of spirit is made manifest in his own private experience, and he attributes the same revelation to everyone else. In short, he apprehends the *subjective spirit*, albeit in a defective form, and so can represent objective spirit only in the guise of religious picture-thinking. Unable to muster even the vaguest concept of the social being of man, the phenomenologist of revelation imagines a political realm based on the crudest politics of identity. The subject is the state and the state is the subject—again we find the sort of nationalistic political thinking that we would expect from a travesty of the standpoint of absolute knowing. But while the absolute knowers did advocate a kind of politics of identity, they at least understood the *concept* of objective spirit. Because the phenomenologist of revelation can picture objective spirit only under the guise of subjective spirit, he envisions not only a politics of identity but also a cult of the individual. Putting these together, he sets his hope on the possible rise of a fascist dictator, who, by force of his personality, will command the self-identifying worship of all the other members of the nation-state. At the very depths of his ethical forgetting, the phenomenologist of revelation actually expects that such fascist politics of identity is the only authentic way of making manifest the being-for-others of individual subjects.

The only thing that can disabuse the phenomenologist of revelation of his delusional thinking is the actual realization of a fascist politics of identity. Subject to the brutality of such a political system, to its contempt for the otherness of others, to the terror of the absolute freedom of an evil leader, the phenomenologist of revelation learns to his incomparable shame that the revelation of being-for-others has been trampled afoot rather than brought to the fore. Yet still he lacks a concept of objective spirit; he imagines that the people have simply fetishized the wrong leader. He is like the evil scientist who sought to create the perfect man and, when he discovers that he has created a man with the mind of a criminal, shakes his head and says, "Well, back to the drawing board!"—still he envisions the ideal of a perfect fascist leader. The phenomenologist of revelation still conflates being-for-others with being-for-self—to the sad and pathetic point that he believes himself to be in real solidarity with those who perish under the evil system he himself has helped to bring into existence. Privately feeling guilt and remorse is for him the only authentic way of actively resisting evil.

The bad faith of the phenomenologist of revelation reaches its most damning point precisely here—when he fails to take responsibility for others. The experience of the absolute evil of fascism is nothing less than a revelation of the error of conflating being-for-others and being-for-self. In failing to attend to *this* revelation, the phenomenologist of revelation betrays his utter incomprehension of what it means to be a subject in the world. Were he to grasp the true meaning of being-in-the-world, he would recognize the absolute rift between being-for-self and being-for-others, while at the same time acknowledging his own absolute responsibility for deciding whether to work to heal this rift or not. The responsibility of calling attention to this responsibility is the task of the true phenomenologist of existence—the *existentialist*.

By relegating the subject to the status of a mere witness of revelation and a mere addressee of language, the phenomenologist of revelation has turned the subject into a being whose highest obligation is to deny that it is responsible for its own intentional acts. To be sure, he does not view the ideal subject as a mere passive observer of experience; on the contrary, he insists that the subject is relentlessly called to the task of an active listening to the revelation of being. But for the phenomenologist of revelation, active listening is opposed to active speaking—one can actively listen to language only when one ceases to view language as a tool to be used by the subject. The subject takes responsibility for listening precisely by giving up its pretense to be responsible for speaking. This false *dichotomy* between speaking and listening corresponds to the false *equation* of being-for-self and being-for-others. On the one hand, the phenomenologist of revelation fails to recognize that the being of language is not a listening-to-oneself but a listening-to-others; on the other hand, he fails to recognize that one cannot *actually* be with others without engaging in conversation—that is, without both listening and speaking. In order to rise to the level of an authentic actualization of being-for-others, it is necessary that the subject take responsibility for its language.

In contrast to the phenomenologist of revelation, therefore, the existentialist begins from the certainty that he—as a particular individual subject—is the only one responsible for the things he says. More specifically, he negates the general claim that the subject "belongs to" its intentional acts, for it is this central tenet of the phenomenologist of revelation which denies the subject's responsibility. In direct opposition, the existentialist maintains that the subject is responsible for all of its intentional acts. But since he, too, views the intentional act as a unity, not divided into separate subject and object poles, the existentialist takes the subject to be responsible not only for himself but also for all of the objects of his intentional acts. In every situation, the subject is faced with only two possible "ethical" alternatives—to acknowledge its responsibility for everything in the world or to hide from this responsibility. To accept one's responsibility is to live authentically; to deny it is to live inauthentically.

As did the transcendental phenomenologist, the existentialist views the subject as the "owner" of its intentional acts. To be sure, he does not turn the subject into an ego existing apart from the world; he accepts the phenomenologist of revelation's description of the subject as existing only in its relation to the objects of its intentional acts. However, by privileging the subject, the existentialist in effect reduces all intentional objects to modes of its own experience. To say that the subject is responsible for the entire world is thus only to say that the subject is responsible for itself—albeit a global expansion of itself. For this reason, the existentialist has no more of a sense of responsibility for others *qua* others than does the phenomenologist of revelation. This is because he has completely reduced all being-for-others to a mode of being-for-self.

That the existentialist's notion of being-for-others is inadequate in this way can be seen from the fact there is no necessary ethical content implied in his conception of absolute responsibility. The subject is absolutely free to do as he wishes. If he chooses to kill, then he chooses to kill: his responsibility consists merely in his having to acknowledge that *he* was the one who decided whether or not to kill. The being of *others* does not in itself alter the nature of the subject's responsibility. Thus, the revelation of the ethical import of being-for-others remains as obscure for the existentialist as it is for the phenomenologist of revelation.

Implicit in the position of the existentialist would *seem* to be the basis for a devastating critique of the phenomenologist of revelation. For what has the latter advocated if not the denial of the subject's responsibility for the world? But in fact the phenomenologist of revelation does believe that the subject is responsible for the world; he is simply unwilling to acknowledge the type of responsibility argued for by the existentialist. Sincerely believing that the only fault of the evil fascist dictator was that he failed to grasp the truth of the revelation of being, the phenomenologist of revelation claims that the possibility of evil arises only when individual subjects believe—as did the evil dictator and as does the existentialist—that they can manipulate the world in accordance with their own whims. Such a view (whose logical conclusion can only be the active nihilism of the psychologist of Christianity) itself represents a shirking of man's true responsibility, namely, to listen to the voice of being which calls the subject to "let beings be," to act as "the shepherd of beings." The phenomenologist of revelation thus accuses the existentialist of advocating a false conception of man's true responsibility; the existentialist, as humanist, is nothing more than an advocate of hubris.

The words of the phenomenologist of revelation are noble ones indeed: in the name of the highest possible "humanism" he criticizes the sham "humanism" of the existentialist. Yet despite the aptness of these criticisms, the phenomenologist of revelation still possesses a woefully inadequate notion of responsibility, which arises from the fact that he himself has no real notion of the meaning of being-for-others. Certainly the phenomenologist of revelation is in no better position than the existentialist to articulate the nature of the subject's ethical responsibility to act on behalf of others. As it stands, the ideal of "letting beings be" is completely abstract and devoid of content. For example, what is a subject called upon to do in the face of a starving child? What exactly does it mean to let this being be? To let it be as it is—that is, as starving? The phenomenologist of revelation's failure to grasp an authentic notion of what it means to be *actually* responsible for others is made most vividly clear by his inability to distinguish between the technological manipulation of objects in the world and the torture and murder of living beings. To the last, he remains committed to a fascist politics, believing that "only a god"—that is, the evil scientist's truly perfect man—"can save us now." It is an offense to the dead that he dares equate the existential humanist to the evil fascist dictator.

The phenomenologist of revelation and the existentialist have both failed to explicate a notion of ethical responsibility because they begin from the subject's being-for-self, on the basis for which they attempt to explicate the phenomenon of its being-for-others. The opposite strategy now emerges as the only viable possibility: in order to describe the revelation of ethical responsibility, one must begin not with the subject's being-for-self, but with the phenomenon of its being-for-others. This is the task of the *phenomenologist of otherness*.

To make primary the task of describing the phenomenon of being-for-others is to reconceive the very project of phenomenology. For one thing, no longer can the subject's perception of objects be primary; rather, one must begin from the subject's encounter with another subject. Moreover, since what is primary is not the subject's being-for-self but its being-for-others, phenomenology can no longer view the face-to-face encounter between subjects solely from the side of one particular subject; rather, it must seek to describe this encounter insofar as it implies the presence of two subjects. Finally, in order to explicate in an authentic way the consciousness of being-for-others, the phenomenologist of otherness must view each perceived subject as irreducible to the subject who perceives it. Hence, the unity of the subject and object in the intentional act is now split into a radical dualism between subject and subject. The perceived other, qua other, is that being which cannot become a mere phenomenal object for the perceiver. As a result, the dual *presence* of subjects qua perceivers in the face-to-face encounter is at the same time a dual *absence* of subjects qua perceived others.

In one way, therefore, the encounter with the other is something which can never take place, for the other is that which, by definition, the perceiving subject cannot encounter. Yet what is primary in the subject's experience is just this encounter with the unencounterable, and to this extent the encounter with the other does take place. Prior to any revelation of its own being-for-self, the subject is confronted with a revelation of its being-for-others. But since being reveals itself to the subject as being-for-self, the priority of being-for-others makes the subject's relationship to others in the face-to-face encounter more originary than its relationship to being. The revelation of being-for-others is "older" than being; or, put otherwise, it *is* in a way that is somehow "otherwise" than the "is" of being.

Since the subject "belongs to" the face-to-face encounter rather than the other way around, his responsibility is, first and foremost, not to himself but to the other. The subject has an *absolute* responsibility for the other. However, insofar as the other is other, the other represents the very limit of the subject's responsibility. Hence, the subject's absolute responsibility for the other is something both necessary and impossible.

Now, of course, the same holds true for both subjects involved in the face-to-face encounter. Each is absolutely responsible for the other. We see in the curious geometry of this relationship the exact opposite of what appeared at the earlier level of the struggle to the death. There, each subject viewed itself as standing infinitely above the other. Here, each sees the other as standing infinitely above himself. Moreover, in the authentic representation of the face-to-face encounter we see revealed the ideal which the absolute knowers attempted to realize in their mutual solicitude toward each other. They were unable to realize this ideal, because beneath their solicitude lurked a narcissistic desire to be recognized themselves. Here, however, the phenomenologist of otherness has posited the absolute priority of solicitude toward others over any possible desire for recognition. Hence, we seem to have arrived at the mediated [I = I] of the absolute standpoint.

However, even if the subject's absolute recognition of the other is reciprocated by the other, the subject cannot recognize himself as the recipient of the other's recognition. On the contrary, the subject's absolute recognition of the other is predicated on him not recognizing himself. For this reason, the "true" absolute standpoint still cannot be achieved. Just as the absolute knowers failed to achieve it because they remained stuck in a one-sided narcissism, so now two authentic participants in a face-to-face encounter fail because they remain stuck in parallel one-sided altruism. Only if these two moments—the moments of narcissism and altruism—could be brought together could the absolute standpoint be attained. But this is just to say that it is necessary to reconcile both the subject's being-for-self and its being-for-others; just as the existentialist privileged the former moment in a one-sided way, so now the phenomenologist of otherness has privileged the latter in a one-sided way.

Hence, the authentic face-to-face encounter remains a mere ideal, and moreover one which seems to have been proven impossible to realize. The beautiful certainty of the phenomenologist of otherness is viewed skeptically as "just a pretty picture," and the irreducibility of the subject's being-for-self is once again affirmed. In every *actual* encounter between subjects, the skeptic declares, there is a struggle for recognition. No matter how solicitous one individual might be toward another, he is, at bottom, doing it for himself.

The truth of phenomenology, therefore, ultimately breaks up into an internal division within the subject. Just as, at the level of perception proper, the thing with its properties split up into force and its manifestations, so here the subject has split up into the force of being-for-self and its various manifestations. This unconscious force manifests itself in various phenomenal guises, but it is always one and the same. Hence, the *truth* of perception is not something to be grasped by a phenomenology of perception, but by an interpretive understanding that seeks to comprehend the truth of that which is merely perceived—that is, by *psychoanalysis*.

C. Force and Understanding of Language. The Analyst/Analysand Dialectic

The face-to-face encounter, which proved to be the truth of the perception of language, manifested itself as an inversion of the earlier struggle for recognition. Since the subject is posited as having its truth in the other, the subject begins not from a certainty of itself but on the contrary from a certainty of the other. Yet just as in the earlier dialectic it proved no simple task for the individual subject to advance from immediate self-recognition to recognition of the other, so in the face-to-face encounter it is difficult for the subject to advance from immediate recognition of the other to self-recognition. Moreover, just as unreciprocated immediate self-recognition disintegrated into the despair of the unhappy consciousness, so here the subject's inability to recognize himself makes his recognition of the other merely immediate and not yet raised to the level of truth. No struggle to the death actually ensues; the face-to-face encounter merely jumps straightaway to an inversion of the stage of the unhappy consciousness. Unable to achieve a mediated certainty of himself, the subject returns to his immediate self-certainty and declares his recognition of the other to be false. However, because he has not actually returned into himself, he posits his own essence as a hidden force, of whose existence he professes to be certain. This is the force of being-for-self. Conversely, the other now also appears as a manifestation of force. The face of the other both is and is not the other; the other is the face insofar as the force of the other is a going-outside-itself, and it is not the face insofar as it is a retreating-back-into-itself.

The force that is the other, therefore, is a dynamic unity of the moments of being-for-self and being-for-others. Yet only one of these moments—being-for-self—is the essence of force. For the truth of the other is that it is infinitely withdrawn from perception; the fact that the other manifests itself in the face-to-face encounter reveals that the other's being-for-others is part of its being-for-self. In other words, it is not the subject that solicits the other to appear as being-for-others; rather, the other itself solicits this going-outside-itself which is merely an inessential moment of its returning-to-itself.

The subject who was unable to recognize himself in the face-to-face encounter now foists the blame for this self-failure onto the other, whom he accuses of duplicity. The other only appeared to be motivated by a force of being-for-others; in truth, he was motivated by a force of being-for-self. In short, the subject accuses the other of precisely what the absolute knowers accused each other of—an irreducible narcissism. Yet the absolute knowers at least held out the possibility of a mutual recognition. Here, the subject despairs of the absolute standpoint's every being reached. He declares the falsity of the face-to-face encounter, maintaining that human interactions can never rise above the level of struggles for recognition. With this cynical thought, the subject who originally entered the face-to-face encounter with so much selfless love and respect for the other, now observes everyone with suspicion and mistrust. When he drops a pen and someone walking by picks it up and hands it to him, the suspicious subject thinks, "He probably wants something from me," or, "He probably wanted to enjoy a good laugh over my clumsiness." It is by being suspicious of the motives of others in this way that the subject becomes a *psychoanalyst*.

However, although the face-to-face encounter failed to lead to a reciprocity of mutual recognition and self-recognition, it failed not because of a one-sided moment of being-for-self but because of a one-sided appearance of being-for-others. For this reason, the psychoanalyst presents a false representation of human nature. Specifically, his certainty that everyone is a selfish egoist presents an accurate picture of the breakdown of the struggle for recognition, but it presents a false picture of the reasons for a breakdown in the face-to-face encounter. In themselves, all subjects exhibit the dual moments of being-for-self and being-for-others. The true task of the psychoanalyst ought to be to figure out how to bring these moments together in a way that does justice to each. But for now he brings them together only by reducing the one to the other.

Now, the realm of civil society continues to be the domain of unbridled egoism, and so long as he confines himself to interpreting egoists, the psychoanalyst can easily find confirmation of his theory. There, it often happens that people offer to do someone a favor only because they want something in return. However, as soon as the individual steps outside civil society and reenters the realm of the family, from which realm he, like everyone else in civil society, has originated, he finds himself confronted with individuals whose solicitude appears to be based upon an unconditioned force of being-for-others. In the dialectical movement whereby the subject starts out from a family, enters civil society, and then starts a family of his own, we find an inversion of the dialectic of force. That is, from the standpoint of the family, the subject is essentially a force of being-for-others. Only when he leaves the family—that is, when this force goes outside itself—does it appear in civil society as a being-for-self. Thus, the dialectic of force as viewed from the perspective of the family appears as a topsy-turvy version of the dialectic of force as viewed from the perspective of civil society. In the family, force is being-for-others; in civil society, it is being-for-self. Each one's posited essence appears to the other as the inessential moment in which force goes outside itself. Put otherwise, in civil society, human interactions are essentially struggles for recognition which fail to lead to reciprocal recognition; in the family, human relations are essentially face-to-face encounters which fail to lead to self-recognition.

The separation between the realms of civil society and the family is one that emerged with the splitting of humanity into two distinct *genders*. As we saw at the level of the ethical order, men have been associated with the family's going-outside-itself into civil society, and women have been associated with the family's returning-to-itself. So long as this distinction between genders remains in place, a reconciliation of being-for-self and being-for-others cannot be realized. A dialectic of recognition must take place between the opposed genders—a dialectic, in other words, between the struggle for recognition and the face-to-face encounter.

Just as earlier, the communists viewed their task as having to bring together the "family" of absolute knowers with the "civil society" of egoists, so here the psychoanalyst will eventually be led to view his task as that of bringing together the realm of being-for-others with the realm of being-for-self. Such a reconciliation, however, will require his recognizing the validity of both the moments of being-for-self and being-for-others. At present, he posits the essential unity of only one of these moments. As a result, he is not yet the great mediator between the dialectic of civil society and the family; as the one who posits the truth of being-for-self, he represents the embodiment of civil society in its struggle with the family. Thus, his aim is to show the falsity of the family's claim to the truth—that is, to demonstrate that all relations of being-for-others in the family have their origin in an unconditioned force of being-for-self. As such, his task is itself a gendered one—he seeks to show that all humans are essentially masculine. Even those who exhibit a feminine gender must, in themselves, be masculine subjects whose being-for-self has for some reason been transformed into a force of being-for-others. The masculine psychoanalyst's task, therefore, is to discover why a force of being-for-self should manifest itself as its opposite in the family.

For the psychoanalyst, even those subjects who appear *for themselves* to be motivated by a force of being-for-others must *in themselves* exhibit a selfish being-for-self. Such subjects—whose extreme degree of femininity wins them the name *hysterics*—collectively represent for the psychoanalyst a type of interpretive test case. He attempts to prove that even the phenomenon of hysterical being-for-others is, at bottom, a manifestation of the force of being-for-self. That is, he tries to show that femininity in general is simply a "symptom" of a force of being-for-self turned away from itself. To "cure" the hysteric of her femininity is to raise the hysteric's being-for-self to the level of self-consciousness—that is, to make her realize that she is, in essence, as masculine as any member of civil society. By proving that humanity is essentially masculine, the psychoanalyst will force the defenders of the law of the family—who, it should be noted, include the communists as well as the Christian humanist—to acknowledge that all apparent face-to-face encounters are really struggles for recognition. With this aim in mind, he enters the one-sided masculine perversion of the face-to-face encounter between the genders—the analyst/analysand confrontation.

Just as the face-to-face encounter recapitulated the earlier struggle for recognition, so now the analyst/analysand confrontation recapitulates the initial movements of the master/slave dialectic. The analyst, like the master, is a self-recognizing subject who confronts an other-recognizing subject. However, just as the face-to-face encounter took place within a dialectic of perception, so now the analyst/analysand confrontation takes place within a dialectic of understanding. The analysand thus appears as the thing whose essence is a hidden force, and the aim of the analyst is to comprehend the nature of this force. For this reason, the psychoanalytic confrontation is not an encounter between two subjects *qua* subjects; it is characterized, rather, by the objectifying gaze of the analyst who views the analysand as a specimen in his psychic laboratory. Their encounter is not face-to-face, therefore, for there is no reason why the analysand should be allowed to gaze at the analyst. The analysand is a mere thing.

This thing's force—the underlying being-for-self of the analysand—remains hidden, but the psychoanalyst is certain that it manifests itself in her apparently selfless speech. Here we see the asymmetry between the analyst/analysand dialectic and the master/slave dialectic. For although the analyst follows the master in putting the other to work for him, he gives himself the task of comprehending this work. The proper work of the analysand is to produce speech; the work of the analyst is to "interpret" this speech—that is, to rewrite its femininity in masculine terms.

Since he begins from the certainty that the hysteric's speech is motivated by the force of being-for-self, yet since this speech appears as if it were motivated solely by her having identified completely with the being-for-self of an other, the psychoanalyst assumes that the hysteric is repressing her being-for-self. To determine the cause of this repression, he has the hysteric describe her life.

Now, as in the case of the subject of the face-to-face encounter, the hysteric's being-for-others appears to be more primordial than her experience of being-for-self. That is, her very sense of self-identity is dependent on her experience of being-for-another. This suggests that her identification with an other must have occurred before her being-for-self manifested itself at all. If this is so, then her being-for-another did not originate out of a face-to-face encounter that she entered of her own free will. On the contrary, as something out of *her* control, her being-for-another must have been forced upon her before her own ego had a chance to develop—that is, it must have occurred in her early childhood. As the victim of an encounter with an other, the prehysterical child would resemble not the free subject of a face-to-face encounter, but rather the unfree slave who has been forced to negate her own being-for-self by a master. Submitting to the master as a pre-self-conscious child could only have been experienced as a trauma, the result of which was to make all subsequent ego-development dependent on this early experience of being-for-another. In order to cure the hysteric, it would be necessary to reverse the effects of this violent experience, so that her being-for-self could develop unencumbered by the memory of the traumatic eruption of the other into her psyche.

With this theory, the psychoanalyst has gone a long way toward understanding the psychic mechanisms whereby not only hysterical subjects, but feminine subjects in general, are traumatically introduced to their lifelong roles of supposedly selfless guardians of the family. However, it is a theory which the psychoanalyst is forced to abandon. The reason for this is that, by appealing to a *real* traumatic experience of being-for-another prior to the formation of being-for-self, the psychoanalyst has posited something which his theory precludes, namely, the possible psychic priority of being-for-others over being-for-self. His certainty rests entirely with the claim that being-for-self is the single psychic force which is at work in all intentional experience. Accordingly, he must deny that it is even possible for a subject to have an experience of an other *qua* other before she has developed a sense of her own self. In place of a pre-self-conscious traumatic encounter with an other, therefore, the psychoanalyst revises his interpretation of the hysteric. He now posits that her early identification with an other must have arisen *after* the emergence of her sense of self. Moreover, since everything must be traced back to an originary force of being-for-self, the hysteric herself must, for some reason, have *chosen* to identify with an other. The traumatic encounter is therefore reinterpreted by the psychoanalyst as something *invented by the hysteric herself*: it is not a real encounter but an imaginary encounter. In attempting to "cure" the hysteric, he now seeks to interpret her speech not as the record of real events in her life but rather as the record of her own fictitious psychic inventions.

In one sense, the hysteric's fantasized trauma continues to play the same role for the analyst that the previously posited real trauma did; namely, it explains why she has repressed her being-for-self. But in another sense it explains nothing, for the source of the fantasized trauma is now nothing other than the hysteric's own force of being-for-self. Thus, the psychoanalyst finds himself back at square one, trying to determine why an individual's being-for-self should negate itself in the first place. What makes this an especially difficult problem is that the underlying force of being-for-self remains something hidden; it is the other's unity insofar as she returns into herself. Unlike the case of normal speech between two self-conscious individuals, where each speaker can simply ask the other to explain what she means by a particular phrase, the psychoanalyst cannot expect the analysand to *comprehend* what she is saying. The reason for this is that the analysand's self-consciousness is itself merely one of the apparent manifestations of her underlying being-for-self. After all, the analysand is for the psychoanalyst truly a perceived *thing*, whose essence is an unconscious being-for-self which manifests itself in this thing's appearing as a self-conscious subject. Being-for-self, in other words, is no longer the self-consciousness of the ego but rather the unconscious thing-in-itself. Yet since the unity of the thing is now identified with its multiplicity, the force of being-for-self is not just the exclusive *one*, it is also the entire process whereby this force goes out of itself into the speech of the analysand and then returns to itself. In principle, therefore, the speech of the analysand must be decipherable; the psychoanalyst merely needs to learn the language in which the unconscious force expresses itself.

Here a problem of self-knowledge arises. Up until now the psychoanalyst has taken himself to be a self-conscious being-for-self precisely insofar as he has perceived himself to be a selfish egoist, and he has taken the hysteric to be an unconscious being-for-self insofar as she identifies her ego with that of another subject. Now, however, he must acknowledge that he himself does not immediately apprehend his own force of being-for-self; that is, his *own* being-for-self as just as much of a mystery as is the being-for-self of the hysteric. With the aim of rising to the level of an authentic consciousness of his own unconscious being-for-self—which he knows cannot be identified with the inauthentic self-consciousness of his ego—he turns his clinically objectifying gaze on the thing that he himself is.

With this shape of the self-consciousness of the self-analyzing analyst, we reach a point of total alienation which brings together the alienation of the object—the infinitely removed force—along with the alienation of the subject—the alienation of the slave. Here, however, we see the dialectic of self-alienation develop from the point of view of the *master*, for although he withdraws into the introspection of self-analysis, the psychoanalytic representative of civil society remains in his dominant relation to the hysterical representative of the law of the family.

From his confrontation with the hysteric and his postulate that the latter does not grasp the true nature of her fictitious psychic inventions, the psychoanalyst has a starting point. Those psychic inventions which appear to subjects to be out of the control of their self-conscious egos exhibit precisely the sort of self-erasing expression that the analyst expects from the appearing-and-withdrawing speech of the unconscious force of being-for-self. Since the individual ego appears to have no control over its *dreams*, these perhaps contain the secret messages that the psychoanalyst is looking for. As the manifestation of force's going-outside itself, a dream would *express* this force; as the manifestation of force's returning into itself, it would simultaneously *suppress* this moment of expression. Since force is both this need to express itself and this need to suppress itself, dreams must be both revelations and masks of force. The psychoanalyst is now in a position to interpret the speech of the unconscious—beginning from the assumption that dreaming is both a representing and a concealing of the true being-for-self of a subject.

An important shift in the perspective of the psychoanalyst has taken place, but it is one which manifests itself in an ambiguous way in his work. The psychoanalyst has discovered that not only must the ego of the hysterical representative of the family be interpreted, but that his own ego—that is, the ego of the masculine representative of civil society—must be interpreted as well. This means that no longer can the work of analysis consist in trying to figure out how essentially masculine subjects become feminine subjects. On the contrary, the work of analysis must consist in asking how force comes to manifest itself in the appearance of both masculine self-serving egos and feminine self-sacrificing egos. It is through this realization that the analyst is led to posit a set of "masculine symptoms" that correspond to the "feminine symptoms." Where the latter—grouped under the generic label of "hysterical neuroses"—characterize egos that appear excessively identified with others, the former—generally grouped together as "the obsessional neuroses"—characterize egos that appear excessively concerned with themselves.

However, this shift is ambiguous because at the same time that he opens up the possibility of a radical questioning of the origins of gender, the psychoanalyst retains his essentially masculine construal of the unconscious—it is still viewed solely as a force of being-for-self. As a result, he fails to rise from the level of psychoanalytic master to the level of, so to speak, the psychoanalytic mediator of the relation between the genders.

Now, in his theory of dreams, the analyst views force as splitting up into a soliciting force and a solicited force, precisely as it did in the earlier dialectic at the level of consciousness proper. As an expression of force, a dream manifests itself as a solicited force. Yet there must also be a force which solicits this force to appear. Hence, being-for-self splits into two, and this split corresponds to the split between the ego's self-consciousness and the unconscious being-for-self. Since the latter is the solicited force, the former must present a soliciting force which calls it forth. The dream itself must express both a conscious expression of being-for-self—that is, a present desire of which the ego is perfectly aware of having—and an unconscious expression of force. Conscious forces solicit unconscious forces. However, the relationship between soliciting and solicited forces reverses itself, for ultimately it must be the unconscious force of being-for-self—since it is posited as the essence of the subject—which solicits conscious forces in the first place. Hence there is a dialectical play of conscious and unconscious desires, or forces, each both soliciting and solicited.

With his discovery of the field of unconscious forces, the psychoanalyst views himself as having revealed a hitherto unsuspected realm of essences, much as did the transcendental phenomenologist. However, where the latter identified these essences with the immediate objects of perception, the former views his essences as wholly hidden from perception. Only with his keen analytic understanding can the psychoanalyst penetrate the appearance of others to comprehend their true being.

Insofar as the unconscious force-in-itself does not itself appear in perception, however, it is easy to view it as unreal. It would seem, in fact, that one can deny the reality of force-in-itself without rejecting the explanatory value of psychoanalytic interpretation. After all, the psychoanalyst purports to explain the appearance of the forces of the ego, albeit in terms of his theory about the hidden reality of the forces of the unconscious. The theory of being-for-self can therefore be reinterpreted simply as a theory of the ego's self-conscious being-for-self, a revision which eliminates the distinction between the unconscious "beyond" and the conscious "here and now." This is the path pursued by the *ego psychologist*.

Conversely, it is possible to accept the truth that the unconscious alone is real, and instead deny the reality of the appearance of the force of being-for-self entirely. This would mean rejecting the reality of the individual ego, and instead viewing the force of being-for-self as a single, all-encompassing, underlying principle of human reality—that is, a collective unconscious. This is the path pursued by the *psychoanalyst of the absolute*.

However, both of these paths are vehemently dismissed by the one who prides himself on his discovery of the *relation* between the unconscious being-for-self and the self-conscious being-for-self. Against the ego psychologist, the "real" psychoanalyst insists that the unconscious is something that exists in and for itself, and that ignorance of this fact can only lead to a superficial understanding of the psychodynamics of force. The possibility of explaining hysteria emerged, after all, only with the distinction between the ego and the unconscious being-for-self. Without this distinction, the phenomenon of a self-denying ego can only be viewed as a mystery.

Against the psychoanalyst of the absolute, he raises a corresponding objection. By reducing the individual to a moment of the being-for-self of humanity, the psychoanalyst of the absolute obviates the distinction between being-for-self and being-for-others. Without this distinction, there is no explanatory work involved in positing the existence of a hidden force, other than the mystical affirmation that the absolute standpoint is something always already achieved. Put otherwise, the being-for-self of force is posited as that stable *one*, which does not actually go outside itself. Such a view, reminiscent of the perspective of the Christian humanist, must deny the reality of conflict among individuals, whereas the humanitarian aim of the real psychoanalyst is to reveal the hidden bases of human aggression. Like the phenomenologist of revelation, the psychoanalyst of the absolute is liable to support a fascist politics of identity.

Distancing himself from these two critics, the psychoanalyst is forced to sustain his dual realm distinction between force-in-itself and force-as-it-appears. For on the one hand, he affirms, as does the ego psychologist, that force is the appearance of forces. Yet on the other hand, he affirms, as does the psychoanalyst of the absolute, that force is something that exists in itself. But this dualistic view is itself unstable. Since each of these two sides is both a soliciting and a solicited force, they are really only one force, for each has its truth immediately in the other. Hence the psychoanalyst must affirm that it is the play of forces itself which is true, a play which is governed by a law which dictates the appearance and disappearance of force.

Since this law is now the essential element of the force of being-for-self, it exists in the subsensible realm of the unconscious. Force is now the dynamic interplay of perceptual appearances and disappearances, insofar as this interplay is governed by an unconscious law. The psychoanalyst now recapitulates the movements of the dialectic of the law of force. He supposes that there must be many unconscious laws, but is eventually led to posit the unity of these in the single law of being-for-self, which law he dubs the "pleasure principle." The problem with this hypothesis is that the subsensible realm of the pleasure principle seems merely a tautological postulate that says only that the laws of the unconscious force the ego to do what the ego does. Hence the psychoanalyst comes under attack by the ego psychologist, who has done away with this apparently tautological realm. Thus, the psychoanalyst is led to posit the existence of a second hidden realm of the unconscious, a supersensible unconscious realm whose laws are the exact opposite of the laws of the subsensible unconscious. The unconscious thus is split into two realms—the subsensible domain of the *id*, governed by the pleasure principle, and the supersensible domain of the *superego*, governed by the antithesis of the pleasure principle—the reality principle.

However, with his doctrine of the split unconscious, the psychoanalyst has now reached a point of implicit contradiction in his theory. On the one hand, he clings to his certainty that the unconscious is essentially a force of being-for-self, and to this extent the innermost essence of a subject is its id. Yet at the same time he has been led to posit the existence of the superego, which represents an inner force governed by principles that are the exact opposite of those by which the ego seems to be governed. The reality principle is, essentially, a law of being-for-others, and as such it is the antithesis of the pleasure principle. Thus, the reality principle bids the ego to satisfy its unconscious force of being-for-self as if the way to do this were by acting contrary to one's being-for-self. So for instance in the case of the ego's desire for revenge against an other who has wronged the subject, the superego inverts the id's impulse to be aggressive toward the other and instead directs its aggression inward. Yet at the same time, the psychoanalyst must make the reality principle a mere derivative of the pleasure principle, in order to maintain his masculine self-certainty that all force is, at bottom, being-for-self. Hence it becomes necessary to declare that the superego's principle of being-for-others is merely a perversion of the id's principle of being-for-self. The supersensible unconscious, in another words, is no longer the true inverted world but the false inverted world. But of course, if the superego is nothing but an extension of the pleasure principle, then once again the entire realm of unconscious law appears as a redundant duplication of the overt psychic phenomena which the ego psychologist can observe through his naive perception.

Hence, if the truth of the unconscious is to be preserved, it is necessary to reverse the psychoanalyst's belief that the primary unconscious force is the force of being-for-self. The masculine psychoanalytic self-certainty is accordingly negated by the appearance of the *feminist psychoanalyst*, who affirms that what is essential in the play of forces is not the force of being-for-self but the force of being-for-others.

The feminist psychoanalyst represents the self-consciousness of the law of the family. Just as the masculine psychoanalyst undertook the work of psychoanalyzing feminity from what he took to be the "normal" standpoint of the law of civil society, so now the feminist psychoanalyst undertakes the work of psychoanalyzing masculinity from what she assumes to be the normal position of the law of the family. Her ideal subject is represented in the figure of the mother, as she has been gendered in her role within the family. Where the self-sacrificing hysteric represented a seeming abnormality to the masculine psychoanalyst, so now the self-centered egoist represents a seeming abnormality to the feminist psychoanalyst. But since she believes that all being-for-self can ultimately be traced to the more primordial force of being-for-others, she assumes that the truth of all egoistic subject positions is rooted in a basic desire to return to the family—and more particularly, to return to that pre-individuated condition when the subject did not experience its differentiation from the body of its mother.

The truth of the feminist psychoanalyst is the mirror image of the truth of the masculine psychoanalyst. With her appearance, she raises the analytic confrontation between a dominant masculine subject and a subordinate feminine subject to a confrontation between two self-conscious gendered equals. The masculine psychoanalyst is naturally surprised to discover that his was a gendered position, and indeed this is something he can be made aware of only when the representative of the family takes charge of her own speech and refuses to accept the masculine subject's truth as her own. Made aware of his false biases, he now declares his alliance with the feminist psychoanalyst.

Yet at first the feminist psychoanalyst resists this overture of reconciliation by the masculine psychoanalyst. As the first self-conscious defender of the law of the family, she sees her truth as the key to reaching the absolute standpoint. After all, she points out, it was the masculine egoism of the absolute knowers which prevented them from reaching reconciliation; and indeed the entire history of failures to resolve the dialectic can be blamed on the emergence of the masculine being-for-self. Taken to its extreme position, the truth of the feminist psychoanalyst gives way to that of the *radical feminist*, who declares that the key to human reconciliation is the elimination of masculinity.

The radical feminist sees herself as longing for the lost truth of the family. But in fact, her desire is for a position before desire; she longs to submerge her self-consciousness entirely. Indeed, since the split between subject and object appears in sense-certainty—or with the separation of the infant from the body of the mother—the radical feminist actually expresses a desire never to have been born. As such, she confirms the truth of the feminist psychoanalyst. But where the feminist psychoanalyst envisioned a return to an authentic being-for-others, the radical feminist's desire to return to the oneness of preconsciousness is in fact a narcissistic desire to be by oneself.

The standoff between the masculine and feminine analysts is not one which can produce a "winner," for the simple reason that both the masculine theorist of being-for-self and the feminist theorist of being-for-others present one-sided truths. In order for the discourse of psychoanalysis to advance, it must rise above the level of a battle over which gender is the essential one. At first, however, the task of carrying out a psychoanalysis of gender is not taken up jointly by the masculine and feminist psychoanalysts. It is, rather, the task of the chastised "reformed" masculine psychoanalyst. Believing that he can tackle the question of gender by himself even though he is himself a masculine subject, he becomes the *masculine psychoanalyst of gender*.

For the masculine psychoanalyst of gender, what is true is neither the masculine force of being-for-self nor the feminine force of being-for-others but the dialectical relationship between the two. What governs this play of forces is the law of gender—the law which splits humanity into the divided realms of the family and civil society. This law is a social law; it exists within the unconscious of a particular subject only insofar as the subject exists as a member of a gendered society. Put otherwise, force proper—the unconscious force which splits into the forces of being-for-self and being-for-others—cannot be located within an isolated individual. The unconscious is itself the hidden truth of social relations. This means that the subject can no longer be viewed as an isolated individual. As a member of a gendered world, every individuated subject is, *in itself*, a differential moment in a network of forces. A subject becomes a self-conscious individual by becoming *for itself* a being who is either a force of being-for-self or a force of being-for-others.

Thus, the masculine psychoanalyst of gender has discovered that the very idea of an isolated person—which, at bottom, was never anything more than the idea of the ego of civil society projected into the unconscious—is merely a symptom of a certain condition of human relations. With this insight, he sees himself rising above the level of the masculine interrogator of the family and becoming instead the genuine mediator who questions the appearance of the masculine/feminine split from a perspective which begins from a pregendered notion of the unconscious force of gendering. As such, he believes himself to be in a position to declare that *in itself* the totality of human relations represents a type of reconciliation of the master/slave and face-to-face encounters. But *for themselves*, gendered subjects—that is, individuals who have not been raised to the level of truth by undergoing analysis—remain trapped at one of these earlier dialectical impasses. The masculine psychoanalyst of gender thus considers himself to be the absolute knower, and his task is to raise the rest of humanity up to his level. Unlike the first psychoanalyst, who viewed human conflict as irreducible, he is certain that the implicit structural reconciliation of human conflict can be raised to the level of self-consciousness.

The truth of the sphere of psychoanalysis now is that the unconscious force is a dialectical interplay of being-for-self and being-for-others. What is true in the analyst/analysand confrontation is neither the essential being-for-self of the analysand (as the masculine psychoanalyst affirms) nor the essential being-for-others of the analysand (as the feminist psychoanalyst posits). Rather, what is true is the dialectical relationship between the analysand's gendered mediation of being-for-self and being-for-others and the analyst's gendered mediation of being-for-self and being-for-others. It is in the network of transferences and counter-transferences between the analysand and the analyst that the analytic encounter has its truth. With this insight, a new consciousness of language emerges. The speech of the analyst/analysand encounter is no longer naively divided into the confessing speech of the analysand and the absolving speech of the analyst. On the contrary, all speech is both the confession and absolution of both the analyst and the analysand. Language is no longer a vehicle by which one individual communicates to another. Since every individual both is and is not other individuals, language is the representation of the unconscious dialectic of transference and counter-transference. Put otherwise, the truth of the unconscious is language; the truth of language is the unconscious.

But the masculine psychoanalyst of gender has attained his certainty of this truth by himself. Dubbing himself the mediator of the dialectical confrontation between the genders, he—this isolated and masculine individual—believes he has raised himself up by his own bootstraps to the absolute standpoint. To be sure, his represents the first shape of the consciousness of language to rise above the split between subject and object to the self-certainty of the truth of language in and for itself. But this truth simply expresses the masculine view of the dialectic of gender.

Once again, therefore, the masculine psychoanalyst is taken to task—this time by the *feminine psychoanalyst of gender*. No longer accepting the feminist psychoanalyst's one-sided defense of the law of the family, she accepts the judgment of the masculine psychoanalyst of gender that both genders are the result of a more fundamental relation of forces. Thus, she rejects the "essentialist" defense of the feminine force of being-for-others. On the other hand, the feminine psychoanalyst of gender agrees that it is the masculine realm of civil society—the so-called symbolic realm—which stands in the way of an authentic realization of being-for-others. Against this realm, she opposes the truth of the "imaginary" or "semiotic" space of the maternal. Recognizing that the truth of society is the dialectical process whereby language leads subjects into the realm of the symbolic, she seeks to underscore the ways in which the realm of the semiotic intrudes into the symbolic, undercutting it and opening up the possibility of a reconciliation of the semiotic being-for-others with the symbolic being-for-self.

Together, the masculine and feminine psychoanalysts of gender reach agreement: the true is the relation between the imaginary and the symbolic realms. In one sense, this truth passes off as a kind of absolute certainty that force splits itself into two distinct realms. But the truth of this certainty cannot by itself "heal" the absolute rift between the forces of being-for-self and being-for-others. As a result, the apparent reconciliation between these two representatives of their genders is no *real* reconciliation at all. Although they share the certainty that one can become "well-adjusted" to society by undergoing analysis, they differ in their assessments of what the precise aim of analysis should be. The masculine psychoanalyst of gender emphasizes that psychoanalysis should ease the process whereby individuals are forced to enter the symbolic realm. By contrast, the feminine psychoanalyst of gender stresses the need for subjects to maintain their ties to the realm of the imaginary.

But this implicit difference will not become explicit until the supposedly neutral ideal of the well-adjusted individual shows itself to be untenable. Despite their latent disagreements, the masculine and feminine analysts of gender have for now reached a mutual recognition which could not be achieved in the face-to-face encounter. Specifically, they have achieved a shared recognition that the truth of the consciousness and self-consciousness of language *is* the play of forces which unites all individuals. To express the absolute standpoint appears to be nothing more nor less than to express the truth of language in and for itself. This is the standpoint of structural reason.

4 (BBB.) • Structural Reason

A. Structural Observation

Structural reason is language raised to the level of self-certainty. As such, it is something universal. Yet it is immediately the possession of the individual subject who knows himself or herself as one element in a network of signifiers. Insofar as the subject has its meaning constituted through this network, it is not just a bare signifier but a sign full of meaning. But since in itself it is just this individual signifier, it has its meaning not primarily for itself but rather for others. Just as the phenomenologist of revelation saw the subject as belonging to its intentional acts rather than the other way around, so now the *structuralist* sees the individual signifier as belonging to the system of language rather than the other way around. The self-conscious subject finds its essence in the structural being of its interrelations with others. Hence the world now appears in a new light, not as something standing over and against a subject who speaks a language; rather, both the world and the subject now have their immediate identity in language itself.

Language raised to the level of self-consciousness in this way is the subject *qua* structural reason. The work of the structuralist is to grasp the interrelated system of signifiers that give rise to the meanings which both constitute and are grasped by the subject. Rather than merely describe language, as the empirical-minded individuals in the sense-certainty of language did, the structuralist sets out to decode language. He interprets language, and therefore apprehends it in an active way, whereas the sense-certainty of language was merely passive. In this way, the structuralist seeks to reconstruct the prose of its world.

Despite the semiotic equivalence of the conscious subject and its various objects, however, the individual act of structural reason is nonetheless divided into the opposite poles of the subject *qua* reader of signs and the object *qua* sign to be read. Of course, both of these have their meaning directly in the other, and to this extent all reading consists in a reading of both the reader and that which the reader reads. Nonetheless, the relation between the reader—that is, the decoder of structure—and the structure to be decoded would give way to a bad infinite of endless reflection were the relation not to essentialize one of the two moments which then becomes the ultimate determiner of meaning. In other words, were structure to consist merely in an interrelatedness of signifiers, there would be no ultimate signified. But of course signifiers without signifieds are not signs; they would mean nothing. Hence, we see at the level of structural reason a need for consciousness to essentialize one of the elements of its relation to the object.

Yet structural reason does not fall back on the division between subject and object as did the consciousness and self-consciousness of language. It knows the truth to consist in the relation, and so it treats the relation itself as the sign to be read. Insofar as it must divide this relation, it splits the sign into two moments—the inessential signifier and the essential signified. The object of consciousness is at first the signified and the subject who intends this object is the signifier. As the inessential moment, the subject could be anyone who observes the world. As the essential moment, the world presents itself as the truth of structure. Hence, the aim of structural reason is to discern the structures of the world by observing and reconstructing the interrelations of natural signifieds.

Structural reason thus sets out on a parallel path to observing reason, recasting each of this earlier shape's truths in linguistic terms. To describe nature now is to discern its systems of codes. Natural laws are gradually recast as systems of language; natural biology gives way to genetics. When structural reason turns its gaze on the subject itself, viewed as a signified object, it raises anthropology to the level of structural anthropology, psychology to the level of depth psychology, phrenology to the level of computational models of the mind.

The limitation of observing structural reason, however, lies with its one-sided privileging of the object as the signified. By relegating the subject to the level of mere signifier, observing structural reason ends up reducing subjectivity to mere thinghood. Yet it contradicts itself in that its measurement of the success or failure of computational models of the mind makes clandestine appeal to the subject qua subject. For instance, in *assessing* the plausibility or implausibility of artificial intelligence projects, the subject does not consider itself *qua* physical object; rather, it considers itself *qua* intentional subject. To this extent, the subject must appear as the signified of its acts rather than as merely their signifier. Ultimately, in other words, one cannot adequately characterize the subject by treating structural reason merely as the equivalent of brain states. Hence, the truth of structural reason is reversed. Instead of viewing the objective moment of the sign as the signified and the subject as the signifier, structural reason now views the subject as the signified and the object as merely being the signifier.

With this truth we arrive at the alienation of structural reason. For although structural reason knows itself as the unity of self and world, in positing the subject as the sole signified of this unity it returns to a position that is the exact equivalent of the alienated rational self-consciousness who expects the world to revolve around it. Viewing the world as something alien to it, structural reason now posits itself as its own antithesis. This is the consciousness of the *anti-structuralist*.

B. Actualization of Structural Reason's Self-consciousness

To the alienated anti-structuralist, the social world from which he derives his identity must be negated. But unlike the slave, who could simply deny that the world had any essential relationship to him, the anti-structuralist knows that he has his identity only in relation to the world. Hence, he cannot negate it—that is, relegate it to the status of mere signifier—without working to recreate himself as an autonomous signified. In order to make himself into an autonomous signified, the anti-structuralist must follow the path of self-actualization taken by the alienated rational self-consciousness of the dialectic of reason proper. His strategies, successes, and failures will thus parallel those which appeared at this earlier stage.

Affirming that his own being-for-self is the only signified of his life, the anti-structuralist seeks to throw off the repressive force of being-for-others—that is, the superego—and to this end he, at first, pursues an unbridled path of pleasure-seeking. The problem with this hedonistic strategy, however, is that in pursuing a life of pleasure the individual is merely acting like everyone else. He remains, as does every other subject, a mere signifier of the world of pleasure-seeking. Hence, the anti-structuralist is led to revise his thinking. Throwing off "the repressive hypothesis," according to which society reduces individuals to mere signifiers by denying them the meaning-endowing act of sexual gratification, he now reverses the idea and declares that society reduces individuals to mere signifiers by forcing them to pursue their own private pleasures.

In order to make himself the signified of his acts, the anti-structuralist now opposes the law of his own heart to this universal law of the social manipulation of bodies. If he, this particular individual, is to be the ultimate signified of his life, the law of *his* heart must be unique. Yet at the same time, the anti-structuralist opposes the universality of structural reason to the particularity of *every* particular individual heart. As the defender of every repressed individual, he is *in himself* a defender of the universal, despite the fact that *for himself* he is the enemy of the universal. Put otherwise, since the anti-structuralist is structural reason in its own alienation, he is in himself the voice of reason, even though for himself he is the enemy of reason. This apparent contradiction, however, is in fact the true expression of the anti-structuralist's consciousness that the totalizing law of structural reason both is and is not the expression of the law of the individual heart. In other words, it is structural reason which is itself in contradiction, which is revealed by the fact that it divides society up into those deemed rational and those deemed irrational. The anti-structuralist accuses structural reason of its duplicity by defending those subjects who are labeled irrational. As such, he himself does not retreat into the frenzy of self-conceit; rather he becomes the defender of those who do thus retreat. In this respect, he resembles more the defender of the law of the family, who insisted on honoring her dead brother, than he does those deemed "irrational" by society. Positing his solidarity with the latter, however, the anti-structuralist does indeed become the defender of the law of self-conceit. Thus, he lauds criminality and random acts of violence as of higher virtue than civic responsibility and human decency.

By defending the frenzy of self-conceit, the anti-structuralist sees himself as preserving the truth of the individual subject over and against the totalizing other-denying force of being-for-self that is society as a whole. Yet in fact it is the frenzy of self-conceit which represents the unbridled force of being-for-self, for it is none other than the violent criminal who seeks to deny meaning to the lives of others. Because he fails to distinguish adequately between criminal revolt against a genuinely oppressive society and indiscriminate criminality, the anti-structuralist proves to be just as hypocritical as structural reason itself.

Realizing the untenability of his contradictory action but clinging to the attempt to affirm that the individual subject alone should be the ultimate signified of its own life, the anti-structuralist now poses as the virtuous consciousness. Instead of defending indiscriminate self-conceit, he now defends the true universal law of the heart. However, this position lapses into a kind of unhappy consciousness. Despite the fact that the virtuous anti-structuralist intends to affirm the integrity of individual experience, he ends up scorning others as following the way of the world. Everyone else is now blamed for trying to force the virtuous individual to show his face, to present himself before the universal. To question the virtuous individual is to oppress him. Like the skeptical consciousness who had no qualms about contradicting anything anyone else said, the virtuous individual refuses to be pinned down.

The hypocritical speech of the anti-structuralist is revealed in his indictment of the way of the world—what he calls the "panopticism" of structural reason. In the panoptical world, individuals are trained to police themselves and one another; thus the way of the world consists in individuals serving an oppressive universal force. The virtuous individual claims to be different; instead of policing others he watches to make sure that no one polices anyone else. But in keeping watch in this way, he acts exactly as does everyone else—as a policeman. Thus, he constantly accuses others of living accusatory lives. To be sure, this is justified by the anti-structuralist's certainty that society is oppressive; however, by indiscriminately rejecting all of the legislated ethical norms of his society, he undermines all possible basis for distinguishing between oppression and liberation. In calling the police evil criminals and criminals good police, the anti-structuralist does not appeal to a genuine alternative. Instead of distinguishing between the oppressive rationalization of society and those structures in terms of which he must implicitly base his defense of individuality, the anti-structuralist ends up equating rationality in general with oppression. As a result, his supposedly virtuous resistance to structural violence merely ends up advocating random, irrational violence.

The faceless virtuous anti-structuralist sees itself as a member of a world in which everyone is at war with everyone else: this is the way of the world. The universal, embodied in the relations of force which assign individuals to their nodal points in the network of signifiers, is nothing more nor less than brute *power*. Now, the anti-structuralist's facelessness, his denial of public subjectivity, appears to represent a position outside of power. But at the same time, the anti-structuralist has to recognize that he, too, is a member of this world. Not only is he an individual on whom power marks its effects, but also he is himself a wielder of power. Since the universality of structural reason has its actuality in the aggregate of individuals who comprise the social order, every individual is as much a potential wielder of power as a potential victim of power. Because there is no position outside of power, the anti-structuralist cannot contrast virtue with the way of the world without appealing to the universal entitlement of individuals not to be *disempowered* by society.

Ultimately, therefore, the anti-structuralist who opposes the way of the world can flesh out in a meaningful way the nature of his virtue only by invoking universal ethical principles. But this would mean acknowleging the moral authority of the *principle* of structural reason, and the righteous self-consciousness of the anti-structuralist forbids him from doing this. Ironically, the critic of the repressive hypothesis is himself stifled by an internal repressive force. Hence, instead of invoking the rationality of a universal struggle against the oppressiveness of structural rationalization, the anti-structuralist can only speak vaguely of the necessity of "micro-struggles" which individuals must engage in if they are to regain control of their lives. Naked individual self-control thus becomes the sole abstract normative criterion that grounds the anti-structuralist's ethic. Care for one's own body—that is, the self-reflexive autonomy of a withdrawn subject—becomes the ideal: the beautiful body as the equivalent to the beautiful soul. Although he himself (in his rejection of the repressive hypothesis) has shown that criticisms of an oppressive society can themselves serve forces of oppression, ultimately he fails to consider how his own rejection of ethical principles might itself be counterproductive.

Instead of discovering a way to further the much-needed work of a gender critique of his society, the anti-structuralist ends up simply being the knight for whom all—and none of—the ways of the world are black. Only by returning to a view of individuals as having something in common—that is, structural reason—can the subject hope to construct a notion of virtuous action that has content. To do this means giving up the one-sided ideal that the subject be the sole signified of its acts. Both the subject and the object of the sign must be viewed as essential—in other words, structural reason must be viewed as a relation between two independent signifieds. With the emergence of this truth, we leave behind the beautiful anti-structuralist and arrive at structural reason's equivalent of real individuality in and for itself, a position that still begs the question of gender.

C. Individuality from the Perspective of Structural Reason

The anti-structuralist, who represented the alienation of structural reason, defended the individual subject against the collective "we" of the social world. But in doing so he was implicitly representing the real virtue of the collective "we" itself. Hence, his struggle against power was in reality a struggle on behalf of a "good" power against a "bad" power. But with this discovery, society itself must be viewed in a new light. It is not something standing over and against the individual; society is itself the substantial result of the work of actual individuals. Since the individual no longer sees its social existence as a form of self-alienation, it returns from its radically antisocial stance to its day-to-day job, contentedly carrying out its socially useful work. The important thing is to do one's job well, whether one's job is shoeshining, mining, nursing, or banking. The now "well-adjusted" individual knows that social change can be brought about only by working "within the system" rather than by trying to stand outside it. If society proves recalcitrant to the sorts of reforms the particular individual attempts to instigate, then this proves that the majority of individuals opposed this particular reform. In the end, therefore, whether or not the individual is successful in carrying out his social reforms, he can feel content that he has played a role in society. Because the "well-adjusted" individual identifies himself with the collective will of society, he posits the truth of *utilitarianism.*

For the utilitarian, the good of society is equivalent to the good of its members. Wherever conflicting interests arise, the function of society is to adjudicate conflicts between individuals to insure that the welfare of each will be taken into account. The fact that society is based on the principle of the greatest good for the greatest number ensures its essential goodness. The individual who believes in this truth goes about his day-to-day business, confident that, should he be wronged, society will compensate him for his suffering.

However, the distinction between society and the individual has disappeared only to the extent that every individual has been reduced to a potentially expendable moment of the social order. Under the pretext of protecting the interests of all individuals, the utilitarian principle in fact articulates the priority of society over any of its particular individuals. The greatest good for the greatest number not only leads to a tyranny of the majority, it also sanctions complete disregard for the insignificant isolated individual.

The great conceit of the utilitarian society, though, is that the individual *can* "make a difference" by working within the system—for instance, by lobbying one's congressman or congresswoman. Moreover, since every particular individual's failure to make a difference is attributed to the fact that there are many other individuals who "made a difference" by opposing the first one's ideas, the individual is led to believe he has made a difference even when he has done nothing of the sort. He lobbies his congressman or congresswoman, his house is torn down for a new highway anyway—and he gets back a form letter applauding him for "helping make democracy work."

The utilitarian consciousness begins from the view that all individuals are interchangeable. Each one is expected not to resent his personal pain if he is shown that someone else has experienced pleasure as a result of it. But in fact the particular individual is not interested in the pleasure of others; he is interested in himself. Thus, he expects from society not rule by utilitarian principles but laws which protect the rights of individuals. The utilitarian consciousness of the just society thus gives way to the consciousness of the *liberal lawgiver.*

The liberal lawgiver begins not from the principle of the greatest good for the greatest number but, on the contrary, from the principle that a good society is one that treats all of its particular members fairly. Whereas the utilitarian protected the abstract notion of individuality at the expense of the interests of real particular individuals, the liberal lawgiver begins from the interests of every particular individual. But no more than the utilitarian can the liberal lawgiver reconcile all the conflicting interests among particular individuals. All he can do is to try to get everyone to agree to the basic principles of a just society. If everyone accepts a basic social structure as just, then everyone will be obliged to treat its actual outcomes as just. However, in order to get everyone to agree to these basic principles without allowing their particular selfish interests to influence their thinking, it is necessary to ask people to abstract from their actual interests and view society from a disinterested "original position." With this request, of course, the liberal lawgiver adopts a notion of individuality that is no less abstract than that of the utilitarian. But unlike the utilitarian, he expects individuals in the original position to arrive not at the principle of "the greatest good for the greatest number," but instead at a principle of "the greatest good for the least privileged individual member of society."

The liberal lawgiver is able to justify only those principles which he expects everyone would adopt. But as a result he does not so much issue absolute laws as he gives expression to commonsensical intuitions shared by the majority of the members of society. For instance, he posits that a just society will distribute benefits in a way that is "reasonably expected" to help everyone. But what counts as reasonable can make a world of difference. In the end, its content will be filled on the basis of what individuals happen to think of as reasonable. But their notion of reasonableness will vary according to the actual social arrangement that they happen to live under. So for instance if they live in a capitalist society they will view one thing as reasonable and if they live in a socialist society they will view something else as reasonable. In the end, the liberal lawgiver does not so much create principles of justice as he gives expression to the ideals already shared by the members of a particular society.

Thus, the liberal lawgiver must really conceive himself as a liberal law-tester. His aim is not to say whether there should be a capitalist society or a socialist society; his work consists in saying whether or not a particular capitalist society or a particular socialist society accords with the principles of justice. But this presumes that he can point to an a priori standard of what a rational person in any society would deem to be just. Instead of beginning from the consciousness of real rational individuals, he must retreat to the completely abstract notion of a "pure" rational subject. Faced with the actual members of particular societies who disagree with his conception of rationality, the liberal law-tester cannot really say why his conception of justice should be accepted over any other notion. In the end, he can only retreat into a kind of faith in a true social order which exists beyond the actual social order.

But since the "we" has its real substantial essence in society, the liberal law-tester's position is a kind of virtuous frenzy of self-conceit. Only by acknowledging the unity of the actual individuals and their substantial embodiment in the "we" of society can he concretize his ethical action on behalf of particular individuals. The liberal law-tester must turn away from the empty abstraction of pure rationality to the concrete reality of his society's particular form of rationality. To do this he must become a sociologist.

The sociologist is the one who knows himself to be the embodiment of the particular "we" that is his society, and he sets out to articulate the truth of this "we." Hence, the sociologist is the self-consciousness of the "we" itself. What has emerged as the truth of structural reason is not spirit, but just the particular word by which this particular society articulates itself to itself in the self-consciousness of the sociologist—"we." It is the same master-word used by the reconciled theorists of gender to give voice to the unity and difference of the unconscious dialectic of forces. But this simple word is, at first, just that—a mere word. Hence, with the sociologist's immediate self-consciousness that *we* are just *"we,"* we have arrived at the ultimate truth of structural reason—the de-spiritualization of spirit that we know ourselves to be.

A. Real Socialism. "We, the People"

The truth of the "we" is posited in the self-consciousness of the sociologist. Where the structuralists attained a consciousness of the structure of their society, the sociologist posits the identity of this consciousness and its object, thereby becoming the individual embodiment of a self-knowing structure. The sociologist accordingly sees himself as having a special insight into the collective beliefs which make up the "we" of his society. Since he himself is the "we" raised to the level of self-consciousness, he does not merely voice an opinion about what is good for society, as did the well-adjusted utilitarian working within the system. On the contrary, the sociologist sees himself as the system itself incarnate; hence when he articulates society's collective beliefs, he believes himself to be speaking on behalf of society.

Yet in order to confirm this view, the sociologist must find another member of his society who agrees with him. Hence, the vocation of the sociologist is essentially a communal one; there are sociologists. By confirming one another's grasp of that particular form of rationality which is embodied in the "we" of their society, the sociologists have raised the structural unconscious of the "we" to the level of a collective consciousness that is for itself in the person of each individual sociologist. In positing the identity of their mutually recognizant self-consciousnesses with that of the "we" of their particular society, the sociologists see themselves as having actualized the certainty of the absolute knowers. Yet this actualization is something accomplished only for those who have been raised to their level. Hence, the sociologists find themselves in the same position as did the communists, who also saw themselves as a privileged group of mutually recognizing absolute knowers. As did the communists, so now the sociologists set out on the basic task of lifting up the rest of society. But whereas

159

the communists faced the task of showing the falsity of the egoism of civil society which pitted individual against individual, the sociologists must demonstrate the falsity of the conflictual model posited at the level of structural reason which pitted individual against society as a whole. Like the liberal lawgiver and law-tester, the sociologists set out to critique the conflictual model of social relations. But what remained merely an ideal for these liberals—namely, a shared consensus—the sociologists now see as an actual reality in their society. Yet this actual consensus is something still only implicit for those still stuck at the level of structural reason. Thus, the work of the sociologists is to lead the rest of their society to see that whatever apparent conflict exists at the level of structural reason is predicated on a deeper reality of social consensus.

With their self-consciousness that society is always in itself based on consensus, the sociologists do not have the same qualms that the anarchists did about the dangers of a communist state. On the contrary, a communist state now represents the ideal of a universal actualization of the self-consciousness of consensus that is the "we." For their part, the work of the communists has not ceased. They have continued their efforts to bring about a dictatorship of the proletariat, which, after the rebuke of the anarchists, they had come to view merely as a transition to a genuinely stateless society. However, with the achievement of the self-consciousness of the "we" as articulated in the doctrines of the sociologists, the communists can now throw off the anti-totalitarian fears of the anarchists altogether and affirm once again, without apology, the intrinsic good of a communist state. The communists now declare themselves to be *state socialists*.

The first substantial appearance of the "we," therefore, occurs with the founding of a socialist state. Proclaiming this state to be the substantial essence of the "we" in which each individual has its identity, the founders of the socialist state deny the very distinction between the state and the people. What is true, they proclaim, is not the communist state as opposed to the people, but the state that is the people, pure and simple—as embodied in the communist party. Put otherwise, the party is the state that pretends not to be a state. The substantial essence of the "we" as embodied in the rule of the party is called "real socialism."

Real socialism is based on the principle that the opposition between the individual and society as a whole is a false one. However, just as the utilitarians reduced the particular individual to an interchangeable component of society, so here the state socialists have imposed an artificial consensus on a people who still remain in conflict with one another. As a result, just as spirit was immediately divided into ethical substance and the actuality of that substance, so here the "we" of real socialism is divided into substance—the party—and the ethical activity of the individual members of society—that is, the people. In order to maintain the pretense that the party *is* the people, every individual under real socialism is given an equivalent title—"comrade." Of course, since only some comrades rule the party, some comrades are more equal than others. Being a comrade, however, is not the equivalent of being a self-subsisting legal person; on the contrary, it is the individual's self-consciousness of having its identity only in the "we." Thus, the comrades, who embody the being-for-self of the "we," carry out their work on behalf of the "we" in a self-sacrificing but self-conscious manner—rather than in the self-interested mode of those who sought to change the system for their own ends.

There is, therefore, a rift between the substantial "we" and the actual "we," but at first it is only implicit. This rift corresponds, moreover, to the division of the genders. The substantial "we" is ruled by the masculine law of the realm of the symbolic; as such it exhibits an unchecked being-for-self. By contrast, the actual "we" is governed by the feminine law of the realm of the imaginary; as such it posits the truth of the being-for-others of the "we." The daylight of the symbolic "we" is revealed in the depictions of individuals sacrificing themselves for the good of the whole—one sees the happy faces of such mythical comrades on posters everywhere. But this world also has its hidden basis in the imaginary nighttime world that is kept hidden from public view. Thus, everyone is forced to live in a glass house so that their symbolic activity will be on public display, though they are granted "personal hours" when they are permitted to pull down their imaginary shades.

The pretense of real socialism is that it has done away with bourgeois individualism. However, insofar as the state represents the sphere of the symbolic, its essence can be found precisely in the masculine realm of civil society. Thus, within the party, all the supposedly "we"-oriented comrades are in fact selfish egoists jockeying for power. Moreover, because the bourgeois state has given way to the state of real socialism, there is no longer a realm of spirit existing over and above the sphere of civil society. In real socialism, it is civil society which rules. But this is just to say that the ascendancy of real socialism represents, in its essence, the ultimate triumph of bourgeois individualism. As in the struggle between the narcissistic absolute knowers, so here a confrontation among the egoistic comrades of the party can be resolved only with the fetishization of a master. The symbolic realm must be ruled by a single masculine subject—the *father of the revolution*.

Now although the party is, in essence, a symbolic organization, the state of real socialism has been posited as the unity of being-for-self and being-for-others in the "we." As such, its coming-to-be is rooted in the support of the feminine keepers of the imaginary realm. Accordingly, a representative of this realm chides her masculine comrades for the contradiction between their self-consciousness of having their identity only in the "we," and the masculine egoistic being-for-self that motivates their infighting. However, because she has herself achieved the self-consciousness of the "we," she is no longer the representative of the family; on the contrary, she is the only comrade with an authentic grasp of what real socialism should consist in. As such, she is the *defender of the people*.

The defender of the people confronts the father of the revolution, accusing him of selfish egoism. For his part, the fetishized father has attained the steely self-righteousness of an absolute knower with power. Completely identifying his own consciousness with the consciousness of the people, he insists that everything he does is for "the good of the revolution." To prove this, he strikes down a fellow comrade with whom he has personally had bad relations, in order to defend his action by declaring that *his* enemy was in fact the enemy *of the people*. Thus, the father of the revolution insists that he alone is the authentic defender of the people.

Of course, to the real defender of the people, the speech of the father of the revolution is sheer hypocrisy. He kills the people and then has the audacity to declare that he does so in the name of the people. She therefore condemns the father of the revolution. And he, now perfectly consistent in his hypocrisy, either puts her to death or sends her into exile—for instance, by telling her to retreat to the realm of the family.

By self-consciously silencing someone whom he himself must recognize as a defender of the people, the father of the revolution has ceased to be a merely self-righteous revolutionary leader. No longer able to hide from himself his own egoism, he has become not the father of the revolution but the *tyrant of the revolution*.

The tyrant of the revolution proclaims himself to be the essence of the "we," but he knows all-too-well that he is just looking out for himself. Publicly, he denies this. But because his hypocrisy is so blatant, the tyrant of the revolution is certain that everyone who looks at him must also be aware of it. Thus, every comrade becomes a challenger to his authority; or, put in the hypocritical speech he still permits himself to indulge in, everyone becomes a suspected "enemy of the people." With a savagery like that of the terror of absolute freedom, but springing from the will of a single individual who enjoins all comrades to suspect one another, the sole work of the tyrant of the revolution is to purge his enemies from the party.

The defender of the revolution has been silenced. But in her place there arises another representative of the political realm of the imaginary—someone who is out of the tyrant's reach—who cries out against the evil of such totalitarian rule. Unlike the defender of the revolution who blamed the father of the revolution for a personal failing, the *anti-totalitarianist* does not attack the personality of the tyrant of the revolution—though, to be sure, her personal contempt for him is unequaled. At bottom, she sees, the tyrant is a "non-entity," an ordinary person who just happens to be the fetishized ruler of the party. Unlike the defender of the revolution, who maintained her faith in the party, the anti-totalitarianist now sees that it is the substantial "we" itself which represents absolute evil. The totalitarian state's evil is absolute because its sole work is the total annihilation of the people. Thus, over and against the evil substantial "we" of the totalitarian state, she opposes the good actual "we" of the people.

But here the self-righteousness of the party loyalists rears its ugly head. These masculine defenders of the substantial "we" now become the *defenders of the tyrant*. They admit, to be sure, that the seemingly indiscriminate purges of party comrades are unfortunate. But, after all, they nervously remind one another, conscious of the fact that the slightest appearance of deviation could make them the next victims of the great purge, the highest work of the individual is to sacrifice itself for the good of the "we." Invoking the truth of the structuralist insight into the unity of the moments of being-for-self and being-for-others in the substantial "we," the defenders of the tyrant look with contempt on the humanism of the anti-totalitarianist. All humanisms, they claim, echoing the phenomenologist of revelation, are opposed to the interests of the people, for they are really just covert attempts to sacrifice the "we" in the name of bourgeois egoism. Sticking as strictly to the party line as possible, the defenders of the tyrant accuse not only the anti-totalitarianist but anyone with the temerity to oppose the tyrant of being an ideological enemy of the people. In contrast to the falsity of ideology, they insist on the scientific character of all party doctrine.

Such a noble sounding defense, which brings together both the supposedly humanistic antihumanism of the phenomenologist of revelation and the earlier communist contempt for those who placed a higher value on actual individual suffering than on the good of the universal, represents the pinnacle of masculine hypocrisy. In pretending that the purges are justified from the standpoint of the substantial "we," the defenders of the tyrant pledge their allegiance to a monolithic force of being-for-self which in its blatant hypocrisy pays only lip service to the moment of being-for-others. Were the tyrant of the revolution to purge everyone but himself and a single one of his defenders, the latter would declare even this justified "in the name of the people"—a point of such gullibility that even the tyrant, forced to see it as mere pretense, would then point his gun at this last remaining participant in "real socialism."

The defenders of the tyrant are able to see themselves as genuine champions of the moment of being-for-others because they do not act as do bourgeois egoists on behalf of themselves. To this extent, they are sincere workers on behalf of the "we" of the people. But by reifying the moment of being-with-others into the substantial "we" of the party, they merely project their own being-for-self onto something else—in this case, the tyrant. By fetishizing the tyrant and working on behalf of the party, they convince themselves that they are other-directed when in fact they are acting solely on behalf of a projected embodiment of a force of being-for-self. Thus, although they accuse the anti-totalitarianist of serving the principle of bourgeois society, it is in fact the defenders of the tyrant who serve this principle.

To be sure, the anti-totalitarianist attacks the very idea of a substantial "we," and to this extent, her critics seem justified in claiming that she is the one who defends a type of bourgeois egoism. However, the anti-totalitarianist attacks the substantial "we" of the totalitarian state not in the name of the isolated individual but in the name of the actual "we" of the people. As such she is a critic of both the egoism of civil society and the egoism of totalitarian rule. Against both of these she opposes the authentic moment of being-with-others that is revealed in the people themselves. Nonetheless, the people whom she defends as a "we" are, as alienated from their substantial unity, a mere aggregated collection of individuals. Hence, her formidable task is to articulate the conditions under which real political solidarity might be forged among individuals who now recognize themselves as self-subsistent individuals.

The actual "we" of the people cannot find its expression in the being-for-self of the party without the latter uniting the people by means of violence. Conversely, the actual "we" of the people cannot remain a "we" without finding its substantial expression in some unitary form of power. Substantial power can replace substantial violence only in a political system based on the collective interests of the individual members who comprise the "we" of the people. The form of this political system, accordingly, must be that of a constitutional democracy which explicitly recognizes the independent existence of each of its individual members. The collapse of real socialism, instigated by the work of the anti-totalitarianist, thus leads to a repetition of the ethical realm of legal personhood.

In the world of legal personhood, "we the people" is no longer posited as "real socialism" but instead as "real democracy," for the universal exists only through the aggregate of legal citizens. As a mere collection of atomistic subjects, however, the substantial "we" remains abstract. But since the individuals under real democracy are conscious of having their identity in the "we," they cannot simply retreat into themselves. As at the earlier level of the legal world of ethical spirit, so here the self-consciousness of the "we" of real democracy splits into the actual world of the "we," on the one hand, and the posited substantial universality of the "we" which exists over and above the world. This supreme other-worldly "we" is itself conceived of as an actual individual. Only through the fetishization of this faith in a supreme God can the isolated individuals of real democracy maintain the pretense that they are, in fact, a United State of "we the people."

However, the possibility of this kind of religious faith has been sublated in the secular egoism of civil society; the philosophical radicals discovered long ago that the people were not shocked to hear of the death of God. Moreover, the age of language is a self-consciously non-spiritual age, and for this reason, the members of even this most necessarily pious of states— the united state of real democracy—cannot believe in the reality of the transcendent God as did the legal persons of the realm of ethical spirit. Yet despite the impossibility of their faith, the individuals' faith is still necessary in order to sustain the pretense that "we the people" is not simply the unchecked anarchy of absolute freedom. Thus, the people of real democracy are pious practitioners of religious life without being pious believers in anything that would truly unite them.

Thus, this lack of faith is, at bottom, a lack of belief in the unity of "we the people." To this extent, real democracy is fraught with splits among the people. To compensate for these rifts, the people redouble their efforts to be religious, even though they cannot do so sincerely. Hiding their bad faith from themselves, they blame others for failing to be pious. In this way, the multiplicity of rival gods which appeared at the level of the ethical spirit appears here as a multiplicity of rival religions. "We the people" splits into numerous competing "we the people" religions, each one claiming to welcome all of the believers of the other "pseudo-religions" to become true believers of their faith. Thus, what fragments "we the people" is religious rivalry, which becomes the more intense the more its combatants become hypocritical. For those who proselytize are simply trying to convince themselves; were any of them true believers in the uniting force of God they would not worry about the apparent diremption of "we the people" into splintering groups.

Corresponding to the splintering of the "we" is a mimetic splintering of the self-consciousness of the sociologists. In place of their consensual model of society these *new sociologists* return to a conflictual model. The consciousness of the alienated anti-structuralist reappears as the concept of the "outsider." The sociologists narrow the purview of their search for consensus, expecting to find it in smaller and smaller pockets of shared religious practice. Increasingly, they study tiny subcultures which they themselves belong to, for at least among "we bee-catchers" or "we heavy-metal enthusiasts" one can expect to find a degree of consensus of beliefs.

With the appearance of real democracy, therefore, the actual "we" of the people becomes completely alienated from its substantial unity. So long as the individual members of this insubstantial state retain their bad religious faith, they can feign a genuine experience of being-with-others. But once they recognize their bad faith, they have left their socialist consciousness behind completely. Whatever insight was gained in the necessity of bringing together the truths of the symbolic and imaginary realms is now forgotten. With the recognition of their religious hypocrisy, the individual persons of real democracy throw off altogether the attempt to bring together the realms of the family and civil society. The two spheres are thrown back on themselves, and so public life appears once again merely as the domain of the selfish masculine egoist. The political dimension of real democracy that has been raised to the level of self-consciousness is masculinity raised to the haughty self-consciousness of being the truth. In place of the tyrant of the revolution who appeared as the logical outcome of real socialism, there now appears the *macho-individualist* of real democracy. And with his appearance we leave the realm of real socialism and enter the realm of the self-alienated "we."

B. Self-alienated "We": The Symbolic Realm

The transition from real socialism to real democracy has given rise to the self-alienation of "we the people," and to this extent the "we" has split into two distinct realms. On the one hand, this split manifests itself in the continued separation of the realms of the family and of civil society. Only the latter has actuality; the former represents the unreality of the substantial "we." But just as at the level of culture the self-alienated members of civil society were conscious of their alienation and took flight in the faith which posited the substantial spirit as something beyond the actual world, so here at the level of the self-alienated "we" the macho-individualists, despite their cynical dismissal of religious thought, are conscious of their own self-alienation. They, too, take flight from themselves, but as self-conscious macho-individualists they posit not the God of religious faith but the God of collective masculine experience. It is thus the symbolic realm itself which is split into two, and the imaginary realm is repressed entirely. To become a "real man" in real democracy's symbolic realm is to rise above one's bare individuality by going through a series of hazing rituals by which the individual takes on the ideal character of masculine culture's faith. The individual attains status in the symbolic realm of masculine culture to the degree that he proves himself in these rituals. Thus, individuals are no longer recognized as members of the "we" simply insofar as they are individuals. In the realm of symbolic culture, individuals count only to the degree to which they become masculine. In striving to realize the ideal of complete masculinity, therefore, the macho-individualists of the symbolic realm must sever completely their connections to the imaginary realm.

For this reason, the family takes on a different status from the one it had at the level of "we the people." There, the feminine subjects who functioned as guardians of the imaginary force of being-with-others were recognized as comrades who performed an important function for the state. Here, by contrast, femininity is completely rejected; the feminine is that which, *by definition*, must be repressed. Anyone gendered more feminine than masculine is accordingly despised in the realm of symbolic culture, not only denied recognition but humiliated.

Yet at the same time, the self-alienated "we" posits the universality of masculine culture, and it can do this only by reference *to* the imaginary law of the family. What unites those with status in the symbolic realm is the fact that each is the lord of his own family; masculine subjects base their camaraderie on their self-consciousness of being a community of lords. Thus, the realm of symbolic culture is based on the most violent ambivalence toward the family—the latter is a realm which must be both utterly annihilated and absolutely preserved.

This violent ambivalence toward the family is the expression of the masculine individualist's own self-alienation. He is, in himself, a split subject. For on the one hand, he sees himself as a self-subsistent individual who exists in utter isolation from all other individuals. Yet on the other hand he has standing in the realm of masculine culture only to the extent that he conforms to its universal rules. The hazing process whereby he learns these rules—that is, his Oedipalization—is supposed to grant him the status of real individuality, but in fact this process represents the actualization of the universal "we" which stands opposed to the individual. The masculine subject attains self-consciousness only as having transcended himself. Bubba is a real man only insofar as he acts like Joe who is a real man only insofar as he acts like Luke who is a real man only insofar as he acts like Bubba. Yet at the same time, the "we" is nothing other than the particular individuals themselves. Accordingly, each transcended masculine subject must retain his determinacy *qua* this particular macho-individualist. Such determinacy can be gained only by the fetishizing of an absolute masculine ideal which then becomes the determinate measure to which others compare themselves.

The work of the macho-individualist consists in striving to attain this absolute masculine ideal. In performing this work, he establishes his real individuality; for instance, the more he can bench-press, the more he is a "somebody" rather than a "nobody." Of course, in becoming a "somebody" he really does become a "nobody," because in the symbolic sphere of masculine culture real individuality consists in its own self-alienation. The subject who can bench-press is valued only as a member of a team. Everything he does for himself he does for the team, and in serving the team he finds himself recognized in the only way possible—as a "team player."

Thus, we see here a recapitulation of the dialectic of state power and wealth. The macho-individualist at first sees the team—that is, state power—as good, and he opposes to the good of the team the evil of the selfish player's concern with individual statistics—that is, wealth. Of course, the distinction is ultimately a false one, since the team will only do well if the individual players do well and vice versa. This follows from the fact that the individual player is interested in accomplishing only those sorts of things which are valued in the ideal of the team player. The work of each macho-individualist is thus both a self-sacrificing being-for-the-team and an egoistic being-for-self. However, the macho-individualist at first holds these two moments apart, declaring the success of the team to be good and the success of the individual to be bad.

The first truth of macho individualism, therefore, is the purely masculine equivalent of the immediate "we" of real socialism. This is the consciousness of the *totalitarian democrat*. In the name of freedom and real individuality, the totalitarian democrat preaches complete self-sacrifice and conformity to the being-for-self of the state. His speech is utterly hypocritical. Posing as the equivalent of the anti-totalitarianist, his real work is equivalent to that of the tyrant of the revolution—to purge all those individuals who affirm their right to think for themselves. Just as in the case of the tyrant of the revolution, so the totalitarian democrat's work is potentially infinite. No one is safe from the charge of being "anti-team" precisely because everyone is an individual. The downfall of the totalitarian democrat comes when he attacks those members of the symbolic realm whose masculinity appears unimpeachable. By attacking the most macho of the macho-individualists, the totalitarian democrat eventually appears as the enemy of macho individualism.

Ironically, therefore, the fall of the totalitarian democrat is no great victory for the still repressed imaginary realm of being-for-others. On the contrary, it is only when the masculine members of the symbolic realm recognize that to defend the state is to argue against macho individualism that they topple the totalitarian democrat. In their eyes, this once ideal team player is now viewed as a feminine subject without standing. Against the truth of the totalitarian democrat, therefore, the values of good and bad are now reversed. It is no longer state power which is good and individual wealth which is bad; on the contrary, it is now individual wealth which is good and team power which is bad. The team exists for the sake of the players rather than the other way around. This is the truth of the *libertarian*.

The libertarian has raised the symbolic realm of masculine culture to a level of self-consciousness by declaring that this realm exists solely for the sake of its individual members. The libertarian resembles the anarchist in that both are enemies of the state; however, where the anarchist attacked the state in the name of the people, the libertarian attacks the very idea of "the people" as a collective. Both the realm of the family and the realm of the state—the only spheres in which a being-for-the-sake-of-others might manifest itself—are negated by the libertarian. Civil society is the only authentic realm of human existence, and egoistic activity is the only authentic work of the individual.

With this truth of the libertarian, the self-alienation of individuals in the symbolic realm reaches its most extreme form. Only with the eventual reappearance of a representative of the repressed imaginary realm will its false consciousness be made explicit. That is, the truth of the alienation of civil society is to be found in the phenomenon of gendering which has divided the "we" into its separate spheres. Until the emergence of a self-consciously feminine gender critique of civil society, the masculine order remains oblivious even of its being gendered. From the perspective of the macho-individualists themselves, the totalization of the realm of civil society signifies that every subject is a masculine subject. They see themselves as the only actual representatives of the "we." At this stage of the dialectic, the speech of every representative of the imaginary realm is summarily dismissed, if it is even noticed at all. Later, it will be possible to hear these silenced voices, but for now this is not possible.

Prior to the emergence of a gender critique of the symbolic realm, therefore, the only reflective challenge to it that arises is itself a masculine one. The good of the libertarian appears as bad to those macho-individualists who retain their faith in the masculine ideal of the team player. The latter now try to recover what they posit as the good moment of real socialism. But since they, too, believe that everything has been swallowed up by the selfish egoism of civil society, their consciousness is without hope. Moreover, since they recall the evil of the tyrant of the revolution, they cannot embrace the one-sided ideal of state power any more than they can the one-sided ideal of individual wealth. Hence, they reject the absolute distinction between state socialism and libertarianism—that is, between state power and individual wealth—and affirm the need for a balance between the two. In place of an absolute guiding social principle, these individuals affirm the need to consider every particular social question on its own merits. Insofar as they posit the need for individual participation in shaping the state, they return to the consciousness of the liberal lawmaker and law-tester. But insofar as they reject the ideal of absolute laws in favor of an ongoing case-by-case balancing of state and individual interests, they are liberal pragmatists.

The pragmatists have a noble consciousness. They seek to serve the people insofar as the people are both socially united and separate individuals. The pragmatists stand opposed to the base consciousness of those individuals—whether state socialists or libertarians—who seek to serve themselves at the expense of the people. This is their equivalent of the "heroism of service" which appeared at the level of culture. The pragmatists pride themselves on being advisers to governments and corporations, informing political leaders and stockholders on how best to use power and wealth to achieve social goals. However, insofar as they are not themselves the actual wielders of power or wealth, their advice is ineffectual; after dinner with and a solemn handshake from the President or a CEO, they are either ignored or used merely as public relations salespersons for whatever it was that power or wealth meant to do anyway. Like the well-adjusted utilitarians, the pragmatists cannot remain true to their ideals while working within the system; only by taking up the stance of the alienated anti-structuralist could they hope to oppose power and wealth in an effective way.

If liberal pragmatism is to continue, therefore, it can do so only in a hypocritical way. The apparent heroism of service is, at bottom, just a form of flattery. But since now the pragmatist is aware of the social *futility* of speech that had once seemed to be of social *utility*, he speaks with self-conscious irony. The liberal pragmatist—though he still hypocritically calls himself a pragmatist—has become a *liberal ironist*. The liberal ironist believes he is doing "all that he can under the circumstances." Yet, in fact, the only sincere thing to do would be to retreat from "playing the game" altogether, to refuse to flatter the bigwigs who invite him to dinner and give him expensive stipends in exchange for his public praise of corporate generosity to the people. Under the pretense of a desire to help the people, the liberal ironist is really just promoting his own career. He defends himself by contrasting his own stance with that of the anti-structuralist and pointing out that it was the latter who failed to rise to the self-consciousness of the true liberal. But, in fact, the liberal ironist himself only pays lip service to such liberalism. Moreover, in the wake of the failure of true pragmatism, the only honest stance for a masculine consciousness who remains oblivious of the need for gender critique is to take up the anti-structuralist's iconclastic attack against this one-dimensional society. But the liberal ironist turns out to be utterly unaware of his own hypocrisy, for he can no longer distinguish between power and wealth that are good and power and wealth that are bad. Clinging to the bad faith of his "good conscience," he goes through the motions of recommending and criticizing various social policies—an activity to which, even he must admit, not much attention is paid by those egoistic wielders of power and wealth. So confused is the liberal ironist that he must give up altogether the idea of saying what "good" and "bad" *mean*—though he attributes this self-failure to a failure in the words themselves. By refusing to define these words, of course, he can justify the vagueness of his own social agenda, as if such vagueness were a virtue. And since he makes no bones about using these undefined terms, the liberal ironist's speech is but a tangled web of noble-sounding, vain discourse.

Insofar as the liberal ironist nonetheless retains a glimmer of his sincere desire to be an effective liberal pragmatist, he proclaims the centrality of one basic rule—that it is wrong to treat people cruelly. Of course, his principle is articulated in such nebulous language that he cannot really distinguish between cruel and non-cruel use of power or wealth. But this glimmer of real commitment represents the moment of hope for the liberal ironist. Faced with the serious speech of those who, because they are actively concerned with cruelty refuse to play the game of flattery, the liberal ironist can be shamed out of his hypocritical position.

But instead of reverting to the position of the genuine liberal pragmatist whose only honest act in the face of unrepentant greed and power-mongering was to retreat to the position of the anti-structuralist, the liberal ironist is in a position to do something different. Specifically, he can use his irony to expose the hypocrisy of the symbolic realm's faith in power and money. Irony has thus become a weapon. Its sheer negativity cuts through the false consciousness—that is, the faith of masculine culture and thereby posits the truth of the individual's pure insight into what is truly good for the people.

The symbolic realm's faith is simply its affirmation of itself, which self-affirmation gets expressed in a variety of masculine myths. This affirmation without negativity is expressed in the slogan, "Love it or leave it." But the "happy consciousness" of this faith is now opposed to the pure insight which posits the possibility of a genuine coming-together of individuals in society. Thus, pure insight draws from the wellspring of the repressed imaginary realm, affirming peace and universal love as its guiding principles. Previously, critics of the one-dimensional masculine culture could not speak their criticisms of it; they could only express their anger and frustration in a tumult of rule-less words or colors. But now the great tools of irony and parody have given the symbolic realm's critics a new medium for expression. In place of the angry riot of colors there now appears the self-conscious mockery of masculine culture's myths—that is, parodies of its own representations of power, money, and masculinity. This ironic culture is accompanied by a new religion—not the sham religions of the symbolic realm but a genuine religion of pure insight. Hence, the self-consciousness of the real "we" is affirmed over and against the sham "we" of the symbolic realm. All that is needed to actualize this real "we" is to participate in the practices of the religion of pure insight—to take part in "love-ins" and "be-ins," and to take consciousness-expanding drugs. Opposed to faith's bellicose "Love it or leave it" is pure insight's "Make love, not war." The work of pure insight is once again, as it was at the level of spirit, the work of Enlightenment, and it is carried out by those individuals who have not been completely molded by the hazing rituals of masculine culture. Those who undertake this work, therefore, represent the *love generation*, and they stand opposed to the *defenders of masculine myths*.

The pure insight of the love generation is opposed to the ideological faith of the symbolic realm in general. But the love generation is principally opposed to the defenders of masculine myths, whom they view not just as defenders but as creators of these myths. Thus, the love generation distinguishes between the sinister creators of masculine myths and the naive individuals who are taken in by them. Hence, they set out to win over the latter by revealing to them the truth of pure insight. Since it naively believes that the naive consciousness is merely waiting to hear this gospel of love, the love generation thinks that all it needs to do is stage a great festival of love to which everyone will be invited.

Resisting its message, however, the symbolic realm stages a counterattack. As at the level of the ethical world, so here the masculine state sends its youths to war, in order to put the members of the love generation through the swiftest and most brutal of its hazing rituals. The love generation resists the war, but it cannot do so without a struggle. The festival of love thus gives way to a violent confrontation between the love generation and the defenders of masculine myths. But by allowing itself to be drawn into a violent confrontation, the love generation resists war precisely by waging war. Hence, it goes through a hazing process anyway, and its pure insight becomes akin to the faith of the defenders of masculine myths.

The love generation's insight into the imaginary realm is the end which they pursue with all of the symbolic means at their disposal. But the distinction between means and ends here is hypocritical, for the love generation sets out to kill for the principle that killing is wrong. Insofar as they are ready to kill for what they believe in, the love generation turns out to be no different from the defenders of masculine myths. Each side believes itself to have insight; each side accuses the other of believing in a false ideology.

Denying this identification, the love generation mocks the defenders of masculine myths, deriding the latter's holidays as a sham coming-together of macho-individualists. Certain that the imaginary realm of being-with-one-another has been completely repressed, the love generation accuses all macho-individualists of being mere hedonistic worshipers of power and money. For their part, the members of the love generation retreat into small family-like communities, sheltered from the symbolic realm.

Although they are right to accuse the symbolic realm of having repressed the imaginary realm altogether, the love generation fails to realize that the alienated macho-individualists are aware of the hollowness of their existence. Although they are insincere religious practitioners, the macho-individualists fervently long to be true believers. At the same time, the self-righteousness of the love generation keeps them from seeing that they, too, have withdrawn into a kind of hedonistic indifference to the rest of society. Their sheltered communities are not political vanguards but merely private families which pose no real threat to the symbolic realm. Where once they took drugs in order to come together with one another, now they sit alone and take these drugs by themselves, unaware of the contradiction in their seeking to "transcend" their individuality precisely by withdrawing into it.

Eventually, some members of the love generation realize that they are not as different as they thought from their alienated fathers. They now see their talk about "universal brotherhood and sisterhood" as half-baked and foolishly youthful. Confessing their guilt, they return to the symbolic realm, positing the unity of faith and pure insight. They represent the *reformed youth*. Like the well-adjusted utilitarian, reformed youth possesses the certainty that one can change the system by working within it. Their fathers, the defenders of masculine symbols, at first expect reformed youth to renounce their earlier views altogether. However, reformed youth can reach reconciliation with their fathers only by extracting a mutual confession, and by clinging to the belief that it is not "selling out" but is "taking it to the streets"—albeit in a three-piece suit.

Both reformed youth and the mollified defenders of masculine myths now set out to be socially useful by "changing the system from within." Now everybody dances to the same music. Just as the well-adjusted utilitarian could feel that all of his works were contributing to the welfare of society, so here everyone feels good about his own personal contributions to the good of society. Everyone is thus entitled—or rather has a social responsibility—to feel good about themselves. The symbolic realm thus becomes a self-consciously narcissistic culture; the love generation gives way to the *"me" generation*. Unlike any of the alienated shapes of the "I" hitherto, the "me" posited here is blissfully unaware of its alienation. Its work is at bottom an utterly selfish one; everything the "me" generation does it does for itself. But in keeping with the truth of the libertarian, whose certainty is the central ideology of the symbolic realm's principle of being-for-self, the individual member of the "me" generation feels no guilt whatsoever about his selfishness. Moreover, since the "me" represents the self-consciousness of wealth, he can allay whatever pangs of social conscience might threaten to interfere with his cocaine-induced euphoria by having the liberal ironist flatter him about how useful to society his selfishness really is. Thus, the "me" goes on naively thinking of himself as the star of the heroic movie that he takes his life to be; he is connected to the "we" solely by way of the massively conceited certainty that everyone in the world would find him the most wonderful thing in it if only they could see the movie of his life.

The more the "me" feels that his work is socially useful, the more he feels entitled to pursue his secondary work of total hedonism. His life is thus divided between the hours he spends doing his supposedly good deeds and the hours he spends rewarding himself for being such a socially useful person. Now, the proper end of the "me's" work is supposed to be to change the system from within. However, precisely by working within the system, he maintains it as it is rather than subverts it. Eventually, therefore, the "me" cannot sustain the pretense that he does his work for the sake of changing the system; the true end of his work, rather, is to be found in the reward he receives—the money which he spends during the weekend when he indulges himself in his narcissistic parody of the love generation's communal celebrations. Thus, the "me" becomes the sole end of his own work, and the truth of the "me" generation is this universal consciousness of the absolute freedom of every particular "me." This truth is expressed in the slogan, "Whatever turns you on."

Unlike the appearance of absolute freedom at the level of spirit which manifested itself as the freedom of objective spirit, what is posited here is merely the absolute freedom of the individual "me" who now comes to know himself as totally isolated from the "we." Instead of seeing the "we" as a threat to his freedom, the "me" sees himself as an absolutely free individual who exists as an anonymous face in a crowd of anonymous faces. Insofar as he posits his absolute freedom, the "me" takes on the consciousness of the existentialist. But whereas the existentialist viewed his freedom in terms of responsibility for everything, the "me" now views himself as responsible only for himself. Yet to admit this—that is, to return to the simple consciousness of the egoist or the macho-individualist—causes him great pain, for he has invested his sense of identity in the pretense that, in his own little way, he has been carrying on the work of the love generation.

Thus, the "me" resembles the philosophical loner, who was certain of his isolation but who longed for human connection. But unlike the loner, who despaired of real connection, the "me" clings to the love generation's insight into the real possibility of creating community. He thus sets out to found a community of "me's," each of whom will possess the sociologist's self-consciousness of the "we." The members of this fabricated *fraternity of sociology* begin from their consciousness that the symbolic realm is devoid of genuine community. They thus appear to themselves to represent the principle of being-with-others of the repressed imaginary realm. However, insofar as they view their community as a gathering of isolated "me's"—that is, self-conscious macho-individualists—they in fact represent the symbolic realm's inevitably futile attempt to forge community solely out of its own anti-communal resources.

Thus, while their group might at first appear as a healthy cure for one-sided masculinity, it quickly develops into something like a cancerous growth of macho-individualism run amok—the body of symbolic culture violently turned against itself. Instead of opposing masculine culture with feminine culture, the fraternity of sociology opposes masculine culture with its own excesses. It thus bases its supposedly anti-symbolic community on hyper-macho hazing rituals; if the symbolic realm requires that a man beat someone up in order to prove his masculinity, the fraternity of sociology goes one better and requires that a man kill someone in order to prove his membership in their supposedly anti-masculine community. Since the individual "me" represents nothing other than the self-consciousness of the macho-individualist, all of the fraternity of sociology's presumably anti-Oedipal excesses are nothing more than an expression of the total hegemony of masculine culture. No longer even bothering to draw on the imaginary realm of the "sacred" in opposition to the symbolic realm of the "profane," the fraternity treats the profane as the sacred. Of course, masculine culture is at its most profane where it violently represses the imaginary realm of the family. Hence, the members of the fraternity of sociology, who seek, presumably, to recreate the conditions for the possibility of something like a genuine family, end up creating an anti-family family—or, what is the same thing here, an anti-feminine imaginary realm. The absolute freedom of its members thus finds its logical outcome in the group's terroristic gynocidal practices.

The sole work of the fraternity of sociology is the death of the imaginary. Yet it pursues this death in the name of overcoming the repression of the imaginary. Hence, its work is absolutely hypocritical. Once the hypocrisy of symbolic efforts to appropriate the imaginary becomes explicit, however, there emerges a new shape of consciousness—one which unmasks the gynocidal ideology which sustains the symbolic realm in general. Thus, we find the earlier position of the feminine psychoanalyst of gender transformed into a new consciousness. Where previously both the masculine and feminine analysts of gender reached the shared certainty of the union of the imaginary and symbolic realms in the self-consciousness of the "we," it has now been made explicit that this apparent reconciliation was in actuality a one-sided masculine affair. Although the "we" of real socialism paid lip service to the public character of the imaginary realm, the party was merely a symbolic arena for the egoistic clashes of civil society. As a result, it found its truth in the merely abstract unity of real democracy. Now, the truth of the symbolic realm's anti-imaginary character has been brought to light.

All along, the symbolic realm has violently repressed the imaginary basis for real community. With its need to maintain the family as the domain of the masculine lord, it has legislated a "proper" place for the feminine. For their part, whenever feminine subjects entered the symbolic realm for any reason, they did so only by undergoing a variety of hazing rituals themselves—some designed to "masculinize" them and others designed to remind them of their femininity—that is, of their unworthiness of recognition within the symbolic realm. But now that the gynocidal essence of the masculine sphere has been made manifest, the feminine subjects who also comprise the actual "we" rise up to reclaim the public sphere. The consciousness of the feminine psychoanalyst of gender now repudiates its previous agreements with the masculine psychoanalyst of gender, and affirms once again the need for an imaginary undermining of the symbolic realm. Instead of viewing the "we" as a unity of the symbolic and the imaginary, the representative of the imaginary sphere now views the "we" as a false uniting of an irreducible difference between these two gendered realms. Viewing psychoanalysis as an essentially masculine project, she rejects the position of the feminine psychoanalyst of gender as a contradictory one. In place of a psychoanalysis of gender, she offers an imaginary perspective of the irreducible split between the genders. This, then, is the truth of the *feminine theorist of difference.*

The feminine theorist of difference begins from her awareness of the gynocidal essence of the symbolic realm, and she sets out to subvert the latter. However, in taking up this stance, she does not pit the imaginary against the symbolic as in a struggle to the death, for she is well aware that the impulse to annihilate the other arises solely from the symbolic realm itself. Her nonviolent efforts to subvert the symbolic realm are, for this reason, *incomprehensible* from the standpoint of the symbolic realm. For the consciousness of the macho-individualists, there are only two sorts of stances that one can take in an encounter with an other—one can try to dominate the other through masculine struggle for recognition, or one can meekly submit to the other in a feminine way. But neither of these is the attitude taken by the feminine theorist of difference. Understanding masculine self-alienation in a way that the alienated macho-individualists themselves do not, the feminine theorist of difference refuses the false dichotomy of the masculine either/or that is based on its masculine idea of the feminine. Instead of "playing their game," therefore, she simply laughs at them. Her laughter is itself the undermining of the proud conceit of the macho-individualists. Yet it is also a laughter which they cannot understand—and for this reason, the question of whether or not an actual reconciliation between the symbolic and imaginary realms is possible is not yet clear.

Nonetheless, in the self-certainty of the feminine theorist of difference, the self-alienation of the "we" is implicitly overcome. With her task of negating the real alienation of the symbolic realm, she reclaims the moral authority and proper work of the defender of the people. Thus, we arrive at the first shape of the "we's" actualized self-certainty—the imaginary view of the world.

C. This "We" That Knows It is Not One

a. The Imaginary View of the World

The self-certain imaginary realm is the sphere of absolute freedom raised to the level of a universal laughter which takes the place of the general will which appeared in the dialectic of spirit. As the *self-consciousness* of the "we," the feminine theorist of difference knows her life-affirming laughter—markedly different from the death-affirming laughter of the fraternity of sociology—as the true undermining of the alienation of the symbolic sphere. However, as the *consciousness* of the symbolic realm, she is aware of this masculine sphere as her recalcitrant other; it represents the irredeemable unfreedom that would annihilate difference. Thus, the symbolic realm appears as the object that is governed by laws of unfreedom. In effect reversing the symbolic realm's association of femininity with nature, the imaginary consciousness knows that it is the symbolic realm of masculine culture that is governed by deterministic laws. However, just as the imaginary consciousness throws off the masculine representation of femininity, so it throws off its representation of nature as well. To say that the symbolic realm is the realm of unfreedom, therefore, is not to associate it with nature; on the contrary, the imaginary consciousness knows the symbolic realm as the most unnatural mode of being. Opposed to masculinity's unnatural mechanical laws of unfreedom stands the self-certain imaginary consciousness that is aware of its own natural and fluid laws of freedom.

In one sense, the two spheres appear as if they were indifferent to each other. However, the imaginary consciousness cannot remain withdrawn in itself. Not only does the symbolic realm threaten it with its gynocidal hatred of flows, but the freedom that is only implicit in the imaginary self-consciousness must be actualized through the real subversion of the symbolic realm. Put otherwise, the certainty of the imaginary self-consciousness must be raised to the level of truth. The duty of the imaginary consciousness consists in its obligation to transform the unnatural symbolic sphere into an imaginary one.

In its efforts to transform the symbolic realm, the imaginary consciousness seeks to undermine the distinction between the genders as this distinction has been posited within the symbolic realm. But this is not equivalent to doing away with the distinction between the genders altogether. On the contrary, the imaginary consciousness itself posits the truth of irreducible difference. Instead of seeking to eradicate masculinity, the individual who embodies this consciousness merely tries to undo the hierarchical relation which places the imaginary in a position of subordination to the symbolic. By reintroducing the imaginary moment within public life, the "we" of real socialism can perhaps be genuinley actualized as the "we" of radical community.

As the inherited consciousness of the defender of the people, the imaginary consciousness knows the essence of the symbolic sphere to consist in its insistence on thinking the "we" as an identity. It is because the essence of the imaginary realm consists in its consciousness of difference that it poses such a threat to the symbolic consciousness. Were the imaginary consciousness to fight the latter's gynocidal logic with its own law of identity, it would merely be conforming to the symbolic realm's ethic of domination. Variations on this flawed tactic have already been seen in the anti-symbolic strategies of the radical feminists, the violently anti-war love generation, and the excessively masculine fraternity of sociology.

At a minimum, the goal of liberating the feminine from its position of subordination would seem to require a radical transformation of the symbolic realm. However, since the symbolic realm is perceived to be *essentially* resistant to the moral insight of the imaginary self-consciousness, it appears to be irredeemably gynocidal. For this reason, the earlier anti-masculine truth of the radical feminist is now reaffirmed by the *liberal feminist*. However, where the radical feminist took just masculinity to be evil, the liberal feminist now takes gender differentiation as a whole to be a product of the symbolic realm. To defend femininity in opposition to masculinity would merely be to maintain the masculine-serving construct of gender differences. In order to resist the hegemony of the masculine, therefore, the liberal feminist now posits the necessity of doing away with gender differentiation itself. Attacking the symbolic realm remains her immediate objective. Just as the communists sought to overthrow the institution of private property by attacking owners, even though both owners and workers were responsible for the fetishization of property, so now the liberal feminist seeks to undermine the fetishization of gender differences primarily by attacking those who benefit from this fetishization—namely, the masculine members of the symbolic realm. In contrast to the imaginary consciousness who clings to her affirmation of difference, the liberal feminist denies that gender differences have any substantial basis at all.

As a certified member of the imaginary realm, the liberal feminist possesses a moral authority that is equivalent to that of the imaginary consciousness. However, by positing the need to eradicate gender differences entirely, she seems to the imaginary consciousness to have been coopted by the symbolic realm's law of identity. The liberal feminist, it would seem, is likely to be the sort of feminine subject who has already passed through the symbolic realm's hazing rituals and survived them without too many bruises.

Questioning the grounds for the liberal feminist's seemingly masculine fear of difference, therefore, the imaginary consciousness distinguishes between two notions of difference. On the one hand, there is a notion of difference as necessarily implying a hierarchy of values. This is difference as it is conceived by the symbolic realm, and the liberal feminist is right to view it as something evil. On the other hand, though, there is a notion of difference that does not entail hierarchy. This is difference as conceived by the imaginary realm. To the symbolic consciousness, which is ruled by the masculine law of identity, non-hierarchical difference appears as something evil, but to the self-certain imaginary consciousness, non-hierarchical difference is intrinsically good. By indiscriminately attacking difference in general, the liberal feminist carries out the anti-imaginary work of the symbolic realm even as she fights against the symbolic realm's hierarchical differences. To this extent, her efforts to overcome gender subordination are at cross-purposes.

In contrast to the ambiguous work of the liberal feminist, the imaginary consciousness attempts to transform hierarchical differences into non-hierarchical differences. However, if the essence of masculinity consists in its law of identity, then it is true that the difference between the genders cannot be maintained without preserving the symbolic will-to-hierarchy. Moreover, since the symbolic realm infuses every difference with its law of identity, the question arises as to whether one can preserve the very *notion* of difference without confirming the symbolic realm's inscription of this notion within a logic of hierarchy. Claiming that the imaginary effort to affirm an irreducible difference between the genders might not be the most effective strategy for subverting the hegemony of the symbolic realm, but acknowledging the force of the imaginary consciousness's critique of the liberal feminist, there now emerges the *deconstructive consciousness*, which affirms the need to defend *radical* difference by subverting the notions of both identity and difference.

To the deconstructive consciousness who would affirm radical difference, all binary oppositions must be subverted—including the opposition between identity and difference. In positing this strategy, the deconstructive consciousness appears as an advocate of the imaginary consciousness. However, since the distinctions between the imaginary and the symbolic, the feminine and the masculine, are themselves binary oppositions, the individual who adopts this consciousness cannot label himself or herself a defender of the imaginary without thereby reaffirming the binary opposition he or she seeks to subvert. Yet neither can he or she claim to represent the unity of both genders, for then he or she would affirm an identity rather than a difference.

Thus, the deconstructive consciousness finds itself in a double bind, which double bind is not, however, the result of its willfulness but which is rather the result of that "divine nature of language" to inscribe all attempts to articulate difference within a logic of identity. No sooner has he or she articulated a trope that expresses the "non-concept" of difference than this expression itself immediately becomes a symbolic coin of conceptual currency; it no longer expresses radical difference but now expresses a hierarchical notion of difference. Therefore the deconstructive consciousness must constantly move from trope to trope, devaluing his or her marks so that they become useless in the general economy of the notion. In sliding along from one expression to the other, deconstructive speech *seems* to resemble the perverted speech of flattery which appeared at the level of culture. But the latter arose because the flattering consciousness was itself duplicitous. Here, the deconstructive consciousness more closely resembles the tranquil consciousness who honestly assesses the truth, for it is *language itself* which is responsible for the hierarchization of difference which forces him or her to express himself or herself in the hidden interstices of words.

In his or her attempts to help the imaginary consciousness articulate a deconstructive strategy for subverting the symbolic realm's law of identity, the deconstructive consciousness ends up critiquing the imaginary consciousness's own self-certainty. Instead of viewing the feminine as something standing over and against the masculine, the deconstructive consciousness argues, it is necessary to affirm "the feminine" solely as a trope to indicate that radical difference which the imaginary consciousness professes to defend.

Although there is a certain undeniable logic in the deconstructive consciousness's reasoning, this conclusion seems to those who identify themselves as feminine subjects to be a flattering masculine perversion of true feminism. The deconstructive consciousness *seems* to say that to be a real feminist one must be an anti-feminist. Both the individual who embodies the imaginary consciousness and the liberal feminist are therefore outraged at the suggestion of the deconstructive consciousness. They accuse this consciousness of being a clandestine agent of the symbolic realm. Now quick to essentialize gender identities, they ask what gives *him* the right to tell feminine subjects that they should not identify themselves as feminine subjects. In this way, the self-righteous moral certitude of the imaginary self-consciousness causes it to forget that it has just finished critiquing the liberal feminist for precisely the same reasons that the deconstructive consciousness now critiques it. By insisting on its "right" to identify itself with the socially constructed place from which it speaks, the imaginary consciousness affirms its own being-for-self rather than the radical difference of its professed flows. Like the Oedipalized liberal feminist, the hypocritical imaginary consciousness stakes out its position within the symbolic sphere and then poses as the radical critic of this sphere. It denies its own duplicity by insisting that one can accept essentialist terms for "strategic" purposes.

The imaginary consciousness becomes hypocritical when a particular individual who embodies this consciousness identifies herself as the privileged "other" of the symbolic realm. In truth, she is only one of many individuals who have been marginalized; and as the self-conscious theorist of difference she should be aware that those who are marginalized do not constitute a homogenous class of identical subjects. So long as she converses with individuals whose social position is exactly like hers, a feminine theorist of difference can remain within her self-righteous certainty of being at the center of the marginalized world. However, no sooner does she resist the deconstructive consciousness by insisting on her authority as an exemplary marginal subject than she finds herself confronted with other imaginary subjects whose particular social status is different from hers. Being an upper-middle-class white lesbian feminine subject, it turns out, is not the same as being a lower-class, Hispanic, heterosexual feminine subject. She discovers, moreover, that the binary opposition between masculine and feminine is an inadequate tool for capturing the wide array of hierarchical exclusions of the symbolic world. This point is made especially clear in the consciousness of those individuals who do not fit neatly into one side of the gender dichotomy. The certainty that there are multiple genders is the truth of the *queer theorist* who *lives* the inadequacy of language which the deconstructive consciousness has brought to consciousness.

But rather than leading straightaway to an undermining of the symbolic law of identity, this splitting up of the once unified imaginary consciousness issues instead in a multiplicity of new identity claims. Since each new group now claims that its own unique identity is marginalized by every other group, it reinterprets the fundamental fissures of the "we" according to the markers of its own identity. Hence, a battle takes place as to whether the exemplary marker is to be determined by class, gender, race, religion, age, and so forth. Just as the self-righteous imaginary subject resented the deconstructive consciousness's presumption to speak on behalf of the feminine, so now every marginal subject who is different from the feminine theorist of difference accuses her of having the temerity to speak on behalf of them. The universal laughter of the imaginary self-consciousness is now dirempted in the bickering of the competing *exemplary others.*

b. *Postmodernist Duplicity*

The imaginary consciousness affirmed irreducible difference but it failed to acknowledge the deconstructive insight that genuinely radical difference cannot be articulated within the language of binary oppositions. As a result, the certainty of duty as the obligation to undermine the symbolic realm's law of identity has reversed itself. Now every individual who claims to embody the imaginary consciousness insists on her own identity. What is true in this great battle for exemplary otherness is that every particular subject is, *qua* particular subject, an enemy of the symbolic realm, which realm now embodies the paranoia that earlier was located in the single person of the tyrant of the revolution. However, what is duplicitous in it is that, beneath the self-righteous mask of the defender of the people which every exemplary other wears, there hides a mere "me" selfishly defending itself. Yet at the same time the exemplary other is conscious of the universality of her position, and to this extent she does indeed affirm not only her own unique position but also the truth of every unique position. The individual who adopts this position is called the "multiculturalist."

By fighting for the right of all marginalized subjects to participate in the symbolic realm's public discourse, the multiculturalist manages to introduce anti-symbolic speech into this previously one-dimensional arena. In this way, he or she—non-exclusive language is important for the multiculturalists, for whom the worst sin is to fail to pay homage to the vast array of identifying social marks—seeks to subvert the symbolic realm. However, as soon as anti-symbolic speech is legitimated within the symbolic realm, it loses its subversive character. Political signs that were once genuinely radical now end up as decorative marks on baseball caps. In its most hypocritical form, the work of the multiculturalist is merely a jockeying for positions of masculine privilege within the symbolic realm—for this is the work of every macho-individualist. Because he or she can win positions of prestige for marginal subjects only by dislodging those particular macho-individualists who already enjoy these positions, the multiculturalist can feel as if he or she is subverting the logic of the symbolic realm even when all he or she is doing is beating someone out for a job. The hypocrisy beneath the pride at "making inroads" is revealed in the indifference to the prospect that the multicultural struggle for recognition may create new marginal groups comprised of those previously marginal subjects who have already managed to win positions of prestige. "Others," in other words, are valued only for so long as they have the decency to remain persecuted.

Thus, the duplicitous multiculturalist consciousness finds itself split. On the one hand, it is the imaginary insight into the intrinsic evil of the symbolic realm, and as such it clings to its righteous self-consciousness, preferring to be an "other" rather than a successful member of masculine culture. Yet on the other hand, its active attempts to "subvert the system from within" lead it to seek recognition within the symbolic realm. The former represents its consciousness of duty; the latter its desire for happiness. Those who fail in their efforts to win prestigious positions within the symbolic realm have the bad faith to deny that this is what they sought; falling back on their pristine self-certainty, they blame those of their comrades who have succeeded for "selling out." So long as the multiculturalist keeps these two consciousnesses separate, such criticisms appear warranted. But by withdrawing from the symbolic realm altogether, the pristine consciousness fails to perform its duty. Accordingly it returns to its work of subversion, but now with the revolutionary fervor of the outsider who will topple the system with acts of violence. Yet by resorting to violence, this supposed friend of the imaginary consciousness merely takes on the stance of a hyper-symbolic latter-day member of the fraternity of sociology. Like the anarchist, but motivated solely by his resentment for having not succeeded in getting that job at Berkeley, the self-proclaimed *subversive terrorist* performs his violent deed, kills a two-year-old child with a carbomb, and believes he has forwarded the work of the imaginary consciousness when in fact he has performed the most brutally symbolic act of all.

The subversive terrorist is not so much hypocritical, however, as he is radically ineffectual. After all, the goal of his action is not to kill a two-year-old child but, on the contrary, to topple a system that is itself institutionally contemptuous of two-year-old children. What the failure of his act demonstrates, however, is the symbolic realm's resourcefulness at reinscribing all attacks against it as justifications for its own existence. The symbolic realm is the sphere of institutional violence, but it thrives on its ability to characterize itself as protection against violence. For this reason it is always quick to remind its Oedipalized citizens of the terror of absolute freedom, a reminder which twists every potential multicultural face-to-face encounter into a struggle between macho-individualists, each of whom is certain that the other is trying to emasculate him. Because the subversive terrorist merely provides a useful occasion for the symbolic realm to perform its own acts of institutional terrorism, his action strengthens the system rather than weakens it.

Since the act of the subversive terrorist now appears to be precisely what the symbolic realm requires, it dawns on the individual who would effectively undermine the system that the only way to succeed would be to deny the symbolic realm its subversive terrorists. However, to act in a way that is exactly contrary to the subversive terrorist—that is, to act like a perfectly content, well-Oedipalized macho-individualist who is proud of his job, even if it is driving a taxi rather than teaching seminars in "Radical Politics" at Berkeley—is an even more contemptible action, since it would clearly confirm the legitimacy of the symbolic realm.

Recognizing that the power of the symbolic realm lies in its ability to use all *real* activity to legitimize itself, it now occurs to the *postmodernist* that the only way to subvert the system is to *pretend* to act rather than to act. By pretending—whether pretending to commit terrorist acts or pretending to act like a macho-individualist—the postmodernist proposes to call attention to the artificial—that is, the unessential—nature of the symbolic realm. Taking up the parodying stance of those liberal ironists who became members of the love generation, the postmodernists now set out to perform the serious work of fighting institutional violence by refusing to take it seriously. In place of actual terrorist acts, they perform such stunts as throwing pies in politicians' faces; in place of blatantly anti-symbolic art, they pretend to try to create art solely for the sake of money.

The desperateness of these attempts reaffirms the difficulty of critiquing the one-dimensional symbolic realm. But it also shows the foolishness of the strategy itself. The idea that one will "bring the system to its knees" by acting childishly is, quite simply, a childish idea. Postmodernists certainly have a lot of fun, which is something, but it is a form of fun of which the system itself is only too willing to approve. It was the insight of the anti-structuralist, we recall, to show that the pleasure principle was itself a universal law, and this insight has been lost on the postmodernist consciousness. As a result, not only do its sham terrorist acts fail to upset the symbolic order, but they also are in fact rewarded by it. The artists who pretend to be trying to become millionaires end up becoming real millionaires—at which point they forget the original point of their endeavors and congratulate themselves on having attained their positions of prestige.

If the successful postmodernist is completely hypocritical, the symbolically successful multiculturalist—the one who did get the job at Berkeley—is sincere enough to acknowledge that by trying to subvert the system from within she can only be partially successful. For this reason she feels guilty about her $75,000 a year salary, even though she knows that those who accuse her of selling out are themselves envious of her success. Accordingly, she continues to carry out her work of subversion, but no longer with the same righteous self-certitude that she possessed before. No longer affirming *absolute* difference but continuing to fight the symbolic realm's logic of identity, she posits the truth of the "we" as the universal consciousness of structural rationality. Certain that it is possible to articulate differences in the common medium of language, this "we" denies the deconstructive consciousness and sets out to jointly construct a communicative model for expressing and overcoming all of the evils of hierarchization. The certainty of this "we" is expressed in the consciousness of solidarity that is embodied in the *theorist of communicative action*.

c. Communicative Rationality. The Differend and its Affirmation

The passage from the imaginary self-certainty to the multiculturalist free-for-all has led to the realization that the binary opposition between the masculine and feminine is itself a product of the symbolic realm. Yet by clinging to its one-sided principle of difference, the multiculturalist consciousness was unable to actualize its consciousness of real difference. For with the dispersal of the imaginary consciousness into separate interest groups, the supposed multiculturalist politics of difference ended up as a politics of identity. Hence, the multiculturalist consciousness threatened to confirm rather than subvert the hierarchical logic of the symbolic realm.

Nevertheless, with the theorist of communicative action there now emerges a consciousness of solidarity among all individual members of the "we," precisely insofar as every individual is an "other" to the symbolic realm. With this return to the sociologists' consciousness of the universality of the "we," the gendered distinction between the symbolic and the imaginary realms is now reinterpreted. The symbolic realm is itself split between its system of culture and the individual members who are trained to perpetuate this system. To this extent, every particular macho-individualist is just as much a victim of the system as are all of the excluded imaginary subjects. Positing the implicit solidarity of all individuals as "we the people" who inhabit the *life-world* over and against the substantial solidification of the "we" in the forms of power and wealth in the symbolic *system-world*, the theorist of communicative action affirms as a universal task the work of subverting the system's colonization of the life-world.

This implicitly universal project is the work of the "we" to preserve itself against its own self-alienation. Thus, the theorist of communicative action reclaims the certainty of the "we" as structural reason, against which he or she opposes the totalitarian "we" that results from alienated structural reason's appearance as the rationalization of society. But since he or she knows that the rationalized system is itself the product of structural reason, the theorist of communicative action is certain that it is possible for the "we" to regain control over it. This can be accomplished, however, only if everyone rises to the level of an explicit self-consciousness of its implicit universal solidarity. To attain this level is not to regress to a politics of identity, but rather to attain a perspective from which a genuine political recognition of difference can lead to a restructuring of the system. The sole criteria to be used for reaching consensus will be articulated out of the shared rationality of individuals.

But, it is impossible for individuals to reach this standpoint without acknowledging the commonality of structural reason which unites all individuals. A *critical feminist* therefore accuses the theorist of communicative action of the same thing that earlier the feminine theorist of difference accused the deconstructive consciousness—namely, of asking feminine subjects conscious of the irreducible difference between the genders to pretend that such differences do not exist. For in reducing all questions concerning the space designated by the symbolic realm for feminine subjects—that is, the family—to questions of how the genderless life-world has been colonized, the theorist of communicative action either deliberately or inadvertently seeks to silence the speech which arises from a consciousness of difference.

Insofar as he is sees himself in solidarity with all subjects, however, the theorist of communicative action agrees that questions of colonization must be discussed in terms that specifically take into account the different ways in which the life-world is experienced by different subjects. His vision of an actualized politics of universal solidarity posits an ideal of an uncoerced open discourse in which all individuals can take part. Hence, he welcomes the arguments of the critical feminist.

At this point, however, the multiculturalist consciousness voices its suspicion. Sensing that the theorist of communicative action posits a politics of identity rather than a politics of difference, the multiculturalists invoke once again the anti-structuralist's distrust of the purported universality of structural reason. But by doing so, they undermine the basis for their own solidarity with one another. The multiculturalist consciousness was, as we saw, a tenuous consciousness of universality which threatened at any moment to degenerate into a mutually antagonistic multiplicity. With its rejection of the very idea of universal rationality, it now does disintegrate into a plurality of competing cultures, each with a tradition of its own. Implicitly hostile to one another but aware of the need for mutual tolerance, the formerly broad-minded multiculturalists withdraw into their own particular cultures, in the hope that such shoring up of walls will enable the many cultures to remain indifferent to one another rather than become openly hostile. Insisting now on the radically particular identity of every tradition, there thus appears the consciousness of the *traditionalist*. The work of the traditionalist is to defend the autonomy of every particular tradition over and against all claims to unification.

For the cloistered but field-surveying traditionalist, every cultural tradition has its own unique form of rationality. It is therefore impossible to find a common ground that would unite them all. Of course in making a sweeping statement about all traditions in this way, the traditionalist purports to say something *universally* true, and to this extent he immediately contradicts himself. However he bases his claim on his own perception of the impossibility of evaluating traditions from an extra-traditional perspective. Hence, his sole universal claim is that it is unfair to evaluate one tradition from the perspective of another. Different traditions are said to be not only incompatible but also incommensurable, so that it may not even be possible for members of one tradition to understand members of another.

In making these claims, the traditionalist performs the important task of clarifying the criteria that would need to be met to insure that the project of the theorist of communicative action does not do violence to members of particular cultures. However, by negating the idea of universal rationality, the traditionalist contradicts his own universal consciousness of what it means to respect different traditions. In the end he can only appeal to the moral tradition of his own culture, whose supposed high-minded respect for other cultures gives it the sheen of the highest universal truth. But this sheen is just that—the reflection of a superficial gold foil covering the dome of the traditionalist's hyper-macho cloister. Naturally, every tradition will see itself as respecting those other cultures which it deems worthy of respect; those it does not respect it feels justified about not condoning. For instance, a meat-eating community will not even seriously raise the question of whether or not animals possess rights. At bottom, the traditionalist is merely a parochial defender of his own community, the extent of whose narrow-mindedness is not even a real question for him. Thus, he merely poses as the advocate of pluralism, whereas in reality he is a member of a particular group that is unwilling to converse with members of those groups who oppose his group for one reason or another. Such a position, moreover, can be advocated only by the supporter of a tradition that enjoys symbolic legitimacy; it is in order to preserve the power of his group that the traditionalist tries to give the impression that separate cultures exist on their own, apart from the rest of the world.

The hypocrisy of the traditionalist's supposed support of multiculturalism becomes clear when he shows that he is perfectly happy defending the autonomy of traditions which are themselves based on an exclusive law of identity. For instance, he sees no reason why the various traditions of the symbolic realm—each with its own set of offensive hazing rituals—should not be allowed to continue on their own. The highest truth of the traditionalist is simply that every community has the right to haze its own children. To this extent he is an enemy of alternative rationalities rather than a friend of them. Instead of taking on the burden of discourse across communities, which discourse alone could enable each side to confront the other's intrinsically antagonistic claim to rationality, he tries to show how unjust it is of any other group to assail his. "What right do women in your community have to tell members of our fraternity that our daughters are not allowed to have abortions?"

The traditionalist is hypocritical in that he pretends to champion otherness while really defending the symbolic repression of others. For this reason, his quietism is rejected by those who remain committed to the truth of multiculturalism. But the latter, since they continue to reject the theorist of communicative action's ideal of shared rationality, now accept the traditionalist's claim that differences which define cultures cannot be resolved through rational discourse. Borrowing a page from the deconstructive consciousness's observation that language can express difference only by failing to recognize radical difference, the hard-core multiculturalist refuses to acknowledge that consensus can be reached without reinstituting hierarchy. This is the certainty of the *consciousness of the differend.*

The individual who embodies this consciousness equates consensus with totalitarianism. Self-righteously inveighing against the work of the theorist of communicative action, he poses as the true advocate of a politics of difference. However, because he interprets all communicative interaction as a battle which cannot be resolved without bloodshed, the consciousness of the differend risks becoming a mere legitimater of the terrorist, despite the fact that he reaffirms the ideal of the face-to-face encounter.

From the perspective of the dead, death by totalitarianism and death by terrorism are six of one, half a dozen of the other. Moreover, the theorist of communicative action at least holds out the prospect of rival sides agreeing to a peace treaty. Hence, this advocate of the struggle to reach consensus accuses the consciousness of the differend of being a conservative supporter of the symbolic realm's conflictual model of human interaction. But the latter responds by insisting that it the theorist of communicative action who would perpetuate the system's institutionalized hierarchies.

With this dialogical impasse—which, of course, the one seeks to overcome by reaching consensus, and which the other seeks to maintain as a differend—we arrive at a recapitulation of the communicative failure that took place between the Christian humanist and the psychologist of Christianity. As did the Christian humanist, so the theorist of communicative action insists that all individuals share a common essence, while the consciousness of the differend invokes the psychologist of Christianity's refusal to acknowledge this claim. Moreover, just as the psychologist of Christianity opposed the humanist for humanitarian reasons which he refused to acknowledge, so here the critic of consensus fears not consensus per se but rather the sham consensus which he expects to result from every multicultural battle. Implicitly, therefore, both sides are in agreement. They both support a politics of difference as opposed to a politics of identity, but each accuses the other of advocating a politics of identity.

Now, the consciousness of the differend can remain within himself just as stubbornly as did the psychologist of Christianity, becoming the beautiful soul who refuses to seek reconciliation because he prefers to judge the evil theorist of communicative action for failing in his efforts to achieve real consensus. Conversely, the theorist of communicative action can withdraw into his own project, but with an uneasy conscience, for he has not actualized his certainty of the "we" as the universal grasp of its own non-unitary commonality. In other words, the attainment of the mediated ["I" = "I"] in the true self-consciousness of the "we" appears to have been missed once again. If everything in history really does occur twice, the first time as seemingly arbitrary occurrence and the second time as definitive truth, then we who have observed the entire dialectic up to this point can only conclude that the absolute standpoint is unattainable.

Reaffirming the position of the psychologist of Christianity, therefore, the consciousness of the differend is tempted to affirm the eternal recurrence of the dialectic. Yet at the same time, this consciousness has now been raised to the level of its truth as essentially anti-dialectical. Saying "Yes!" to the differend is not the same as saying "Yes!" to the dialectic. It is a yes-saying to the end of the dialectic, but to the end not in the sense of a telos but in the sense of an interruption. The machinery of dialectic stalls with the consciousness of the differend. But this is just to say that the consciousness of the differend becomes self-conscious when it assumes the standpoint of the *anti-dialectician.*

In one sense, the truth of the anti-dialectician is simply a reaffirmation of that of the psychologist of Christianity. But it is a position that has been mediated by the gender critique of the feminine theorist of difference, who here renews the position of the true lover of humanity. But whereas the psychologist of Christianity was unable to acknowledge the position of the true lover of humanity, because the latter represented a teleological endpoint to the dialectic, the anti-dialectician must acknowledge immediately that the position of the feminine theorist of difference is, essentially, identical to that of the psychologist of Christianity. Therefore, *on behalf of the psychologist of Christianity,* the anti-dialectician confesses to the feminine theorist of difference precisely insofar as the latter represents the position of the true lover of humanity. The latter reciprocates, acknowledging that *her* position ought to be that of the true lover of humanity. With this, their shared certainty of the unattainability of the absolute standpoint, the anti-dialectician and the feminine theorist of difference arrive at a new "truth." But this "truth" is, simply, the truth of the untruth of truth.

Hence, the dialectic of the "we" does not end with the same impasse that the dialectic of materialist spirit ended. It ends, rather, with the resounding *Yes* of the anti-dialectician and the feminine theorist of difference. For both, the differend remains as the difference that cannot be dialectically inscribed in a "we" which captures both identity and difference. Since they both affirm that every difference is, in its essence, a differend, they deny that the dialectic has given rise to any identities. To the concepts of identity and difference, they oppose the concepts of *multiple becomings,* and of the *flows* that stand in contrast to the rigid identities of the symbolic realm. Insofar as they are non-dialectical, these multiple becomings or flows do not represent a coming-together of the forces of being-for-others and be-ing-for-self; on the contrary, the latter are merely unreal shapes assumed by these non-dialectical movements.

The only truth that can be attained by way of dialectic, therefore, is the truth that the dialectic is itself untrue. And with this paradoxical result we reach the highest achievement of dialectical reasoning. The fact that it is a *paradoxical* result can always lead to a resumption of the dialectic. But to the consciousnesses that affirm the anti-dialectical *as such,* the revelation of untruth is not itself to be taken as a truth. And in fact just *this* is the implicit nature of their certainty. Hence, all that remains is for their consciousness of the *truth of untruth* to be made explicit. Since what is true is now, precisely, *nothing,* there is nothing to represent here. There is no religion of untruth. Thus, the sphere of religion does not reappear here, except as the blank space of a blank page, although, to be sure, a dialectician can make a religion out of any possible position. We jump, instead, to the explicit self-knowledge of the essentially *non-religious* philosophers— that is, of those who say, "I know that I know nothing." This is the anti-dialectical truth of the *Satyagrahis.*

6 (DDD.) • Satyagraha

"There is nothing tht comes as close to truth as *boundless reverence for all that exists*."—Lou Salomé

To say that the sphere of religion does not recapitulate itself here is to demarcate the difference between Satyagraha and absolute knowing. For the consciousness of the absolute knowers, the relationship between philosophy and religion was, as we saw, an ambiguous one. It was ambiguous not so much due to the mere logic of dialectical sublation, according to which religion would be both negated and preserved in philosophical thought. Rather, it was ambiguous in that the hierarchical ordering of the many religions both was and was not recapitulated in the consciousness of the absolute knowers. This ambiguity, which remained only implicit for the absolute knowers themselves, became explicit in the consciousness of the Christian humanist—specifically, in his anti-Semitism. For the Christian humanist who posited an essential link between revealed religion and absolute knowing, Jews—as exemplary non-Christians—had to be both affirmed and negated. The Christian humanist "solved" this problem by affirming Jews as Christians, but not as Jews. In doing so, he revealed the latent contradiction in absolute knowing's dual claim that, on the one hand, every religion was true in and for itself, but that, on the other hand, only the Christian religion was true in and for itself. It was just this hypocrisy, revealed in the consciousness of the psychologist of Christianity, which undermined the sphere of spirit altogether.

Now, however, the dialectical confrontation between the theorist of communicative action and the consciousness of the differend has recapitulated the opposition between the Christian humanist and the psychologist of Christianity—but without the theorist of communicative action basing his humanism on an appeal to religion. On the contrary, the theorist of communicative action has thrown off all transcendent appeals to grounding

the discourse of structural reason. In doing so, he has severed the connection between the spheres of religion and absolute knowing, positing the
latter as the ideal of a universal, noncoercive discourse. Hence, although he
clings to the ideal of universal truth, an ideal to which the consciousness
of the differend can never agree, he nonetheless recognizes the falsity of all
claims to absolute truth. For this reason, a reconciliation between the
theorist of communicative action and the consciousness of the differend is
not only something possible, it is something already implicit in their shared
ideal of a just recognition of real differences. But it is something whose
untruth must be made explicit by the feminine theorist of difference. Her
"Yes" with the anti-dialectician is thus implicitly a "Yes" to the difference
between them which unites them even as it divides them.

   As the truth of *both* of these anti-dialecticians raised to the level of
self-consciousness, Satyagraha is philosophy that has returned to its origin
as the love of non-dialectical wisdom and given up its pretense to possess
the truth. Like the consciousness of the differend, the practitioners of
Satyagraha—the Satyagrahis—say "Yes" to the differend, but in a self-consciously non-dialectical way.

   To the consciousness of the differend, dialectical conflict is viewed
from the duplicitous perspective of the understanding. The relationship
between two competing "others" appears to him as a relation of forces. He
does not see in this relation of forces the appearance of the notion—that
is, the "I" that confronts another "I." Instead, the Satyagrahis view conflict
from a perspective which affirms both commonality and irreducible difference in all relations. Yet in truth, the Satyagrahis merely make explicit
what was implicitly true in the very concept of the differend. For this
absolute impasse which unites individuals insofar as it differentiates their
positions is nothing less than the actual identity of their identity and difference. That no absolute reconciliation is possible says only half the story;
the other half is that they are implicitly reconciled in their mutual affirmation of the impossibility of reconciliation.

   Put otherwise, the Satyagrahis have negated the sphere of religion
altogether, while recognizing the plurality of religions. By contrast, the
consciousness of the differend posits the irreducibility of religious conflict.
To be sure, the latter is right to notice that every previous position will be
a religion for the individual who adopts it. To this extent, the sphere of
religion has not really been negated. However, the Satyagrahis embrace the
anti-dialectician's insight into the falsity of all religious identification, thereby
reversing the absolute knowers' understanding of the relationship between
philosophy and religion.

   In this respect, the Satyagrahis take up the position of the philosophical radicals, who also believed that religion must be negated for the abso-

lute standpoint to be reached. In attacking the faith of religion, however, the philosophical radicals saw themselves as possessing the pure insight of the Enlightenment. As such, they opposed falsity with truth. By contrast, the Satyagrahis oppose all pretensions to truth with their own philosophical humility. In negating the sphere of religion, the Satyagrahis do not oppose falsity with truth; they affirm, instead, the fictitiousness of all positions. What the Satyagrahis reject, accordingly, is religion's claim to truth. Considering them as self-conscious fictions, however, the Satyagrahis can respect the positions of all religions.

We recall that it was the philosophical radicals themselves who turned out to possess a religious faith. By contrast, the egoistic people appeared as the Enlightened individuals who had thrown off religion altogether. These secular masses appeared again for themselves in the symbolic sphere of masculine culture. Previously, when "we the people" embraced religion only in bad faith, it seemed as if the sphere of religion had been negated. However, the symbolic realm was itself the embodiment of a religion of macho individualism. Only by throwing off their absolute faith in their masculine idols would it be possible for the macho-individualists to hear the voices of the imaginary consciousness and the multiculturalist.

To negate one's religious attachment to a particular position is to defetishize that position. It is not, however, to throw off the position entirely. The Satyagrahis therefore teach not self-irony but self-humility. In saying "Yes" to irreducible difference, they recognize and respect every previous position—but only insofar as it is not turned into a religion. Differends become irreducibly violent when they are fought over by religious *believers*. Put more succinctly: *truth claims and violence go hand in hand*.

As something whose resolution is always deferred, the differend of religion prevents dialectical closure from occurring. To the theorist of communicative action, religious violence is something to be negated; to the consciousness who opposes resolution, it is something to be affirmed. But for the Satyagrahis, both of these judgments are reconciled in the ideal of a commitment to nonviolent struggle. Insofar as one commits to *nonviolence*, one acts as if the theorist of communicative action's ideal speech situation can be achieved. Insofar as one commits to *struggle*, one accepts the need to affirm irreducible difference rather than to settle for a resolution that would do violence to particular individuals.

If the Satyagrahis know anything, it is that there is no way "out" of the dialectic, and yet they also know that, at any point within the dialectic it is always possible to act as if the *impossible* absolute were itself a regulative ideal. To become a Satyagrahi is not to withdraw from the dialectic but to insist that the means to be used in dialectical struggle must coinicide with the ideal end to be attained—even if this end can never be actualized. Thus, the Satyagrahis do not, as did the Christian humanist, sit complacently above real struggles. Sometimes, to be sure, they judge it better to remain outside particular conflicts; this is something that can be learned only through attention to the dialectical struggle under question. But sometimes it is not, and the Satyagrahis do not hesitate to fight for one side in a struggle over a differend. Satyagraha is the work of eliminating violence from all struggles for recognition—precisely by way of *face-to-face struggle*.

Now, it was the psychologist of Christianity who first taught the great Yes-saying to dialectical struggle. However, he was unable to make explicit what was implicit in his affirmation—namely, the humanist's declaration of universal love. What kept the psychologist of Christianity from making explicit his universal love was precisely the differend that separated him from the Christian humanist. What he could not tolerate was the latter's pretension to possess the truth, whether this pretension was expressed in the language of religion—that is, insofar as he appeared as a *Christian* humanist—or in the language of philosophy—insofar as the Christian humanist was willing to become a *true* humanist. For both of these metaphysical humanists, the absolute standpoint was still a "true" position which they had attained, outside the historical exigencies of dialectical struggle. In opposing this fictitious "truth," the psychologist of Christianity plunged straight back into the violence of the dialectic, instead of recognizing that his own type of humanism was, at bottom, a love only of non-cruel—that is, nonviolent—struggle.

With the consciousness of the anti-dialectician, however, the pretension to truth has been negated. In saying "Yes" to the differend, one does not affirm a universal truth. *Truth* is merely a word; moreover, it is a word which belongs to the hierarchical language of the symbolic realm. To say "Yes" with the anti-dialectician is to laugh with the imaginary consciousness and to voice the impossible expression of irreducible difference whose impossibility the deconstructive consciousness sought to articulate.

Insofar as the ideal speech situation would involve a mutual "Yes"-saying among all others, what the Satyagrahis affirm is nothing less than the actualization of the face-to-face encounter that was articulated by the phenomenologist of ethical revelation. It is also the proper goal of all struggles for recognition. That such struggles are unavoidable is to be expected; the inevitability of struggle is precisely what is affirmed in the idea of the differend. What the Satyagrahis affirm is not that there are easy solutions to such struggles, but that genuine recognition is only possible when the violence of dialectical confrontation gives way to the nonviolence of Satyagratic confrontation. In other words, the Satyagrahi teaches that struggles for recognition should be conducted as face-to-face encounters—without denying that they are struggles for recognition.

But in order to teach individuals the virtue of this practice of nonviolent struggle, it is necessary to teach them the highest affirmation (not *truth*) of the Satyagrahis—philosophical humility. The Satyagrahis, we have said, remain lovers of wisdom, but their sole "truth" is the certainty that we do not possess truth. In this shape of *absolute unknowing*, the individual *imagines* himself or herself as a lover of wisdom, whereas in all previous shapes we have *believed* ourselves to be possessers of truth. So long as one claims to possess the truth, the will-to-violence is inevitable. But once one acknowledges one's ignorance, the will-to-violence can *perhaps* disappear—though not the will to struggle.

This form of self-knowledge—the philosophical humility of knowing one knows nothing—is itself, paradoxically, the highest form of knowing. It is the wisdom which teaches Satyagraha as the rightful practice of philosophy—to go out into the world to confront all pretenders to the truth who do violence in defense of their positions. The work of the Satyagrahis, in short, is to be the gadflies of the symbolic realm, the teachers of philosophical humility.

But the Satyagrahis must also refuse to make a religion out of this anti-religious stance. "Let a thousand flowers bloom" could express the highest moral imperative. But were this imperative to become a religious dogma, it would degenerate into a call for a cultural revolution designed to eliminate rather than promote radical diversity.

The Satyagrahis are not dialecticians. Thus, they appear as/at the "end" of the dialectic. But to the extent that every concept of a telos is dialectical, the Satyagrahis represent not the fulfillment of dialectic, but the interruption of it. To interrupt is not to negate. The Satyagrahis are involved, essentially, in the work of remembering. But memory is not nostalgia.

The *meaning* of community is always in danger of reappearing as a dialectical problem. The "death" of religion can appear to be a new absolute truth. The word "absolute" can be retained "under erasure." The *religious* Satyagrahi will speak of an absolute "beyond" the absolute. Of a "community" beyond community. Of "compearing," and so forth. The bad infinite of the dialectic knows no bounds—especially when faced with those who seek to deconstruct it. This is the risk of all deconstructive politics.

A politics of Satyagraha would need to oppose all forms of violence, including the sort of institutional violence which the consciousness of the differend emphasizes. Yet just as obviously, the precise nature of such a politics still needs to be explicated. The *merely immediate* self-consciousness of the Satyagrahis articulated here gives rise to the project of systematically articulating a politics of Satyagraha. Such a "system" can only be provisional, for it must take as its point of departure whatever ongoing dialectical struggles remain unresolved in some way—including, of course, those that have been "resolved" only by way of violence. In setting out to articulate the details of this politics, the Satyagrahis must take into account the work of those involved in these struggles. Not a politics of community, Satyagraha is not simply a politics of anti-community either. It is an undefinable work of friendship.

To commit to such a politics of Satyagraha would not require us to believe that we will ever exit the dialectical violence of history. But it is to be certain that, if violence can *perhaps* be eliminated, it can be only through non-violent means. Satyagraha is a position that is in principle open to everyone at every time; from a dialectical standpoint, this means that one can leap from any previous position to this "absolute standpoint." But to take up the burden of Satyagraha is not easy. It is an enormously difficult burden, all the more so for those who suffer from extreme forces of domination. In fact, it is the impossible gift itself. Its wishes and expectations are extravagant and incapable of supporting any claim to certainty. Yet the only other alternative to the perhaps Sisyphean struggle for a politics of Satyagraha is to celebrate the eternal return of violence—an option which, though sublime, cannot compare to the intense beauty of Satyagraha.